The Making of the TVA

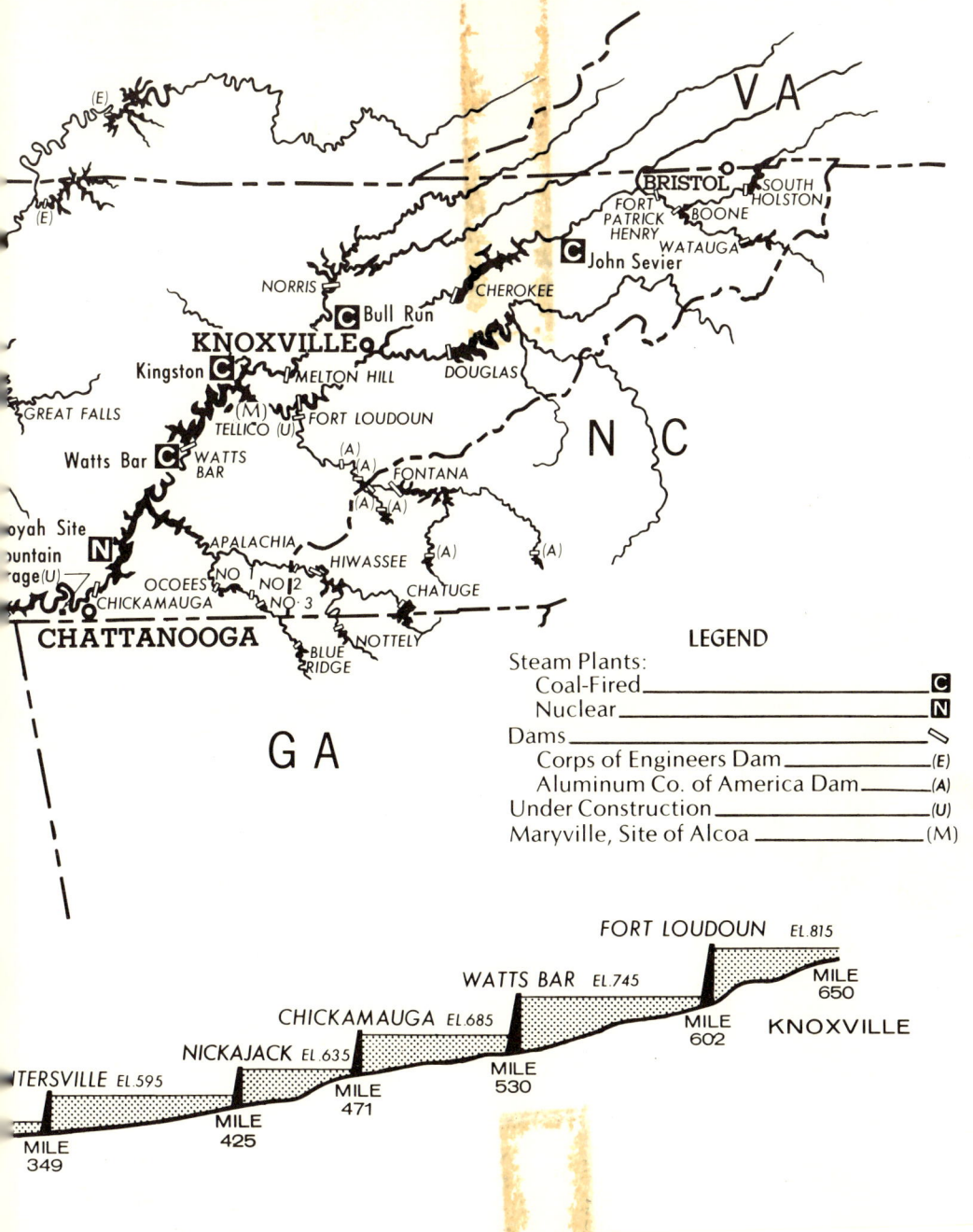

A meeting of the original TVA Board of Directors, (from left) Harcourt A. Morgan, David E. Lilienthal, and chairman Arthur E. Morgan.

A construction man, Senator George Norris, and Arthur E. Morgan at Norris Dam construction site.

President Franklin Roosevelt, Eleanor Roosevelt, and Arthur Morgan at Norris Dam.

Washday at Stooksberry homestead near Andersonville, Tennessee. This land was submerged by construction of Norris Reservoir.

Construction work on a TVA dam.

Norris Dam.

Sevierville Pike, located in a timber and farm area in East Tennessee, showing the condition of some of the land.

Arthur Morgan at work in his study.

Arthur E. Morgan

The Making of the TVA

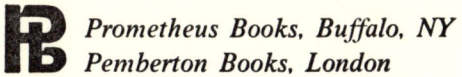
Prometheus Books, Buffalo, NY
Pemberton Books, London

Acknowledgment is gratefully extended to the following for permission to quote from their works:

Harper & Row, Publishers: From *The Journals of David E. Lilienthal, Vol. I: The TVA Years, 1939-1945*. Copyright © 1964 by David E. Lilienthal.

Holt, Rinehart and Winston, Inc.: From *The Tennessee. Vol. II: The New River, Civil War to TVA* by Donald Davidson. Copyright © 1948 by Donald Davidson.

J. B. Lippincott Co.: From *TVA and the Power Fight* by Thomas K. McCraw. Copyright © 1971 by J. B. Lippincott.

Loyola University Press: From *Morgan vs. Lilienthal: The Feud Within the TVA* by Thomas K. McCraw. Copyright © 1970 by Loyola University Press.

Praeger Publishers, Inc.: From *The TVA* by Marguerite Owen. Copyright © 1973 by Praeger Publishers.

University of North Carolina Press: From *The Tennessee Valley Authority: A Study in Public Administration* by C. Herman Pritchett. Copyright © 1943 by C. Herman Pritchett. Reprinted New York: Russell & Russell, 1971.

University of Tennessee Press: From *TVA: The First Twenty Years*, ed. by Roscoe C. Martin. Copyright © 1956 by the University of Tennessee Press.

Published 1974 by Prometheus Books
923 Kensington Avenue, Buffalo, N.Y. 14215
and Pemberton Books, London N1 8EN, England

Copyright © by Prometheus Books
All rights reserved

Library of Congress Card Number 74-75350
ISBN 0 87975 034 0

Printed in the United States of America

Contents

PREFACE	xiii
Chapter 1. THE PRESIDENT'S MESSAGE TO CONGRESS	1
Chapter 2. PRELIMINARIES	4
Chapter 3. EARLY ORGANIZATION	18
Chapter 4. EARLY TVA BOARD MEETINGS	25
Chapter 5. MY BACKGROUND IN ENGINEERING	38
Chapter 6. VAGARIES	53
Chapter 7. MULTIPURPOSE ENGINEERING	93

The Making of the TVA

Chapter 8.	THE FONTANA DAM	104
Chapter 9.	THE PERSONNEL AND TRAINING PROGRAM	118
Chapter 10.	THE FERTILIZER PROGRAM	131
Chapter 11.	THE POLITICAL CONDITIONS OF POWER NEGOTIATIONS AND SALES	136
Chapter 12.	"LIFE TO ALL FORMS OF HUMAN CONCERNS"	154
Chapter 13.	THE BASIS OF CONFLICT AND ITS RESOLUTION	164
Chapter 14.	THE LONG ROAD	183
	INDEX	201

Preface

This book is an account of my activities in the establishment and early years of the Tennessee Valley Authority and of my sustained effort to develop and carry through to fruition the purposes of the TVA, especially those somewhat unconventional purposes that President Franklin D. Roosevelt emphasized so strongly in messages to Congress and in private discussions with me.

I have also undertaken to express my own life purposes, particularly as they relate to social concepts in practice in the TVA. Underlying this account of my stewardship as chairman of the Authority is a discussion of the ideals, objectives, and patterns of operation that I had hoped might characterize it and be adopted eventually by other governmental agencies. I have, in addition, pointed out some developments during the later years of the TVA that represent a continuation or renewal of my hopes and intentions for the Authority.

At the beginning of my service as chairman of the Tennessee Valley Authority, it became apparent that the President's and my philosophy and method differed unmistakably from that of the other board members. These differences seriously impaired the ability of some elements of the TVA to function as a unified body and finally culminated in my separation from the Authority.

I endeavored at first to omit all criticism and adverse comment concerning the other board members. But it is neither possible nor desirable to give a comprehensive account of my participation in the TVA without making occasional reference to the divisive relationships existing within its board of directors. Without some such comment this account would be so incomplete as to be not fully accurate. It has, however, been my aim to exclude personal references except in those instances where they are necessary to provide clear understanding.

In spite of the difficulties I encountered, those years of opportunity and challenge in the early life of the TVA provided one of the most significant experiences of my professional career.

In completing this volume in my ninety-sixth year, I have had to call on the help of relations and friends in Yellow Springs and elsewhere. Although I could write, I could not read what I had written, and it has been necessary for them to transcribe the manuscript and then to read it to me.

Among those I called on for help were my secretary, Margot Ensign; my son, Griscom Morgan; my former associate in the Tennessee Valley Authority, Harry Wiersema, who joined me after a period of service with the Morgan Engineering Company; Albert Fry, who also came from the Morgan Engineering Company and in time became the chief of the TVA Research Laboratory; Charles Hoffman, former keeper of TVA official records; Dudley Dawson, former head of the training program for employees at TVA construction sites; and Walter Kahoe, who served for a time as my secretary at the TVA and was very cooperative and helpful.

The staffs of the TVA in Knoxville, Norris, and Chattanooga, Tennessee, were also most cooperative and helpful, as were former TVA employees, in making me acquainted with recent TVA work.

Arthur E. Morgan
Yellow Springs, Ohio

Chapter One

The President's Message to Congress

Broad currents of legislation reflect, in general, the times and the pressing needs of particular regions. The theory of the economic determination of history has much validity. Those things that happen are almost destined to happen at the time, place, and under the existing circumstances; but within that broad determination a great variety is possible.

In the area of legislation, the general course of development may be determined, but the inner genius of men is to some degree independent of outward circumstances. Given the conditions preceding Franklin Roosevelt's inauguration as president, social change was inevitable. As people find old methods and old conditions producing disaster, they naturally seek new methods and new approaches. That exploration is experimental, and its direction will be affected by the genius of the leadership of the time. Still, those who had been aggressively working for change might have found the government's response limited to eco-

The Making of the TVA

nomic questions. The electorate, by accident of personality or drift of circumstances, might have chosen a less far seeing leader than Franklin D. Roosevelt. The fact that he had a wide range of interests and that he was fundamentally a planner was, it seems to me, over and beyond what the public consciously asked for. It was because the man who became president in 1933 happened to be a man of imagination, a man who thought in terms of planning, that the Tennessee Valley Authority was created and exists today.

President Roosevelt was determined that the hydroelectric project at Muscle Shoals, Alabama, initiated by the government during World War I, reach fruition and that it be supported by additional projects. He wanted the fertilizer project powered by Muscle Shoals to go ahead; this might have been carried through as the sole purpose and intent of the legislation he proposed, but the President did not let the matter rest there. In his message to Congress on April 10, 1933, proposing the bill to create the Tennessee Valley Authority, he said that the great development at Muscle Shoals was only a minor part of his plan; he looked forward to a project for bringing industrial and social order out of the haphazard growth that had characterized our national life. He hoped the Tennessee Valley project could serve as a model for the application of similar policies and methods in other parts of the country.*

In his message to Congress concerning the Muscle Shoals development on the Tennessee River, President Roosevelt transmitted a request for legislation to create a Tennessee Valley Authority, "a corporation clothed with the power of government but possessed of the flexibility and initiative of a private enterprise."

> The continued idleness of a great national investment in the Tennessee Valley leads me to ask the Congress for legislation necessary to enlist this project in the service of the people.
>
> It is clear that the Muscle Shoals development is but a small part of the potential public usefulness of the entire Tennessee River. Such use, if envisioned in its entirety, transcends mere power development: it enters the wide fields of flood control, soil erosion, afforestation, elimination from agricultural use of marginal lands, and distribution and diversification of industry. In short, this power development of war days leads logically to national planning for a complete river watershed involving many States and the future lives and welfare of millions. It touches and gives life to all forms of human concerns.
>
> I, therefore, suggest to the Congress, legislation to create a Tennessee Valley Authority—a corporation clothed with the power of government but possessed of

---

*These remarks are taken substantially from a speech I made to the Central States Forestry Congress, Knoxville, Tenn., May 30, 1934.

The President's Message

the flexibility and initiative of a private enterprise. It should be charged with the broadest duty of planning for the proper use, conservation, and development of the natural resources of the Tennessee River drainage basin and its adjoining territory for the general social and economic welfare of the Nation. This authority should also be clothed with the necessary power to carry these plans into effect. Its duty should be the rehabilitation of the Muscle Shoals development and the coordination of it with the wider plan.

Many hard lessons have taught us the human waste that results from lack of planning. Here and there a few wise cities and counties have looked ahead and planned. But our Nation has "just grown." It is time to extend planning to a wider field, in this instance comprehending in one great project many States directly concerned with the basin of one of our greatest rivers.

This in a true sense is a return to the spirit and vision of the pioneer. If we are successful here we can march on, step by step, in a like development of other great natural territorial units within our borders.*

There was a period of great difficulty in the TVA, approximately during its second decade. After that the spirit that was in evidence in its earliest years was reasserted. I feel that, as to the Authority's record of the past quarter-century or more, the following statement by its current directors, Aubrey J. Wagner, Don McBride, and William L. Jenkins, is largely justified by the realities.

> The people of the Tennessee Valley Region joined a unique partnership forty years ago when Congress created the Tennessee Valley Authority and began the transformation of a river valley.
>
> This cooperative partnership, involving hundreds of institutions, thousands of individuals, and the TVA, has rebuilt farms and forests, controlled a mighty river, electrified a region, created industry and commerce, provided new recreational opportunities, and revitalized the human spirit.
>
> This joint effort of people and an agency to restore a region has not been easy, but under any measurement of success all of us have accomplished a great deal, laying a strong base for continued progress in the years ahead.**

The present life of the TVA reflects in no small degree President Roosevelt's life, his broad range of interests, and his hopes, so strongly expressed in the early months of the TVA.

The Public Papers and Addresses of Franklin D. Roosevelt, 1928-1945, vol. 2, Samuel I. Rosenman, ed. (New York: Random House, 1938), p. 122.
**"TVA News," May 18, 1973.

Chapter Two

Preliminaries

When President Roosevelt sent his message proposing the TVA to Congress, I read it as a piece of news but said to myself, "That is the kind of job in regional development that I would like." I was very much moved and had a vision of great possibilities, exactly in line with my interests and experience and with my boyhood dreams of what I hoped would be my career. The President's proposal resembled what I had been practicing in education and in engineering for some twenty years.

More than a decade earlier, in 1920, in a declining village of twelve hundred people, I had taken over Antioch College, which was about to disappear, and designed an innovative educational program with national appeal and distinction. In that connection I had helped young men start small industries, which developed business of more than a million dollars a month. (Incidentally, while Roosevelt was governor of New York, he and Mrs. Roosevelt visited Yellow

Springs when I was president of Antioch, but I was not at home at this time. The Governor was interested in having an Antioch professor, William Leiserson, serve as a labor-relations manager for him. He later appointed Leiserson to serve in that capacity in the national government.)

At that time, in 1933, while still at Antioch, I served as chief engineer of a fifty-million-dollar water-control project, the Muskingum Conservancy District, in Ohio. This project was primarily for flood control, but it offered the opportunity to combine flood control with the storage of water for navigation on the Ohio River and the development of a beautiful recreation area in a region of second-rate and somewhat rundown farms.

This was a period of extreme depression, and the government was striving to find ways to increase employment quickly. The Muskingum District seemed to me just the sort of project the government might need to increase employment. I therefore made a trip to Washington with some county officials to meet the congressional representatives of the area and to explore possibilities for financial help in constructing the works of this conservancy district. I talked to several representatives from the Muskingum District to see if that project could be included among similar relief projects. Some of these congressmen urged me to talk to the President and ask for his help, but I felt that imposing upon the President when he was so heavily burdened would be poor citizenship and refused to try to see him.

About a week after my return to Ohio, I received a letter from the White House asking me to come to see the President. As a matter of course, I supposed that some of the representatives from the Muskingum District had ignored my hesitancy and had made arrangements for me to visit him in the interest of our project.

On the train to Washington I met an attorney with whom I was acquainted. In the course of our conversation he said, "Mr. Morgan, have you ever considered entering government service?" I told him that I had spent two brief periods in government service more than twenty years before but that I had decided to remain in private life where I would be free from the compulsions of politics that are so common in government service.

After the Dayton flood in 1913, I was made responsible for plans for a flood-control project in that area. I followed my usual course of acting independently of current practice and of examining every engineering possibility, whether or not it was currently in good standing. My investigation led me to choose flood-control reservoirs, which for more than half a century had been strongly opposed by the Army Corps of Engineers. At that time, not a single flood-control reservoir of any size existed in the United States. With the help of a lawyer to provide legal terminology, I drafted the law that provided an opportunity for such construction.

The governor of Ohio, James M. Cox, asked that he be given the power to appoint the governing board for the conservancy district. Because Governor Cox generally made appointments for political reasons, I insisted on stipulating that they be governed by the judges in the counties included in the district. The Governor reluctantly agreed to such a provision. Later, when construction was about to begin, the Governor told me that he was politically obligated to a manufacturer of construction equipment and asked that equipment for the work be bought from this firm. I was opposed to political influence in public works and did not honor his request.

Previous to the time that the Tennessee Valley Authority was being formed, Governor Cox and Franklin Roosevelt had been associated as presidential and vice-presidential candidates. Because of my disagreements with Cox over the political-appointments issue during my service as chief engineer of the Miami Conservancy District, I assumed that he might have an adverse opinion of me. I was told that when the President talked with Governor Cox about me, the Governor, referring to my refusal to make political appointments, told him that I could be very stubborn but that he was impressed by my honesty.

On reaching Washington I went to the President's office. Supposing that he had sent for me with reference to the Muskingum District, I began at once to outline the conditions and needs of that district. He let me talk for about ten minutes and then interrupted me to say that he had not sent for me to talk about that but about the Tennessee Valley Authority, which was in the process of being formed. Then he announced that he would like to have me serve as chairman of the organization. I said, "But, Mr. President, you do not know me." He responded, "Haven't I been reading *Antioch Notes* all these years? I like your vision." (I recall on one occasion seeing a copy of *Antioch Notes* on his White House office table.) He spent about an hour and a half giving me his picture of the proposed TVA. He did not speak at length concerning power development or fertilizer, but talked generally about the total improvement of the area. He said that as a young man he had traveled through that region and had been struck by the backwardness of its development. Now he hoped he could advance a policy that would have practical results. He spoke of a community in northern New England, in either Vermont or New Hampshire, that had undertaken to advance its condition. It had used its timber supply for specialized wood products, making a given amount of wood produce far more income than when sold as lumber. He told of other communities that had developed technologies that were valid for their area and that were making social and economic progress. He hoped that similar results might be achieved in the Tennessee Valley. The fact that I was an engineer in water control and that my writings showed a concern for the economic improvement of community life seemed a fortunate combination.

When the President talked with me about the TVA, he seemed to be talking in the spirit that I associated with Eleanor Roosevelt, and not in the spirit of partisan politics. I told him that I had reservations about public service, because of the usual necessity for following the dictates of political patronage, and that I did not want to be associated with that process as I thought it had long-range harmful effects on the course of government. He pounded his fist on the table and said, "There is to be no politics in this!" I felt then that I wanted the job. When he spent most of our time together talking not about dams or electric power or fertilizer but about the quality of life of the people of the Tennessee Valley, I was quite certain of it. He said that I could appoint the other directors on the condition that one was a southern agriculturalist and the other a man competent in power development. I told him that under those circumstances I would appreciate the opportunity of working in the TVA. He said he would submit my name to Congress.

A brief reference to my impressions of FDR's life patterns may be appropriate. There seemed to be two distinct influences on him as president. The first was his wife, Eleanor, who cooperated with Marvin McIntyre, a family friend and later secretary to the President, in encouraging the President during his long siege of infantile paralysis. Mrs. Roosevelt told me that the President had considered his career to have been ended by the disease, which had apparently left him a helpless invalid. His life expectations were gone. But those two people took upon themselves the difficult task of recreating in him a spirit of life and hope.

Eleanor Roosevelt was a remarkable woman of great and sustained spirit. She had a broad sense of purpose, and was patient and persistent in meeting life. She carried the President's life purposes and hopes during periods when he was discouraged and, little by little, succeeded in transfusing some of her spirit into her husband until gradually his own spirit and courage returned.

Eleanor Roosevelt also had another aim. Although she had been born into the upper class, her heart was with the lives of all people, excluding none. During her husband's recovery she aroused in him a genuine interest in her concerns.

The Making of the TVA

That interest was a real part of his revival, and during the days of his slow recovery, Franklin's hopes and those of his wife seemed to be one.

It probably was she who acquainted him with *Antioch Notes* and with my work. As a member of the Antioch Committee in New York, she had taken a marked interest in the program for Antioch and Yellow Springs.

Eleanor took a lively interest in a girls' school in New York where she had taught. At her invitation I once gave the graduation speech at the school, after which there was a general request for her to speak. She seemed to be under deep emotional stress, and she "let her hair down" and opened up her heart to the girls. She told a story of unfulfilled hopes, of long-time effort and meager success. She closed by saying that in a difficult situation there was only one course to take: "Keep up your courage and hope, and do your best."

The other influence on the President was the prevailing political pattern. There was enough of the practical politician in him for him to be elected governor of New York and president. In politics it is good to have common everyday honesty so that in ordinary affairs men can trust you, yet according to a popular view of political wisdom, honesty is not always politically advisable; occasions arise when sheer, unadulterated honesty seems to be political suicide.

FDR was a man of insight and imagination and was sensitive to the suggestions of others. He threw out ideas and suggestions along the way, but so far as I know, he seldom if ever thought them through carefully. He left his ideas to be filled out by others, which was certainly true of the TVA project. One of his limitations was his inability to give effect to his big, but not clear, ideas. But in each of the few cases that I suggested a good man to him, he gave that person something important to do.

While Franklin Roosevelt was a man of vision, with a desire to contribute to human welfare, his political life was also, as Eleanor Roosevelt commented to me, a game that he played. He had the emotions and used the language of ethics and human aspiration. Yet I sometimes asked myself whether there was any point at which his ethical standards would restrain him from taking such action as seemed necessary to gain his ends.

I often wondered how such contrasting qualities could live within him without tearing him to pieces. In my opinion, he worked out a philosophy that made ethical considerations secondary to the possession of power, and on the basis of that philosophy there was consistency to his course. I did not observe in him any of the inner tensions that one might have expected, and it seems to me that only such a philosophy could have kept his personality from being disrupted by these conflicting elements.

After I recognized this trait in the President, I decided that I could not depend on his support where ethical issues were involved. But I was determined to make the most of my circumstances, and I believe I achieved nearly as much as was possible with the TVA under those limitations.

Many of my engineering projects had been for public bodies; however, with only a few exceptions, these political bodies had been my clients, not my employers. I could maintain my pattern of life and action, and they could take me or leave me, as they liked. In general my services were called for in cases of practical need—sometimes extreme and exceptional need—where conventional patterns of political compromise would be temporarily set aside to accommodate me. I could carry through projects according to my own standards, without compromise. I tried to increase the range and number of cases in which the saying "politics is the art of the possible" did not imply expected and easy compromise of ideals that through centuries have been looked on as unquestionably desirable, but commonly not practicable.

A recent visit (June 1973), during which I undertook to appraise the TVA as it exists today, indicated that there is concern for the overall quality of life. There are, for example, health programs that reach out into the communities, a practice that originated in our concern for the health of employees forty years ago.

Naturally, one of my major interests was to accomplish the task of controlling the Tennessee River. The execution of that work was a part of my life purpose as surely as the seemingly more incidental activities. But a life purpose properly expressed should include a wide range of concerns and activities and should not be limited simply to physical developments.

MY FIRST CONFERENCE WITH FARLEY

When President Roosevelt asked me to be chairman of the Tennessee Valley Authority, I accepted the appointment with his distinct promise that there would be no political patronage. However, he arranged for me to see Postmaster General James A. Farley, who was the chairman of the Democratic National Committee. Mr. Farley and his three assistant postmasters general spent a long session forcefully urging me to give the Democratic organization authority to make or at least to pass on appointments. I refused. Senator George Norris had introduced into the TVA bill a prohibition of patronage appointments. (Without my knowledge, two or three such appointments were made, yet such appointments were so few that the TVA was relatively free of them. I consider

The Making of the TVA

this to be a substantial contribution to good government.)

Before the conference with Postmaster General Farley, I had not met him, nor had I met any of his assistants. I wrote the following memorandum almost immediately after the interview.

> Today, Wednesday, June 7, 1933, I was called to the telephone in my room in the Willard Hotel from the Post Office Department. The person who called said that Postmaster General Farley would like to see me at his office at my convenience. We agreed on 3:30 p.m. as a time of meeting. On arriving at his office waiting room I waited fifteen or twenty minutes, and then was asked into his office.
>
> Postmaster General Farley introduced himself and then introduced me by name to three other men, who he said were the First, Second, and Third Assistant Postmasters General. Except for occasional entrances of his secretary and persons behind me whom I did not turn round to see as they entered and left, we five were the only ones in the room. Mr. Farley said he thought he had met me before and we then "passed the time of day" with a few casual remarks.
>
> The Postmaster General asked the nature of the work of the Tennessee Valley Authority. I started to explain very briefly. After perhaps half a minute he said that he would come directly to the point and would speak plainly, that he wanted to talk about appointments. He said that appointments should be made so as not to embarrass the administration. I asked what he meant, and he said that we should get good men but should get men recommended by congressmen and senators and should get Democrats or Roosevelt Republicans.
>
> The three Assistant Postmasters General entered into the conversation from time to time. I said I believed that we should get the best men available regardless of party affiliation. They said that the Republicans had prostituted the merit system and Civil Service and that we should appoint men who were supporters of the party that had elected the President.
>
> I said that the law specifically stated that no political test be required. (They brushed that aside as though it were unimportant.)
>
> The four men were very vigorous, very forceful, and very insistent that I appoint Democrats. There were plenty of good Democrats, they said, and since the Democratic Party had elected President Roosevelt, Democrats should be given the offices. They said that there were about fifty thousand postmasters in the country and that in three years they would nearly all be Democrats. They said that the Republicans did the same thing.
>
> I told them that I had not asked for this appointment, had not expected it, and that I had accepted the appointment, but without any such conditions. I said that as long as I was connected with the office I would continue to look for the best men. If there were two good men available, but the better man had no political influence, I would appoint him.
>
> Mr. Farley warned me emphatically and repeatedly that such a policy would get me into a great deal of trouble. (The Second or Third Assistant Postmaster General said very disapprovingly that many of the more important positions in the

department were still manned by Republicans, and that Democrats should be there, since it was the Democratic Party that had elected the President.)

First Assistant Postmaster General O'Mahoney said that I should be willing to make some concessions in nonessentials like patronage in order to get the main end achieved. I replied that to follow the method of appointment they suggested and urged would, in my opinion, defeat the main end, that it is at the heart of the matter.

There was much expression of appreciation and agreement with my aims, but it was always coupled with insistence that the party that elected President Roosevelt should get the appointments. We need not consider this in the case of common labor, they said, but should give the executive jobs to Democrats. In one instance Roosevelt Republicans were included among those who could well be appointed.

I said that I had taken this office with the understanding that politics would not enter into it, and that as long as I was associated with the job it must be carried on on that basis.

They said President Roosevelt might lose control of Congress and the country if such methods were used. I replied that I had been overwhelmed with letters from all parts of the country from people who said that such an obviously nonpartisan appointment gave them renewed faith in government. I said that I believed that the policy I was following would win President Roosevelt ten votes for every one it would lose him. I said that President Roosevelt had shattered the Republican Party and that I believed my policy of absolute impartiality would help me to keep it shattered by maintaining confidence in the President.

At one point I thought that Mr. O'Mahoney (I believe I have the right Assistant Postmaster General in mind) made a definitely unsportsmanlike and unfair remark. He said I had come into the room as though I were in a mood to resist and rebel (I am not sure of the exact words used, but the idea was that I had entered with an air of suspicion and antagonism). This was not true. I did not know what was wanted of me and for a very few minutes we chatted very pleasantly. It was only in reply to the very plain, unequivocal statement of Mr. Farley, who prefaced his remarks with "Let us get to the point and speak plainly" that I spoke clearly and positively. I did not begin by objecting in general. I told them, in answer to their demand for appointment of Democrats, that in the building of a dam I wanted to look through the hills and find the most intelligent and most teachable young people and, while they were at work building the dam, furnish healthful living and recreational facilities and provide optimum training in skills they could take back home, while at the same time improving their effectiveness as TVA employees. In reply to this, Postmaster General Farley said they were not concerned with labor but with the executives. He said it is particularly important that the personnel manager in charge of employing labor should be satisfactory.

There was much righteous indignation from all four of the men against Republicans who dropped Democrats and appointed Republicans. He said that in the Veterans Service, which grew up under a Republican administration, Republicans predominated over Democrats seven to one.

Except for the one remark about my entering the room in an antagonistic mood, which I believe was made for future use, I thought the remarks of these men were brutally frank and cynically direct. They talked much sophistry about saving civilization through supporting the party that elected President Roosevelt and about overcoming the evil deeds of Republicans, but for the most part it was a straightforward demand that appointments be given to Democrats. One of the men—Mr. O'Mahoney, I believe—said I seemed to lean backward, as though it would be a disadvantage to be a Democrat. I told them "no." I said that I realized the great odds against President Roosevelt and that I was trying to be careful in every way to give full courtesy and attention and consideration to each senator and representative. I am fully determined, I said, to have each recommendation carefully examined to insure that no good man is overlooked and a poorer one chosen. I said that I felt a very human responsibility to add no burden of any kind to President Roosevelt and that I believed every employee could be counted on for such loyalty if our policy and intent could be fully carried out.

I said, in an attitude of friendliness, that it seemed improbable that in a short meeting our philosophies of government could be made to harmonize but that my intention was clear to meet fully the letter and spirit of the Tennessee Valley Authority Act and not to allow political considerations to have any weight in appointments. (I told them that if I could say it in any plainer language I would do so.)

Postmaster General Farley genially agreed on the improbability of our agreeing on political philosophy. He said that the suggestion for the meeting did not come from him but from President Roosevelt and that I had better see the President. I told him I would do so. I said that I had spoken far more directly to him than I did to senators and congressmen because with him I was somewhat at the source of power and policy and I wanted to be fully and unequivocally understood.

(Mr. Farley remarked that what had been said would not go beyond the four of them in the room. I said, "You may make such use of it as you wish." He repeated that it would not go beyond the four of them. I repeated, "You may make such use of it as you wish.")

We parted with friendliness and expressions of goodwill. Except for the one comment by First Assistant Postmaster General O'Mahoney, the conversation throughout was lacking in any suggestion of irritation or ill feeling on the part of the Postmaster General. Nevertheless, I felt that I had been very definitely and explicitly told what to do, and that there would be trouble if I did not comply. Nothing explicit was indicated as to where that trouble would come from except that in one or two of the several instances when trouble was energetically predicted, senators and representatives were mentioned as the source.

The interview lasted perhaps forty minutes. I did not look at my watch as I entered. Mr. Farley and Mr. O'Mahoney did most of the talking from that side. The other Assistant Postmasters General often interpolated remarks but did not long sustain the conversation. At one point I said that I found in Eastern Europe that Czechoslovakians greatly distrusted the Hungarians and in general hated them, while the Hungarians felt the same toward Czechoslovakians. I said that the same hostility existed between Germany and France. The Postmasters General had expressed the same relationship between Republicans and Democrats. The work of the Tennessee Valley Authority, I said, is not political, and we should surmount this bitterness with fairness and nonpartisan dealing. I said that pro-public power and anti-public power was a similar alignment in the Tennessee Valley and that I would be looked upon as an enemy of both sides because I was trying to be objective and fair. I said that I intended to be the same toward Republicans and Democrats.

This memorandum was begun within thirty minutes of this interview and finished at 7:40 p.m., June 7, the day of the interview.

Postscript: Within about half an hour of the time I returned from this interview a young man came in who said that he came from Democratic National Headquarters, that he had the endorsement of both his senators and of the congressman from his district, and that he wanted a job. I suspected that Mr. Farley had sent him to me as a perfect test case to see how I would act. The young man said he had graduated three years ago from Massachusetts Institute of Technology in electrical engineering, that his only job had been in highway engineering, and that he wanted a job as assistant to the chief electrical engineer at Muscle Shoals. I told him that appointments were not being made on a political basis, that his application would be given consideration along with others, and that we should endeavor to secure the best available person for each position.

This postscript and some of the interlineations in the handwritten copy were added June 10 when I was rereading the handwritten copy. Such interlineations are enclosed in parentheses.

MEMORANDUM OF A CONFERENCE WITH ROOSEVELT

About 10:30 a.m., June 8, pursuant to the suggestion of Postmaster General Farley made on June 7, 1933, I called the President's secretary, Mr. McIntyre, at the White House and asked for an appointment with the President. I held the telephone while he spoke to the President. He returned and asked me to have lunch with the President at 1:15 p.m. today (June 8).

I went to the White House office at 12:45 in order to get some information from one of the President's assistants, Mr. Foster, as to the form of an executive order for the construction of the Cove Creek Dam.

While I was waiting in the outer office Postmaster General Farley came in. I went up to him and spoke to him. I said we had been swamped with mail but that I was doing my best to give considerate attention to letters and requests from senators and congressmen. He said that I should give particular attention to all senators and to congressmen from the districts directly involved. Other congressmen, he said, were not so much concerned. This policy, he said, would cut down the number of people to be seen.

I told the Postmaster General that I had come to see the President in accord with his suggestion, but had not seen him yet. Mr. Farley was called away just then and said that he would talk with me again later.

After a time—it was about 2:45 when my turn came—Mr. McIntyre said that I could go into the President's private office. Secretary Woodin, who was in the outer office, and Postmaster General Farley started in ahead of me. I stopped and turned back, whereupon Mr. McIntyre remarked to me, "This is just a house party! Go right in." I then went into the President's office. His lunch had just been brought in on a tray and set on his desk in front of him. On the far side of the desk from the entrance was another tray for me. As I sat at the desk with the tray in front of me, I faced the President and whoever had entered the room.

Secretary Woodin and Mr. Farley talked standing up—I think about appointments. It was not my affair and I did not try to pick up the thread of the conversation. After a time the two went out and then Mr. Farley returned, so that the President, Mr. Farley, and myself were alone. Mr. Farley and the President talked for a few minutes. None of us mentioned the reason for my visit. I did not do so for I did not know whether it would be acceptable to each of the others for me to do so.

When Mr. Farley was gone, I discussed one or two Tennessee Valley Authority matters with the President and then told him approximately as follows:

"Yesterday Postmaster General Farley asked me to come to his office. With him were the First, Second, and Third Assistant Postmasters General. They discussed patronage with me and told me in brief that they wanted jobs on the Tennessee Valley Authority to be filled by Democrats, as those in the post offices were being filled. They were rather open and direct and forceful in their suggestion to me."

When I finished my statement, or rather before I had finished and gone into detail, the President said in effect: "No, that is not the case. But there are two things we do want. First, that men are not appointed who would be particularly offensive to prominent Democrats. Second, we should prefer not to have appointments fall into the hands of politically active Republican politicians, as this would be embarrassing."

I told him that I was with him 100 percent on these points and that I thought they would not interfere with a thoroughly nonpartisan policy. I indicated that I was deeply committed in my mind to a thoroughly nonpartisan administration. He showed no signs of disapproval and definite evidence of approval.

He added, "We recently had this case. In starting the administration of the farm-relief bill, we placed local appointments in the hands of county agents. In Missouri, in some part of it (I believe that was the state he mentioned), of eighty farm agents, sixty (I think) were part of the Republican state political machine. Within a week, notices went out from the Republican county committees in these counties that employment under this law would be in the hands of the Republican county chairman." The President wanted to avoid such developments.

He suggested further about as follows: "I would suggest that you appoint a man—he may be in a subordinate position—who will watch out for such mistakes." He said that with such precautions as this he approved the employment of Republicans as well as Democrats. He said that he wanted us to have assurance of nonpartisanship. Then he smiled and said, "The appointment of good men who are Republicans may have a desirable effect upon Republicans." (My quotations are not exact but are from memory. The thoughts, I believe, are fully accurate, but the wording is only approximate.)

At the close of our talk on the matter I said, "May I go to Mr. Farley and tell him of our talk and of your position?" Without a moment's hesitation he said, "Yes, do so."

We then went on to other matters.

During the earlier part of our conversation, when a caller was in the room, he said, "I should like a sort of second cabinet, with about four cabinet members, Mr. Morgan here, the director of the budget, and about ten others to meet here once a week to talk over policies."

During our talk I said that I was getting together a fine lot of men, some of whom were willing to come at great financial sacrifice, and who could put their whole hearts into a clean job. When I arose to go, he detained me to talk generally about the project for a few minutes.

This memorandum was written the evening of June 8, 1933.

Postscript: (Written on June 9) On reading this I observe that I did not make it clear that in former meetings the President, on his own initiative, twice impressed upon me that the Tennessee Valley project is not to be partisan or political.

MY SECOND CONFERENCE WITH FARLEY

On Friday, June 9, I called Postmaster General Farley's office and asked whether I could see him. The reply was that he was busy but would call me.

About 10:30 this morning, Saturday, June 10, Mr. Farley called me on the telephone and said, "This is Jim Farley. I was told that you want to see me." I replied, "Yes, may I come over?" He said, "Yes, come over any time." I said, "I will be over in half an hour." (I was in my room at the Willard Hotel.)

I arrived at Postmaster General Farley's office at about eleven. His secretary was very courteous and said that he would speak to Mr. Farley at once. He came back saying that Mr. Farley was busy dictating but would see me in fifteen minutes. I waited perhaps twenty-five minutes, and then was ushered in through a hall and by a side door through another office. Mr. Farley explained that his office had announced that he was in New York for the day. During the first part of our talk he was constantly interrupted by telephone calls. Then he called his telephone operator and told the operator to tell callers he was out of the room for thirty minutes. The office was the same one as that in which we had the former conversation. Mr. Farley and I were the only persons in the room. When someone came in the door during our talk, Mr. Farley waved him to leave the room.

Mr. Farley left his desk and sat in a chair about eight feet away. He mentioned the welcome change from excessive heat, and we talked pleasantries for about a minute.

Then I said that President Roosevelt had told me of some developments I had not heard about before. I repeated President Roosevelt's account of how in certain parts of Missouri an effort to be nonpartisan had resulted in the farm-relief work being put into the hands of the local Republican organization and used as their political tool. I said that I was determined that the Tennessee Valley Authority work be genuinely and completely nonpartisan and that I did not want to make any such mistake as the one in Missouri. I said that if he should find me making any such blunder I should like to have him tell me about it. I said that I had very definitely in mind what I wanted to do but might not always know how to do it and that I would appreciate his advice and counsel in preventing me from making blunders.

Mr. Farley then recounted to me the same story I had heard from the President, except that in his version it was a state game and fish warden who was the Republican boss and who, on being appointed to a position under the farm-relief bill, used his appointment to distribute jobs through the Republican Party machine. He said he agreed with me fully that the Tennessee work should be nonpolitical and nonpartisan and that all he wanted was to protect the administration from criticism on the part of senators and congressmen. He said that he felt that appointments should not be made of persons who were particularly obnoxious to senators.

I replied that I agreed with him on that. I added that the Tennessee Valley Authority law required that the work be entirely nonpartisan and that I intended to fully comply with that law in letter and spirit.

I told him there were persistent reports around town, apparently coming directly from the Democratic National Headquarters, that jobs on the Tennessee Valley work were to be filled by the Postmaster General. I told him it was not good for such reports to be passed around. He said that he wholly agreed with me that the Tennessee work be nonpartisan and that he would not have us appoint any but the best-qualified men (or good men—I do not recall which expression was used).

He said it might be well for us to have a man who was well acquainted with things, perhaps an assistant personnel man, to keep us out of trouble. He said that he had no one in mind but that he might find someone in a few days. I said such a man would be good but that I should want to appoint him myself. I said that if I should find a man to keep me informed, I should want him to stop in and see Mr. Farley from time to time. During our talk he came back again to the matter of this man to keep us out of trouble and indicated that he could find such a man for me. Again I stated very definitely that I should want to choose that man myself.

I spent a little time in saying that recent legislation put unprecedented power in the hands of the administration. I said that the country was very sick when it began to take President Roosevelt's medicine. We seemed to be recovering, but if we should have another relapse the results might be very serious and the government and the country might disintegrate. I said that under the circumstances the best available men would be needed and that to appoint any others would be dangerous. I said that for the Tennessee job I was finding exceptionally able men who would come if they believed the job could be handled absolutely on a merit basis but that any compromises would spoil that setup.

Mr. Farley replied that he fully agreed with me, that he picked his own men for quality, though they were all Democrats, and that he had not employed any of his friends. He said that he only wanted to support the President and to protect him from embarrassment. He asked whether, in case he found well-qualified men, he might send them to me to consider as I would any others. I said, "certainly," that such men would receive careful consideration.

Preliminaries

My quotations are not literal, but I think they are substantially correct. We talked for about half an hour, but I think I have here reported the substance. On leaving I told him that I should want to come to see him from time to time. This memorandum was written on the train, Saturday evening, June 10, 1933.

Postscript: Toward the close of the talk I told Mr. Farley how I had faced the Republican political machine in New Mexico, how I was laughed at by the Democrats for my innocence and was called "a babe in the woods," and how I completely carried the day almost alone. I used this case as an illustration of the fact that I was not wholly a tenderfoot and was not giving aid and comfort to the Republican machine.

Chapter Three

Early Organization

Soon after my first conference with the President, I asked him whether I might meet with the Conference Committee of the House and Senate, which had under consideration the bill for the organization of the TVA. The President unreservedly gave me permission. I was also informed that the committee would appreciate my participation. Shortly afterward, I met with them, and in several sessions, we went over the bill in considerable detail.

Inasmuch as I had drafted drainage and flood-control bills for Minnesota, Arkansas, Mississippi, Ohio, Colorado, and New Mexico, I had developed some adeptness in formulating legislation. I made approximately one hundred changes in the draft of the TVA bill. Some of these were simply slight changes of wording to make clear its intent, but several of the changes were very material. For example, the bill stipulated that the planning of the work be in the hands of the TVA board but that its execution be in the hands of the Army Corps of

Engineers. I changed it to place construction in the hands either of the Corps or of a person selected by the President.* Also, while the bill provided for the generation of power at the various dams that were to be built, it did not provide for the distribution of that power. I changed it to provide for the construction of transmission lines. A number of other changes that I suggested because they would result in more-efficient operation were adopted.

A member of the committee asked me whether I would prefer to be a member of a board composed of several persons or to serve as an individual. The question surprised me, and I hesitated to answer. In his talk with me President Roosevelt had assumed that there would be two other directors, and I had accepted that assumption without much further thought. The congressman's question, however, forced the matter to my attention again, and I quickly reviewed my impressions on the subject. I had quite clear ideas as to what should be the policies of the Authority, but on the other hand, I thought that three good men serving as equals could greatly strengthen one another. I wondered whether an administration under a single individual would have public acceptance or whether it would be better for its policies to have the support of a board. On the spur of the moment, I told the committee that I believed it would be better if the policies of the Authority were in the hands of a board of about three members. The committee also asked me whether, as chairman, I should have a larger salary than the other directors. I said that I preferred equal salaries, as I wished the board to be men of full equality. I began my service determined to maintain substantial equality among the members of the board.

I discussed other aspects of the bill with the committee, but there were some provisions with which I did not venture to differ. One dealt with water transportation. At that time, American rivers were improved for navigation at federal expense, but no charge was made to those using the streams. I thought that no one means of transportation should be subsidized while others were made to bear their entire operating cost. A change in this policy would have wide effect, not only on the Tennessee River, but on the Ohio and Mississippi Rivers as well. To attempt to reverse the policy on the Tennessee would be somewhat like making the tail wag the dog and might place the entire project in jeopardy. I therefore said nothing about it.

My sessions with the committee were very harmonious, and the members seemed to give considerable attention to my suggestions.

*Up to the time of this writing every president has appointed a non-Corps engineer to be chairman and chief engineer.

The Making of the TVA

There were, however, issues that arose after the law was in operation that I had not anticipated when the bill was being drafted. For instance, a major purpose of the bill was to control the flow of water in the Tennessee River and below it in the Ohio and Mississippi. If private companies built large dams on some of the tributaries of the Tennessee, they could control the rate of flow and might let down too much water in flood season or too little during low water. The position that I later took and that ultimately prevailed was that the TVA should construct and control storage dams on tributary streams and thus not be subservient to any private organization.

The TVA bill was passed fairly promptly, and my position as chairman of the Authority was confirmed. It remained to appoint the other two directors. When the TVA was being planned, the President had told me that I would have that responsibility, provided that one director was a southern agriculturalist and the other a man informed on the public-power issue. We wanted to find men with a variety of strengths; no single strength would do. In addition to being strong in his special field, each should have strengths that would contribute to the TVA as a whole. The President had mentioned with marked approval two men informed on public power and had asked me to look them up, but he did not suggest anyone whose field was agriculture.

I turned first to finding a southern agriculturalist. In general, persons of property in the South who were interested in agriculture did not share the President's concern for the interests of the average people who populated the farms and mountains of the Tennessee Valley region. Race relations, too, were rigidly fixed there. I inquired of every source I knew in the area without much success. I considered the editor of the major agricultural paper in the South—published, I believe, in Atlanta—for whom I had great respect. Although he edited an agricultural paper, he was not a practical farmer, and I decided that he would not be very successful in the TVA job. I was also interested in the former president of a southern steel company who had given up his business career to devote his time and money to trying to improve southern agriculture. I discussed him with the President, who told me quite firmly that anyone who had been identified with a large steel company would be inadvisable because the President's supporters would assume that such a man must be representing the steel companies. I asked myself if there were men in the North who were familiar with southern agriculture and might know of persons who had achieved more than local prominence.

I wrote to Cornell University's agriculture experts and asked their advice. They suggested a Canadian biologist, Dr. Harcourt A. Morgan, who upon moving to New Orleans had established his reputation by working out the life cycle of the boll weevil. That achievement had earned him recognition, and he had later been made president of the University of Tennessee. His was an unusual story, but he had made his way among practical men in southern agriculture. Local inquiries showed that he had considerable status among people in the agricultural colleges. The president of the nearest large educational institution, Peabody College, gave an unfavorable report, describing him as a person of great energy but undependable actions, but I suspected that this opinion might be the prejudice of a less-successful educator whose field was higher education not agriculture. A rapid but widespread search did not disclose any other strong candidate who was interested in the poorer elements of the population.

When I asked Dr. Morgan whether he would be a director, his response was extremely modest. He said that I had been chosen as a person competent in the field and that the TVA should be primarily my responsibility but that he would be honored to make whatever modest contribution was in his power. After such an excessively modest statement, it did not occur to me that I should first work out a program point by point with him, especially with regard to those activities in which the President was most interested.

I considered spending time with Dr. Morgan and becoming acquainted with him immediately, but decided against that course. For us to become intimate before he had met the third director might put the other man at a disadvantage. It would be better, I thought, for the three directors to be strangers until we met together.

The President had suggested two powerful and effective public-power men—one in Los Angeles and the other in Seattle—either of whom would suit him. I went to the Pacific Coast and looked them up. Each of them, however, had personal traits and methods of operation that led me to conclude that I would not want either of them involved in decisions about programs and policy.

That left the field open. Time was short, and I searched intensively to find a person suitable to me and to the President. I found another man in the state of Washington, Llewellyn Evans, who had done a fine job of developing public power for Tacoma. He had an excellent knowledge of the theoretical and technical phases of electric power. He was a person of integrity and with a pleasing personality, practical and not a crank. Although working actively for public power, he had gained the respect of the private-power people on the Northwest Coast. In most respects he seemed almost ideal.

But Evans appeared to be a somewhat reflective, mild-tempered man, not particularly tough in makeup. I questioned whether he had the ruggedness of personality to stand up to the private-power men he would have to deal with as a member of the TVA board. I talked with the President about Evans and decided to pass him by. At that time I believed that somewhere in the United States we would find a man with *all* the major qualities we sought. Later, I sometimes wished I had chosen Evans. Given his technical expertise and practical experience, I might have been able to help him hold the line in case of unusual stress. (After David Lilienthal's appointment, I recommended Evans to him. Lilienthal employed him, and Evans provided a large portion of the technical judgment, skill, and experience in the power job; but he had relatively little to do with the formation of policy and did not become a major administrative or personal assistant to Lilienthal.)

In my search for the remaining director, I tried to discover every promising prospect. I had become acquainted with Justice Louis Brandeis of the Supreme Court through my *Antioch Notes,* and I went to him, as I had gone to many others, for suggestions. He was active in many causes affecting the public interest, among which was the support of a publishing effort for literature concerning social motivation. Without my knowledge that he was behind the venture, he published in 1936 an edition of two hundred thousand copies (I was told) of a small book of mine, *The Long Road.* During our conversation he remarked that his daughter in Madison, Wisconsin, had mentioned very favorably a young man, David Lilienthal, on the Wisconsin Public Service Commission. Justice Brandeis told me that he had little knowledge concerning this man except what his daughter had told him. I added Mr. Lilienthal to my list of persons to be considered.

As there was not time for me to become personally acquainted with all the prospects for the job, I asked the help of my friends. Algo Henderson, dean at Antioch College, was helping me investigate prospects. I asked him to go to Chicago, and if necessary to Madison, to see a number of prospects, including Lilienthal. Edwin Cassells, a trustee of Antioch College and head of a Chicago law firm, was a man I greatly respected for his integrity, sound judgment, and freedom from bias. Since Lilienthal had been a member of a Chicago law firm, I asked Henderson to consult Cassells about him. Cassells said he knew Lilienthal quite well as a member, or partner, with Donald Richberg, of a law firm specializing in labor law. Cassells thought Lilienthal to be quickminded and vigorous but said that Lilienthal had overweening personal ambitions and that if he were made a director of the TVA, to use Cassells' exact words, "He will steal the show!"

The other reports concerning Lilienthal that Henderson brought back were

Early Organization

quite favorable. He also had talked with Lilienthal and was favorably impressed, though he too observed evidence of strong, active ambition. He said that Lilienthal had recently visited Washington and, according to Henderson's informant, was the source of newspaper publicity that mentioned him as a possible member of the board of directors of the TVA.

After receiving Mr. Henderson's report, I arranged to meet Lilienthal in Chicago. He seemed a fresh, young, vigorous person, who in some respects appealed to me. There was one fact about him, conventionally thought of as a disability, that made me desire all the more to find him acceptable: He knew that I had made the trip to Chicago to see him, yet after we had talked for only a short time, he said that he had an out-of-town engagement and excused himself. I wondered why, with so large a personal matter at stake, he could not find time for a longer interview. As he left he said almost effusively that if he were considered for the position he would be honored to make his small contribution under my leadership.

At that time, Mr. Lilienthal was a member of the Wisconsin Public Service Commission, to which he had been appointed by the La Follettes. He was thirty-three years old and had graduated from the Harvard Law School.

I visited the President again to tell him of the prospects I had not yet reported on. When I mentioned Mr. Lilienthal, he at once said, "I shall appoint him." Roosevelt leaned heavily on the support of Senator Robert M. La Follette of Wisconsin, and Lilienthal was La Follette's protégé. The President did not mention La Follette to me, nor did he indicate that he had ever heard of Lilienthal. I had reservations about Lilienthal, which I made known to the President. But under the circumstances I was not in a strong position to raise questions since I had no unqualifiedly superior prospect to suggest, and he had said that the appointment must be made very soon. He therefore took the matter as settled. Two or three exceptional prospects whose names I would have liked to present to the President had declined to be considered, and he did not care for the one or two other possible appointees that I had suggested.

Although the President had unequivocally stated that I could select the other directors, I am inclined to think, in view of his relations with Senator La Follette, that his method was to avoid settling on any prospect until it was time to make the appointment and then to turn to the man La Follette wanted. On the other hand, it seems reasonable that he should have had a prospect in reserve in case I did not find one suitable to both of us.

*The Journals of David E. Lilienthal** contain material supporting the view

---

*Vol. 1: The TVA Years, 1939-1945 (New York: Harper & Row, 1964).

The Making of the TVA

that Lilienthal had been much in the President's mind and that Senator La Follette had discussed the matter with Lilienthal. The President is quoted as saying, "If we could get Lilienthal, it would be a ten strike." It is curious that, while the President suggested several persons for me to look up, he never mentioned Mr. Lilienthal.

Chapter Four

Early TVA Board Meetings

At the time of the first meeting of the TVA Board of Directors, the nation was in an economic crisis. About the first of June 1933, we met in a Washington hotel, nearly complete strangers, with the TVA still an idea and a mass of important correspondence to handle. It was against this background that I asked the board to take action on some urgent matters that could not wait for the development of overall policy. I proposed to David Lilienthal and Harcourt Morgan that our relations might be made easier if we had a general manager who would report to each of us. While I was searching the country for the other directors, I had also looked for a man who would do well as general manager. I asked one man, whose career I had carefully studied and who had much experience in such work, to come to our first meeting, but at the meeting he told us that he had already committed himself to another of the new agencies. With that prospect closed, the board did not at that time pursue my suggestion further. Later, a

The Making of the TVA

manager-coordinator, of whom I expressed strong disapproval to the board and to the President, was hired.

During the period after their appointment and through the first part of July, the other directors were at the temporary office in Washington for only a few days; unfortunately, neither had been prepared to begin work at once. Harcourt Morgan had wanted to complete his vacation, and Mr. Lilienthal said he had other matters to consider and could not immediately join the board. At our last June meeting I went through temporary and emergency procedures with them as best I could and asked whether I should act as manager until they returned. They agreed that I should.

For a while I acted alone as general manager. By early October, I had assembled a supervisory and construction staff and had begun work on one of the country's largest dams, the Cove Creek (Norris) dam. Shortly thereafter construction of a second dam (Wheeler) was begun. At times, as both engineer and builder, I had work worth more than one hundred million dollars under construction. The creation of a large administrative apparatus and labor force in three months called for strenuous effort. Harcourt Morgan protested that he had expected the directors to spend considerable time discussing objectives, policies, plans, and working arrangements; he felt that I was precipitate.

But the country was in crisis. Millions of people were unemployed. Men have to eat, and they needed jobs. The President was urging quick action to get employment programs under way. Was it possible to move quickly, yet in line with permanent values, or would the work be only make-do, inefficient? A large part of the TVA program was clearly defined, to be worked out before employment could begin. I was qualified by my past accomplishments to get that work under way: the dams, the power plants, and flood-control and navigation programs, beginning with Norris Dam. The other directors had not the faintest qualification for that work nor awareness of what it involved. The near perfection of that vast project and the near perfection with which its multitudinous parts, large and small, were carried through to complete the whole, in the period of stress, is now generally recognized.

Before the President had even signed the bill creating the TVA, I had two geologists at the Norris damsite exploring for possible difficulties in constructing its foundation. To make headway while assembling our own design staff, we turned over to the United States Reclamation Service the design of the concrete structure. (The Army Corps of Engineers had previously been put to work designing the structure in their St. Louis office, but at that time they had had little experience in dam design. Before the TVA bill was signed, I sent an exceptionally able engineer to St. Louis to report on the work being done there. He concluded that it was "pretty naive" and that we should begin anew, which we did.) The Reclamation Service staff were already old hands at dam design. While they were designing the superstructure, we could be working on the foundation, approach roads, employee housing, and other projects.

We had set up the temporary office in Washington with the approval of the President in an effort to keep up with the thousands of letters that were being received.

The man I put in charge of this office, Dr. Floyd Reeves, was a member of the faculty of the University of Chicago. In the previous year he had played a prominent role in the North Central Association of Colleges and Secondary Schools as a member of a three-man commission to examine the quality of the work being done in the universities and colleges of the North Central Association, which extends from Minnesota and Iowa to Ohio and Kentucky. Membership on the commission involved a major responsibility. Some of the changes in administrative rules and policies recommended by this commission were borrowed from Antioch and became particularly valuable characteristics of the colleges and universities of the North Central Association. I considered Dr. Reeves creative and competent in appraising educational administration and in practical administration.

Structuring and classifying the great mass of mail was a considerable responsibility, which Dr. Reeves shared with me. For instance, there were letters from the President, the Army Corps of Engineers, and from many members of Congress. As an illustration of the urgency of the situation, the Corps wanted to know what their relation would be with the TVA since within a few days they would have to know whether they were to continue developing plans for the Cove Creek (Norris) dam. There were also thousands of applications, some from persons of very exceptional ability, whom it would be unwise not to consider for employment.

Since Mr. Lilienthal had relatively few duties except those relating to the transmission and distribution of TVA power, the technical aspects of which were admirably administered by Llewellyn Evans, whom I had found for him, and the management of the legal department, which was chiefly concerned with the sale of power, he had much time for contacts in Washington. After he had been in the Washington office for a few weeks, Dr. Reeves came to me and said, "Mr. Morgan, there is nothing for you to do but to resign. Mr. Lilienthal is going from man to man in the office discrediting you. I have perhaps been around more than you, and I know that this situation will never work. If you resign, all the office staff will go with you."

The TVA was just being born. The President's mind was crowded with projects. Even to mention the situation to him might be a serious disturbance. I hoped that this first action of Lilienthal's would change as we became further acquainted and decided not to mention it to the President.

For almost the entire first year of the TVA's operation, I was so successful in keeping to myself any sign of lack of harmony that even my own personal secretary, a young woman of marked insight and judgment, was not aware of any embarrassment on my part and from time to time felt it necessary to call my attention to petty strategy and manipulation. She assumed that the absence of adverse reaction on my part was evidence of lack of perception.

Earlier in our association, each of the other directors seemed interested in exploring whether I would ally myself with him, in effect dividing the TVA between us and putting the third director in a minority position. For instance, on a rare occasion when I had dinner with Lilienthal, he began the conversation by saying with reference to Harcourt Morgan: "What do you make of that old duffer? He sits in meetings and mumbles, and you cannot make out what he is saying. What can you make of that old duffer?" I did not reply but changed the subject. Similarly, Dr. Morgan once came to me in apparent great distress and said, "David Lilienthal's behavior disturbs me very greatly," but I cut the conversation short by changing the subject. Although I refused to become involved in this practice, I could anticipate that my refusal would likely lead to their forming an alliance that would place me in a minority position.

Harcourt Morgan was nearly twice the age of Lilienthal and it seemed natural for the younger man to act like a son to the elder. Lilienthal brought Dr. Morgan to the office in the morning, took him out to lunch and home in the evening. He arranged for his office to adjoin Dr. Morgan's, with a connecting door between, and for Dr. Morgan's office to be the farthest distance from mine. I seldom had conversations with Dr. Morgan. While the other two directors were extremely intimate, their relations seemed to be mostly for practical purposes. The arrangement of their offices constituted a somewhat exclusive board headquarters for the two of them, and they soon became the working majority of the board, almost invariably voting together.

There were few meetings of the full board during the period when the central office of the TVA was temporarily in Washington. The other two board members indicated that they needed to be away most of the time on their own affairs, so I was left with responsibility for matters that needed attention.

The other directors soon decided, with no notice to me, that the main office should be in Knoxville, Tennessee, but that a Washington office should be maintained because of the need for working relations with Congress, the White House, and other federal agencies. The head of the Washington office was envisioned as an important person in the total TVA program. Our personnel director, Floyd Reeves, had been trying to locate a suitable person for the position but had not as yet found one.

Even at this early stage, I began to sense a strain in my relations with David Lilienthal. His style of operation was decidedly different from mine, and a lack of mutual trust and understanding was developing. In my endeavor to build a foundation of trust and mutual respect with him, I deliberately put in his hands power that could be used against me. I hoped that the younger man's fear of the older, more experienced person could thereby be relieved and that he would not then regard me as a threat to his career. But I did not accurately gauge the extent to which personal ambition would make my overtures appear to him as weaknesses to be exploited, rather than openings for mutuality and friendship.

I thought that the appointment of a head of the Washington office presented a good opportunity to trust Mr. Lilienthal and share with him responsibility for the overall administrative functions, which I carried. I told Mr. Lilienthal, "You mentioned that you had someone suitable to do this job. I will leave the appointment to you." He chose a young woman he had in mind, Marguerite Owen, who had been the secretary to a Colorado congressman who had not been reelected. He had Miss Owen turn over most matters of importance to him rather than to me. Mr. Lilienthal assumed the major elements of direction, rather than referring them to Miss Owen, who was, in fact, a woman of excellent caliber and experience. She might have done a far better job had more responsibility been assigned to her and if her relationship had been with the whole board rather than primarily with Lilienthal.

Before the Washington office was established with a separate head, I had assembled a number of competent men for work there, and they were in the habit of reporting to me. After it was established, Mr. Lilienthal failed to include these men as Miss Owen's actual assistants. There also were several persons whom he should have put under her direction, but who were almost wholly neglected. This left our Washington office with a variety of general office men who were forced to try to find work for themselves.

Shortly after Miss Owen's appointment, I received a letter from Arnold Kruckman, whom I had appointed an assistant in that office on the high recommendation of an outstanding government chemist, Dr. C. G. Cottrell. Mr. Kruckman told me that men and women who were earlier appointees of mine were left without direction to roam about the Washington office because Miss Owen had not been given adequate relationship to the office staff that had previously been developed. He further told me that this situation was being used to alienate my support and to promote Mr. Lilienthal's interests, and he outlined in detail his knowledge of this process. I did not reply to his suggestion for tackling such subversion in the office because I did not want the TVA to descend to internecine strife and because from long experience I had found that I could sometimes turn adverse human relationships into good ones.

A second letter from Mr. Kruckman told me of the appointment of two men who would act in opposition to me, one of them a congressman's cousin and the other a congressman's secretary. Both turned up in Mr. Lilienthal's office in Knoxville, without his having introduced them to me, and proceeded in enmity toward me. Their appointments were contrary to the advice of the Personnel Department, which had previously found each unsuitable for a position with the TVA. This violated the no-patronage provision of the TVA Act.

One of the most serious consequences of having turned the appointment of the head of the Washington office over to Mr. Lilienthal was that it gave him the opportunity to interrupt the line of communication between the President and me and to use the office against me. I discovered that this was being done soon after the office was established, when I received in Knoxville a telephone message from the White House wanting to know why a communication to me of a week earlier had not been given attention. Since I had never received the communication, I went at once to Washington and asked Miss Owen about it. She said it was not available, but it became available a few hours later when Mr. Lilienthal returned to the office. Inquiries meant for me were commonly handled by Mr. Lilienthal, who would tell congressmen and others that I was incompetent or uninterested or both. He pictured to people the need for eliminating me. The following letter from Arnold Kruckman, dated May 31, 1938, shows the serious disarray in the office under Mr. Lilienthal's assumption of sole authority. Kruckman was not aware that this office was no longer under my direction and therefore wrote to me personally.

> A little preface of history will make this statement eventually clearer as to purpose.
>
> Either late May, or early June, 1933, a friend telephoned asking that I come to the Interior Building to help with some emergency work. It was clear that it was a call for volunteers who would give service without pay. At the Interior Building I found Mr. Helsley and Mr. David. I understood you either were in the city or were expected. Mr. Bock also was expected. Apparently you had just been appointed as

Chairman of the TVA. No other members of the Board had been either announced or appointed by the President. The quarters of the TVA consisted of three offices loaned by the Secretary of the Interior. Mr. Helsley, as an experienced and trained procurement expert in Government, was engaged chiefly in securing furniture and supplies for the offices.

There were somewhere between 100 thousand and 150 thousand accumulated letters, I was told, and more coming in at the rate of approximately one thousand per day. There were also queues of people in the halls, people who in some mysterious way had heard that the TVA was swinging into action and that this was the place to come to put in an early bid for a job. Those were the days when every place that remotely offered a chance for employment was besieged by the newly poor. The human deterioration that followed the operation of relief on a gigantic scale had not yet set in. People apparently still wanted to pay their own way, and strove to maintain self-respect.

David and I set to work sorting letters. Other persons also had been summoned to give a hand. Helsley managed to get more room space, more supplies, and some of your earlier associates began to interview the job hunters. Draper came on the job; then came Gillingham and others. It was not until after July 4, 1933, some seven weeks later, that your Commission, which had just recently organized, came into funds. Until that time, as I recall, the very considerable staff at work was giving service without pay and with the hope of employment when the money was available.

On July 3, Mr. Bock offered me a job with pay. He did not know what I would do, or what I might be supposed to do, but he suggested that I might find it interesting to work with you in whipping into shape some of the announcements that would have to go to the public. Aside from that definition I don't think anyone ever made clearer just what I was to do. You gave me a number of manuscripts to study and to work over, and, of course, I found abundant other work that was waiting to be done. At that time it was naturally difficult to have proper consultations with the members of the Commission; and the various executives who either had been appointed, or were in the process of appointment, were as much at sea as the rest of us. We were all trying to orient ourselves on the unique TVA job.

Not long after Mr. Lilienthal came to Washington permanently,* I was summoned to see his secretary, Mr. Littell. My impression was that the inquisition was designed to determine whose man I might be. I tried to make it clear that I was not and would not be anybody's "man," that I enjoyed the scant opportunity for acquaintance with Dr. H. A. Morgan, and that under the circumstances then existing it appeared to me that a responsible attaché of the TVA must feel that the Chairman was the personification of the TVA to whom he must report and be responsible, unless otherwise instructed. Just exactly how it came about I can't clearly recall, but immediately after this interview I learned that I was regarded as an "A. E. Morgan man."

---

*Mr. Lilienthal's permanent office was in Knoxville, Tenn., not in Washington.

The Making of the TVA

This clotting up, or ganging up, into groups, attached to this Director or that one, seemed to develop very rapidly. Everyone seemed to know that Lilienthal was at odds with you. And the work of the whole organization, so far as I knew it when it still was located in Washington, was unhappily affected by this partisanship. It seemed to me that most employees took sides involuntarily, and that their work, from office boy to section chief, was adversely affected by their surreptitious efforts to keep abreast of current palace politics, to keep in the wake of the most prosperous faction leader, as it were. Jobs were rare as diamonds, then as now, and most of the people in the TVA organization were eager to be on the "right" side, regardless of the principles or equities involved, in order to keep those hardly won jobs.

But I think I have never been so conscious of intense unhappiness, uncertainty, and frustration as I was in the TVA at that stage. There was no consciousness of loyalty either to a principle or to a person. The conflict at the top made unhappiness, distrust, suspicion, insecurity, and furtive unsocialness prevail throughout the organization. And obviously, at least to my mind, you can't make a silk purse out of a sow's ear, or build an organization devoted to the making of an Ideal out of a group of people who fear their neighbors may be hatchetmen. It is quite possible I may be wrong and that it can be done. Maybe Mr. Lilienthal can do it and is doing it. In all honesty I merely say I don't see how it can be done.

So far as I could ascertain, Miss Owen was in a position in which she was subservient to Mr. Lilienthal. He was very firm that people working in the office should have no dealings with me, and in general he took over contacts that naturally related to the manager of the Washington office. With the active campaign against me carried on by Mr. Lilienthal, who dominated the functions of the TVA Washington office staff, I did not see how I could bring about a workable administration. On the other hand, it would not be easy to undo my mistake of asking Mr. Lilienthal to select the head of the office. Almost all of Mr. Lilienthal's engineering duties were carried on by Llewellyn Evans, and his responsibilities as attorney for the TVA served admirably as the basis for political influence.

I was busy planning the TVA overall design, supervising the design and construction of dams and reservoirs, building electric-power plants, navigation locks, and directing the general research work of the TVA. I had no time for political conflict, even if I had desired to spend my time in that way. Because of the completely fictional accounts of my political intrigues, which in fact were nonexistent, I was left in a poor position on a board wholly dominated by two practical politicians. The President and Senator Norris were regularly and deeply impregnated with untrue stories about my disloyalty, which eroded and eventually eliminated their warm friendship and trust for me. Senator Norris expressed himself as being so disturbed by these many stories concerning a man

Early Board Meetings

whom he had fully trusted that he wished he were dead.* President Roosevelt came to be similarly convinced of my total dishonesty, depravity, and disloyalty to the New Deal in favor of the private utilities.

Mr. Kruckman's description of the disorganization of the Washington office under these circumstances continues:

> I think those who were employed in the TVA at Washington—and probably Knoxville—during 1933, while I was either on or off the payrolls, will acknowledge, if they are candid, that it was a distressful and harassing experience, because there was a sharp consciousness of a lack of direction and of a lack of harmonious guidance. We worked to keep busy, not because we were doing something in which we had either pride or confidence. We did not know whether the work we were doing today would have meaning tomorrow. Looking back I can understand the reasons more clearly. You and your associates had, of course, a broad sense of your objectives, but you were badly adrift apparently in regard to the details of the chart. We rocked about more or less aimlessly, but we did not realize how serious was the condition that paralyzed the leadership until you personally made your statement to the Congressional Committee recently.
>
> During the five or six months I worked in the TVA I never had definite instructions about the work I was to do. I determined we needed more data about the human history of the Tennessee Valley and its people during recent years, and I proceeded to get in touch with the editors of all the small weeklies, semiweeklies and dailies within the area or just beyond the borders of the area. Also, we broadcast a letter to all chambers of commerce and similar organizations. In the course of time we assembled a really very valuable collection of data about all phases of the life in the Tennessee Valley, which was classified and digested by the men on the staff. I understand this material was finally refused by the permanent office of records in the TVA in Knoxville. For a long time the material was allowed to moulder in the old Temporary Building F. What happened to it after that building was torn down I don't know. We also made a survey of all public nongovernmental agencies focusing in Washington whose activities in any way directly, or indirectly, affected the TVA. And we made a special study of Census data, mostly unpublished material in Government records, of immediate value to the TVA. We made contact with all libraries in Washington, either governmental or nongovernmental, general or special, to list all literature that might be required in prospective TVA developments. There were at least three men engaged in this work, which included various undertakings not here enumerated. I think there were three young women in the Library itself, which we had, in the meantime, gradually assembled. Our object was to provide for the TVA itself, and for its clients, a broad and sweeping assembly of information that might be available in the most useful form.**

*Letter from Norris to the President, quoted in Thomas K. McCraw, *Morgan vs. Lilienthal: The Feud Within the TVA* (Chicago: Loyola University Press, 1970), p. 23.
**I was not adequately informed of the existence of this material and, with the help of Senator Norris, had undertaken to assemble my own.

The Making of the TVA

In the course of organizing this work our office became the nerve center for most of the information and gossip that either was afloat in the organization itself or affected the TVA and came from the outside. We perforce became host to many visitors from all parts of the world, students, writers, editors, artists, scholars, educators, and others, who were shunted off from other sections because they sought probably a broad picture of TVA as well as a picture of the facets that affected their specialized interests. Members of Congress, Government officials, and others in Washington having a special interest in some of the multifarious angles of incidence upon TVA came to us. Either the young men, or young women, or I heard much that seemed interesting and important to the welfare of the TVA.

My relations with you had remained practically as they were in the beginning—very casual and fleeting. It was my impression—I think mistaken, in the light of subsequent events—that you mistrusted me. I don't mean that I felt you mistrusted me as an individual personalized, as that you mistrusted the whole machine. I gathered that it was a proceeding that was new in your experience and that you misunderstood our objects and our earnestness and probably our methods. And we did not quite know what to make of you. We had no idea of the extent of the conflict in the Commission, and we probably mistook your natural preoccupation for a lack of warmth and a lack of interest in our efforts to serve the TVA. We sensed the fact however that you represented the only element in the Commission that seemed fair, sound, and sincere, and that you were striving to make the job work to the eventual advantage of *all* elements affected. Therefore, we addressed ourselves to you as an individual as much as we addressed ourselves to you as the Chairman. Often, when information that seemed important, either to the organization as a whole or to you as an individual, came to us through the many persons with whom we had relationships, we transmitted the facts to you. Sometimes they were given to Len Broughton, your Assistant; at other times they were written to you, personally, either here in Washington or at Knoxville. Broughton advised us that some communications sent to you at your office in Knoxville had a mysterious way of either not reaching you at all, or reaching you after they had first been communicated to others. To prevent any miscarriage of important data he suggested that such matter be sent to your home. I do not remember the exact address, but it vaguely comes to me it was on some Circle, in Knoxville.

It seemed to me that you as Chairman, and as an individual in a peculiar situation in relation to your associates, should be fully informed of all news, verified or unconfirmed, that came our way. My thought was that such information indubitably was useful to the officer commanding a military operation. It seemed to me our business to forward the data to you, and that it was your business to use it as you saw fit.

I, therefore, was nonplussed to receive from you in the Fall of 1933, probably late in September, a letter requesting that, henceforth, I send nothing to you that might be construed as a confidential communication. I gathered that you did not wish to be in the possession of any information which you could not "fully and freely present to the other Board members," as you subsequently declared in a conversation. You apparently considered some of the information we had transmitted to you as of such nature that you could not fully and freely discuss it with your associates. It was my impression that this referred particularly to the fact that we had heard that efforts were to be made to initiate organized proceedings to discredit you, in order that you might be superseded as Chairman by Mr. Lilienthal. At this writing, I don't recall who gave us this information. It is possible that Kendall K. Hoyt, who worked on the Hill for us, may have more exact facts. The letter in which you instructed me to cease sending "confidential" information was written in longhand to you. When I left the TVA I left the letter in its files.*

It was my understanding that senators and representatives were being told that I was opposed to them and that I was making decisions that adversely affected their efforts. As a result, a widespread antagonism to my attitude developed in the Congress. Because of the strict requirements that I had provided for in evaluating applicants, care in appraisals and appointments were very thorough, and the casual choices of congressmen commonly were not approved.

Though more extreme in its implications, the case of my asking Mr. Lilienthal to appoint the director of the Washington office was just one of many attempts I made to show confidence in him, in the hope that he would come to respond in kind. But since he seemed to regard such conduct on my part as stupid and an invitation to his dominance, it resulted only in largely closing my avenues of communication with the White House and Congress.

I did not hear from the other directors after the first few meetings of the board in Washington in early June until I received a telegram in mid-July asking me to meet them in Knoxville. I was later told that Mr. Lilienthal had in the meantime been writing letters to political associates and members of Congress in which he stated that, on becoming acquainted with me, he had found me to be incompetent and had therefore withdrawn to Knoxville to prepare a suitable program for the TVA. I went to Knoxville as they had requested and they laid before me—a little more than a month after their appointments as members of the board—an overall design for operating the TVA. Under their plan I was to operate the office and to build the dams, powerhouses, reservoirs, and navigation locks, for which they had no training or experience. They also gave me responsibility for programs that they considered minor aspects of the TVA, such as forestry and recreation. Harcourt Morgan was to direct the fertilizer program, including distribution without charge to selected private farms, maintain

---

*Arnold Kruckman's letter carried the following notarized statement: "The above signature acknowledged before me this third day of June 1938." (Signed) G. H. Schulze, Jr., Notary Public, Washington, D.C.

contact with the executives of land-grant colleges, and take care of any related matters that might arise. Mr. Lilienthal would administer the legal apparatus and operate the electric-power sales program.

C. Herman Pritchett, in *The Tennessee Valley Authority*, describes the situation as it was reported by the board majority:

> According to H. A. Morgan, he and Mr. Lilienthal were finally led into open objection by the elaborate program of activities which the chairman presented at the board meeting of July 30, 1933. This list included some of the immediate and proper objectives of the Authority but it also contained items which H. A. Morgan considered "impracticable and highly visionary or clearly outside the scope of our responsibility under the law." He was particularly disturbed to learn that the chairman had apparently made a number of commitments prior to submission of these proposals to the board. H. A. Morgan concluded that he could not continue on the board unless some method was adopted "whereby each member of the Board would be limited in individual action to those with which each was intimately familiar and whereby there would be reserved to the Board as a Board the prerogatives of review and decision with respect to the broader policy questions." Since Mr. Lilienthal felt the same way, the two directors agreed on the plan of dividing responsibility already described. Chairman Morgan apparently accepted this check in good spirit at the time.*

Mr. Pritchett was mistaken in attributing the events he reports to a board meeting on July 30, 1933. The important board meeting called by the other two directors at which the responsibilities of the board were divided among the three directors was earlier in July.

They assumed that each director's area would for the most part be his individual responsibility and the other directors would not be involved with it or informed about it. The single exception would be my overall responsibility in general administration. Thus the power policy was to be Lilienthal's work. As chief engineer, I would handle the construction of the plants for generating power, and would turn them over upon completion to operate under Mr. Lilienthal's direction. With these two functions assigned and the legal problems in Mr. Lilienthal's hands, it seemed to me that the management of the TVA could be reasonably effective under the design that had been handed to me.

Later Harcourt Morgan and David Lilienthal each drew attention to the fact that in the first three or four years there was not a single negative vote in the board. But I had followed a policy of abstaining from voting on matters with

---

*C. Herman Pritchett, *The Tennessee Valley Authority: A Study in Public Administration* (Chapel Hill, N.C.: University of North Carolina Press, 1943), pp. 187-188.

which I did not agree. I continued to follow that policy until the division of responsibility earlier dictated by the board majority was ended on May 19, 1936, when without discussion they took out of my hands my responsibility as chief engineer for one of the two most important projects in my own field, the development of Fontana Dam.

The action of the other members of the board removing me from this responsibility in my own field was unprecedented. At the initial meeting I was summarily told of the decision of the other members of the board. Two critical meetings that followed on the issue were held without me and without notifying me that they were to be held even though on each occasion it was known that I would be in my office within a day or two. The reason subsequently offered for meeting without my presence was that I was away on an extended vacation. On one of these occasions I had been away for a couple of days visiting dams under construction. After this change in the division of responsibility by the majority of the TVA board, I began putting on record my disagreements with them.

The TVA was just being born and was an unprecedented new element in government. Other elements of the President's vast program were in trouble. I had decided not to disturb him about the matter. With cooperation, such a division of responsibilities might be made to work and work well, though some of my strongest supporters warned me that the course I was taking of avoiding open conflict would be the catastrophic end of the TVA.

Chapter Five

My Background in Engineering

This account of my experience in the TVA can be better understood if reference is made to my background before I joined the TVA and to the life philosophy that I had developed. I shall, therefore, depart briefly from this narrative to discuss those earlier years.

When the average person undertakes an activity, he usually gives little thought to its ultimate purpose in his life or to its ultimate benefits to mankind. He concerns himself primarily with the immediate activities required to fill his needs and desires and with those questions most immediately related to such activities. Yet a man's every act has some effect, however insignificant, upon humanity's destiny.

Although most people have some degree of commitment to living in a way that will serve ultimate values, their commitment is often insufficient. In addition, the conventional values to which they are committed are often ill conceived or obsolescent. The prevailing patterns of action are generally misunderstood as approaches to the ultimate values. Yet, humanity repeatedly reaches toward the ultimate value. There is a constant though very slow approach to clearer purpose and more definite patterns, though insight is frequently mixed with error.

The actions of men in everyday life tend to follow definite patterns. In general, one's own way of doing things becomes so habitual as to seem to be the natural way, and any other way, whatever its merits, seems so unusual that it is just as habitually disregarded. Sometimes, however, a person or a group of persons will make a conscious effort to work out and follow a way of life that to them is more purposeful and not just "the way things are done." In the long run, it is by the intensive, conscious efforts of such persons that a higher sense of purpose gradually emerges. Most significant human purpose has survived and increased through the efforts of people of moderate ability but extraordinary persistence. In spite of the large degree of failure involved in such efforts, human purpose gradually is improved and strengthened. That is true of the great historical movements that from time to time augment prevailing conceptions of human purpose. Progress usually comes through the successful fragments of efforts that on the whole were failures. Since such efforts are not in accord with common practice, they may sometimes cause difficulties for the individual who persists in them.

When I was very young, I had an attack of cerebral meningitis that nearly ended my life. The attack persisted until my mother, as she told me later, wished that I would die soon and end the agony. Gradually, however, the spasms ceased and I began making a slow recovery, which continued for several years. During that time I watched older people to see how they maintained their health. I watched plants in the family garden in order to learn their capacity for survival and renewal, since I felt it might be similar to my own.

My sister was a member of a group of people from fifteen to thirty-five years old, students and faculty at the St. Cloud, Minnesota, Normal (Teacher's Training) School; who met each Sunday evening with other active minds, to discuss and to try to determine their life purpose. My mother, in an effort to help my recovery, required that I go to bed at seven o'clock each evening, but when I was attending the meetings of this group, she would allow me to stay up late. I was treated as a member of the group from the time I was about seven years old, and I stayed in it until I was about eighteen. This association was an important factor in my life and led me to a deep concern with ethical standards.

I began very early to search for the values that would govern my life. At the age of seven or eight, I was as serious as any of these young people and was asking myself questions. Where did leaders of the group get the profound wisdom they expressed? What proof was there for the miraculous "truths" in the Bible and the dogmas of religion? At the age of nine I was "immersed" into Baptist membership, much the youngest member of the congregation. By the time I was ten, I doubted such powers as omnipotence and omniscience attributed to God, which I heard about in Sunday school. How could any creature be omniscient or omnipotent? Could he bring it about that I never had existed? If not, there was something he could not do. Why would a good God create a hell and put people in it for eternity? Had God made a mistake?

Through the years my health improved. As I watched older people to learn what insight and mastery they had acquired, I saw that different people had different strengths and excelled in different areas of life. Some excelled in physical strength, some in mental development, some in the management of practical affairs, some in theoretical knowledge, some in careful development of health, and many in several respects. I asked myself what men and women would be like if every person would strive persistently for excellence in everything that he did. By the time I was eighteen I had decided that every individual should, within reasonable limits and allowing for specialization in some field, strive for such all-round development.

One important influence on me was an address by a Buddhist from Ceylon, who came to speak in St. Cloud at the time of the World Congress of Religions in Chicago in 1894. This was my first encounter with a highly intelligent person who was outside the Christian tradition. I began to depart from orthodoxy and slowly to create my own patterns of values. At the age of sixteen I became acquainted with the theory of evolution, which challenged the idea of a static creation and emphasized progressive development. The evolutionary process after three billion years of gradual development had produced patterns of value that resulted in humanity, with perhaps unlimited time to continue and perhaps unlimited possibilities of future development. I was critical of the doctrine of immortality, which seemed to me not only unrealistic but also less than ideal. The infinite continuation of one's own personality had limited appeal for me. I did not think of humanity as made up of individual existences but as a total unity, just as the cells of our body are not ultimate individual entities but are parts of a larger whole. I gradually formed the conclusion that my daily life in a natural world must be the focus of my endeavors.

We cannot, therefore, fulfill our lives as individual beings; we must instead recognize that we are part of this larger unity of life. The joy an individual takes in life should not be limited to satisfaction of narrow, personal desires or goals, but rather in contributing to the possibilities for growth and fulfillment of all men, present and future. Thus, the measure of my life will not be primarily what I have achieved in personal satisfaction, but what will be achieved through me for humanity as a whole.

In keeping with this view, I have tried to make my life a positive force in the struggling emergence of new human purpose. I found encouragement in this effort in the teachings of Christianity, Buddhism, and from some of the Greek Stoics. The teachings of Jesus were not just traditional Jewish doctrine, however much they had their roots in Jewish tradition. They were inevitably influenced by the great range of cultures surrounding Jesus in the province of Galilee. Nazareth was a village just four miles from the capital of Galilee, Sepphoris, a Greek-speaking city that was on the caravan route to India. Within twenty miles were a number of Greek cultural centers, including Gadara, then the home of Syria's greatest poet, Meleager. Some of the great religious traditions of India and Persia were becoming widely known throughout the Mediterranean area after Alexander the Great's conquest of India. In Syria and Galilee the great Stoic religion was culturally dominant, and the ascetic Essene cult was only one of the powerful influences beyond Jewish orthodoxy by which Jesus must have been greatly influenced.

This area where Asia, Africa, and Europe join was a natural center for the collection of the new cultural elements from all these sources, and the far-flung Roman empire brought a new flux of change. It is significant that Jesus would sometimes begin a statement with the words "Ye have heard it said by them of old time, but I say unto you . . ."

I came to see that mankind was in the process of gradual emergence, and that Christians, Buddhists, Zoroastrians, and Stoics were evolutionary breakthroughs to a new and better order of living, but the deeply embedded heritage from mankind's animal ancestors repeatedly corrupted and obscured these promising advances. The rise of humanity to higher levels of social consciousness depended on such breakthroughs becoming established and dominant. The best aspects of modern life seemed to be furthering this gradual emergence.

Ethical principles appealed to me. I could see how universal honesty, friendship, and fair play would be fundamentally practical. These principles would help make life worth living. Experience would help me distinguish good judgment from poor. The advice of other men would be helpful, but it must be tested by experience and reason. This became my religion.*

---

*There is an excellent recent statement of this old doctrine in a little book by Michael Polanyi, *The Study of Man* (Chicago: University of Chicago Press, 1959).

It seemed to me that the ethics of human unity, honesty, goodwill, sound physical and mental condition, and other emerging traits of excellence should be the major concern of society and of individuals. I could be a part, however small, of that troubled but promising emergence of a new and better society, and I decided to make that my life purpose.

Many persons live in such a spirit. The parents who work to see their children given advantages in life, whose fulfillment they will not live to see, the citizen who contributes to the welfare of his community, and the man or woman who guides his or her life by the standard of what is good for the whole nation are living by this faith.

If we observe the motivations of the individuals who make up human society, we will see that only in part are the efforts of their lives contributing to the fulfillment of the whole through the generations; they are much more committed to the instinctive action bred through animal evolution, to primitive purpose, to individual satisfaction, and to values of limited groups than to a sound relationship to the whole. Insofar as human aspiration aims toward the increase of total value, the progress of human evolution and fulfillment of unending destiny will increase.

Human destiny and even the cosmos may have no limits so far as the ultimate development of men and their powers are concerned. Even in our present circumstances we find that many of the factors of life are not limited by the capacity of present human possibility. The scope of human achievement and development may enlarge indefinitely in the future as the overall capacities and purposes of mankind increase.

This is a crudely expressed concept of my conviction of where value lies and how it may increase. I have attempted to live by this conviction throughout my own life, with limited results and with frequent serious failures. But I feel that insofar as I have followed this purpose, I have done well.

I was born in Cincinnati, Ohio, and lived most of my boyhood in St. Cloud, Minnesota, a town of five to ten thousand in a part of the state largely populated by recent immigrants from Germany, Poland, Holland, Austria, Scandinavia, and Ireland, but with a small minority of old-line English settlers. In each of these ethnic groups there were individuals or small groups who went far toward fulfilling their dreams, but there were many others who fell short. For instance, in our town there were thirty saloons, frequented by a considerable part of the population. While there were elements that were petty and sordid, cultural habits were on the whole fairly decent. The most serious crimes, like stealing and robbery and murder, were rare. Yet the manner of life left much to be desired; a considerable part of the activities of the community did not advance its well-being.

As a boy I believe that the reason was that our community was one of underprivileged immigrants. I imagined that in the city the people were like those I had read about in Emerson's essays or had seen in pictures of ancient Greece. When my Sunday-school teacher took our class to the annual Minneapolis Exposition, I was surprised to find that the people looked much as they did at home.

Of course, I outgrew these childish notions and became acquainted with the larger world. But I retained a boyhood trait of imagining what people would be like and how they would act in more favorable settings. I often thought about ways in which living conditions might be improved. Later, as I traveled around the state working on land-reclamation projects, I habitually took notice of the cultural traits of the various communities that I visited.

My father had no theological affiliation. He was an agnostic—although he never used the word to describe himself—who retained the ethical outlook of his Quaker ancestors. He was a land surveyor with some limited training in that field from the Lebanon Academy of Surveying near Lebanon, Ohio. My mother was a member of a newly emerged denomination, the Christian Church. She "took boarders," students at the Normal School (now St. Cloud State University).

Our home in St. Cloud, a somewhat primitive four-room cottage (which grew to eight rooms, including the unfinished attic), was near the edge of town. A garden lot gave me the opportunity to help feed the family and to peddle vegetables to earn spending money and buy clothing. I attended the local high school for part of each year for three years and graduated. Except for a few months in the Preparatory High School of the University of Colorado, followed by about two months as a student at the university, this was the extent of my formal education.

In my youth, as I explored the woods or attended school or worked in my garden or observed the daily life of our community, I often created mental pictures of how human affairs might be rearranged for the better. Some passages in the New Testament struck me as unusually significant, as for instance, "Whatsoever ye would that men should do unto you, do ye even so unto them." Such passages implied the possibility of social and individual existence on a far higher moral plane than we experienced. There was a small community in central Minnesota of settlers from New England that impressed me with the high quality of their community life, which was of the kind that characterized the best New England towns. The image of that community stayed in my mind as a hint of what might someday become the general character of social groups. I also imagined technological improvements and advances in man's knowledge that would contribute to greater social well-being. By the time I was seventeen, for example, I had developed a mental picture of education in an ideal village where teachers, pupils, and workers lived together.

I gave attention to questions that are generally considered trivial and quixotic. For instance, I was concerned with nutrition and physical condition, and avoided tobacco, intoxicants, coffee and tea, since the best of health is necessary for full effectiveness. My early attack of cerebral meningitis had made my way much more difficult, and my best efforts with regard to personal fitness would be none too much.

When after high school I left home and started on foot for Colorado, I endeavored to work out in my own mind standards of action that would help in improving human standards. I decided that I would not undertake to make a living at any work that in its essential character was not a contribution to human well-being.

My way was not easy, yet the venture never seemed impossible. Sometimes I slept in straw stacks or empty boxcars because I did not have the price of a bed. In Colorado I worked on fruit farms, as a delivery man, in a print shop, in a coal mine, and at various other occupations. The most appealing job I held was cutting timber in a lumber camp high in the mountains. The scenery was beautiful, the geology varied, and the botanical specimens new and interesting to me. I also appreciated my association with the rough timbermen. I had seldom enjoyed life more. Then I learned that my employer, a small sawmill operator, had contracted to supply the lumber for building a large gambling house in a mining camp. This did not harmonize with the life I was trying to live. After I had confirmed the report by a personal visit to the mining camp, I decided to give up my job, much as I enjoyed it. After a few months at the Preparatory School and the University of Colorado in Boulder, I returned to Minnesota, where I apprenticed myself to my father and through private study became a land surveyor, with some experience in drainage projects.

From that I turned to engineering. Lacking any training, however, I wanted to find a field of engineering in which my own inexperience was matched by a general lack of knowledge among professionals so that I might start on somewhat even terms with them. I settled upon the field of control of water resources.

My Background

As I carried through one project after another, I became aware of the imperfections of the drainage laws of my state. I decided, for three reasons, to work at revising those laws. First, I wished to improve the legal structure of the Minnesota laws on water control. My second motivation was to increase the number of my acquaintances and associations in order to increase my employment opportunities. The third reason grew out of my desire to make my current work, so far as my skill and judgment would allow, consistent with my ultimate values.

I assembled drainage laws, especially those from states with the best-developed codes, and some Supreme Court decisions. I was surprised to find that the engineering profession was not even consulted about many unusual situations that arose around drainage and water-control laws. I undertook an extensive study of engineering codes in the field and of recognized engineering principles, and in the course of a year, I formulated a legal code for water control in my state. In the process, I carried on a widespread correspondence with engineers, lawyers, and public officials.

The state engineering society of Minnesota became interested in the undertaking, and at their annual meeting in January 1907, the code was made the principal order of business. The society held its meeting in the state capitol building in St. Paul, where the discussions were observed by state senators and representatives, who enacted the draft into law after finding the engineering profession in general agreement about its merits. In succeeding years I rewrote or revised the flood-control laws of Arkansas, Mississippi, Ohio, Colorado, and New Mexico.

My work on the Minnesota water-control bill greatly expanded the number of my acquaintances and led to increased professional associations. It also gave me freedom to refuse employment by those whose methods of operation I did not approve. Within a few months of the enactment of this legislation, officials in my county began a water-control project that I could not have supervised with a clear conscience. I had thus established my grounds for freedom of action none too soon. This incident illustrates, I think, that forethought can sometimes save a man from having to compromise his standards in order to hold his position. As a result of my authorship of the bill, the governor of Minnesota offered me a position as a state engineer, but I declined because of other plans.

One man who attended the meeting at the state capitol, but whom I did not meet at that time, was C. G. Elliott, head of the Office of Drainage Investigations of the U.S. Department of Agriculture. A few weeks later he wrote to me inviting me to take a Civil Service examination to see if I would qualify for a position as a supervising engineer in that agency. I was one of about 150 persons who took this examination and one of four who received an appointment.

During the three or four years that I held the position of supervising engineer in the Office of Drainage Investigations, there were several occasions that required a definite effort on my part to maintain my professional standards. I had asked the Office of Drainage Investigations to make my early appointments in the Northwest, where I had some experience. Instead, they assigned me to a project in the San Luis Valley in Colorado to solve a problem of removing the harmful salts that cause "alkali land." The project was located in the Colorado desert, and the nearest helpful literature that I knew about was in Washington and had to be sent for.

This was a new field for me, but I began to make some headway. My advance toward a solution of this problem was far from abstruse. It was to establish rather deep subdrainage of the land and then to irrigate it as liberally as possible, thus draining the contaminated ground of its harmful chemicals. Tile drainage would not work because the leakage from gravel through tile joints would throw them out of line, and ordinary timber would decay in a few years. But I found remains of pitch-pine logs that had been buried for many years without decaying. With channels constructed with pitch-pine boards, which would be free from decay, and with overlapping joints, which would allow groundwater to leak in, the problem could be solved by a single structure.

After several months, however, my chief ordered me to Washington to another job. I told him that I was making progress and that if I left the job at that time, my efforts would be wasted. He replied that the allotment for the job had been exhausted and again told me to return to the Washington office. I told him again that I felt I should not leave a job in that condition and that he should find some means for me to remain on it a few months longer. He did, and as soon as it seemed feasible I offered to return to Washington.

He next assigned me to a job in the lower Mississippi Valley, in Louisiana, where other unsolved problems waited. Once again I was ordered to return to Washington before I had found an effective solution. Again I postponed my return. I feared that I might be dismissed for this stubbornness on my part, but to my surprise, they appointed me to be in charge of the largest project that had ever been undertaken by the Office of Drainage Investigations, on the St. Francis River system in Missouri and Arkansas.

On the whole that assignment went well. One important element of the project was a proposed large earth dam, which was quite beyond my experience. When I asked my chief for permission to hire consultants, he replied, "We do not employ consultants. We *are* consultants." Not being satisfied with my own

My Background

findings, I went to the large lumber companies who would profit from the work. I told them that I was not sure of my conclusions and asked whether they would put up money for consultants. They agreed, and I again raised the question of consultants with my chief. He provided the services of the two leading hydraulic engineers in the central United States, Isham Randolph, chief engineer of the Chicago Drainage Canal, and Anson Marsden, dean of engineering at Iowa State College. These two men examined my plans and gave them unqualified approval. I still had doubts, however, so the plan was never used.

At one point the chief of the Office of Drainage Investigations made a trip to the Pacific Coast and left me in charge of the Washington office. At that time there existed a nationwide organized effort to sell wetlands of the Florida Everglades to people of small means. A group of three men, including the head of the legal section of the Department of Agriculture and the son of the secretary of agriculture, had united in supporting the completely unsound land-development proposal of a real-estate syndicate. During the absence of my chief this matter came to my desk for final official approval before being given national circulation. I wired my chief that I was holding up the bulletin because I believed that the project was unfeasible and that the public funds committed to the reclamation of the wetlands were entirely inadequate to fulfill its advertised purpose. My chief replied that he was aware of the shortcomings of the report but said that he had added qualifying paragraphs to each chapter to protect the reader. He directed me to give final approval to the report for distribution. I again wired him that I considered the report wholly improper and suggested that he return. He returned, read the report, and withdrew it from publication.

At about this time, a member of the Department of Agriculture who had overspent his agency's appropriation for that period persuaded my chief to make him a short-term loan from our office's budget. The head of the legal section of the Department discovered this, charged my chief with committing an irregularity and had him dismissed, and then approved for publication the report on the Florida Everglades that had been previously withdrawn.

I wrote to the secretary of agriculture about the impropriety of the land-sale project and suggested his intervention. When I received no response after a considerable period of time, I gave an interview to the *Memphis Commercial Appeal* and to the Associated Press, telling of the exploitation of people of small means by this nationwide real-estate promotion. The interview created a national stir and was followed by a congressional investigation of the matter. I was the first witness called, and my questioner was the head of the legal section of the Department of Agriculture. He had evidently gone over my accounts and correspondence for the past three years, hunting for evidence of improper conduct. His tactic consisted of taking single sentences or paragraphs out of context from my letters and asking if I had written them. I would in turn ask him to read the entire letter to restore the context. In this manner he kept me on the witness stand for a day or two, until the chairman of the committee finally said that enough time had been spent in that way and called on me to testify. As a result of the investigation, the report was again withdrawn from publication, the head of the legal section and the engineer who was his associate in promoting it were allowed to resign, and the entire real-estate promotion collapsed. Mr. Elliott, my chief, was reinstated with an increase in salary.

A few months after this incident my appointment to the Office of Drainage Investigations was quietly cancelled. A Florida congressman who had protested publication of the bulletin to the secretary of agriculture received the response that the Department of Agriculture was not in the business of protecting ignorant people from promotion literature. Presumably, that attitude was behind my dismissal.

Shortly after I left the Department, I became involved in another incident relating to the Florida Everglades. The governor of Florida had decided to drain Lake Okeechobee. From what I knew of the situation, that would prove fatal to the Everglades ecology and damaging to the public interest in other ways. A group of Florida citizens implored me to help them oppose the governor's contemplated action. When I spoke to the governor, he replied, "When I have an illness, I do not consult a blacksmith, and where state government is concerned, I do not consult an engineer." In the meantime the governor had sold a state bond issue to a New York investment banker.

The citizens who had employed me had previously consulted about a dozen bankers and investment attorneys whose names I had provided as references. In every case, they were told by my references that I was in the first rank of water-control engineers. This citizens' group then sent copies of those letters of recommendation to the banker handling the bond issue. He came to Memphis, Tennessee, to discuss the matter with me, and decided as a result of our discussion to withdraw his bid. The governor tried to find other bidders, but since the issue had become publicized, he was unsuccessful, and the project collapsed for lack of funds.

An experience that occurred early in my engineering career influenced my method of handling engineering problems. The University of Minnesota, through coming into possession of land rich in iron deposits, had large financial resources. The engineering school of the University was a high-ranking institution and its dean a man of considerable standing. The dean criticized the methods that I was using in a water-control operation. I had great respect for his opinion, yet I thought that I had found the right solution. I went over my solution to the problem with great care and decided that he had made a mistake simply by having overlooked some essential facts.

This experience made a great impression on me. With less than three years of high school, I had correctly solved a problem about which the dean of a great engineering school was in error because he did not have all the facts. This clearly demonstrated to me the importance of mastery of the facts concerning a problem. I made it a rule of my engineering life that on large issues that justified the effort I would make sure of my facts and principles before reaching a final conclusion. I decided that in such cases I would examine even unpopular and commonly discredited solutions, an approach that I called "conclusive engineering analysis." As my work progressed, I expanded the application of this principle. Often I found men employing methods and policies in business or in other areas of life that were so common as to be rarely questioned, but that neglected important principles of action.

In view of my limited education, my commitment to this principle required much added effort. I shall mention two instances in which I used conclusive engineering analysis. The first concerned the Little River Drainage District, consisting of half a million acres in southeast Missouri, which was, I believe, the largest organized drainage district in the United States. The engineers and attorneys of the District had spent ten years in perfecting its engineering designs and its legal structure. When the plans were completed they were submitted to Isham Randolph and Anson Marsden, the two foremost water engineers in the Midwest, who unreservedly approved them.

Then, to raise the money to construct the system, the District sold bonds to a broker. It is usual in such cases for the broker who purchases the bonds to arrange for an independent examination of the plans so that he can announce to the public that they have been reviewed and approved. I was appointed to make such an examination of the Little River Drainage District.

It was clear that the plans would do what was demanded. The drainage district, which was once the upper tip of the Gulf of Mexico, was now a huge tract of fertile but flat and undrained land. The Little River flowed from the Missouri hills and emptied onto this plain as it used to empty into the Gulf of Mexico. In ordinary seasons the proposed drainage system would effectively drain this land and produce large crop yields. But the District did not have enough money to make provisions for drainage of the Little River basin in the event of a great flood of the type that occurs only once or twice in a century. While ordinary floods on the Little River might have a discharge of twenty thousand cubic feet per second, a great flood might have a discharge of more than a hundred thousand cubic feet per second.

The construction of flood-control reservoirs, having been condemned for half a century by the Army Corps of Engineers, was dismissed from consideration. Under the proposed drainage system, the land could be settled and might prosper for a generation or two, only to be stricken by a devastating flood, with vast destruction of property and great loss of life, and the settlers on the land would be left to shift for themselves.

Only five million dollars was available for the project, whereas a channel large enough to carry a great flood for fifty miles through the District would cost twenty million dollars or more. A conventional design would require an equally large expenditure to carry floodwaters downstream for another fifty miles in Arkansas to where there was a natural discharge opening into the Mississippi at the mouth of the St. Francis River. (The Little River is a branch of the St. Francis.) Could I report that the proposed plans were adequate? And if not, what could be done? That was the dilemma that faced me. But the engineers of the District had probably considered all the designs normally used in such cases. If there were to be a solution, it would have to be found among methods that were not usually considered. Were there such possibilities to be discovered?

I had made it a policy not to rest content with the conventional answers that were described in engineering textbooks, and in this case I found a solution that was as simple as it was unconventional. The Little River left the hill country and entered the plain about twenty miles from the Mississippi River. But since the Mississippi overflowed its banks frequently, sometimes to a depth of ten feet, it did not seem to provide a workable outlet. It was held in its channel by levees more than ten feet high. The solution I arrived at was to construct an extension of the Mississippi River levees to where the Little River came out of the hills, thereby using the hills and the levees to confine the Little River. The earth removed in making the channel could be used to build high levees far enough apart to take care of the most extreme flood. Since the length of the proposed channel under my plan was much shorter, the cost of the project would be only four and a half million dollars, or less than the cost of the original proposal. The engineers of the District reviewed my plan and approved it. A few years later Morgan Engineering Company was made chief engineer of the Little River Drainage District, which is still in effective use today.

Another instance in which I used the principle of conclusive engineering analysis was in the design of the well-known Miami Conservancy District in Ohio, the first time in American practice that reservoirs were used for flood control. During the time that I was chief engineer of the Miami District, I visited Princeton University, and the engineering school requested an audience with me. They told me that their reason for asking for the conference was to inquire how I was able to secure such uniformly excellent technical design of engineering plans. I replied that it was because I had secured Walter Smith, an engineer from a small and largely unknown technical school in North Carolina, to direct that work. That seemed to the Princeton engineers a rather crude joke. Yet that was the case. When I was searching for key men to work on the Miami project and inquired about this man of his employer, I was told that the prospect was a troublemaker. When I became acquainted with him, I learned that because of his persistence in excellence he was sometimes in trouble with conventional engineers who worked for him. I made further inquiries concerning him, found him to be a very creative person, and employed him. When there was conflict between him and his assistants, I told them that they might well bear with his exactions and acquire some of his rare skill, which they did. When the Miami Conservancy District construction was approaching completion, he left to become chief engineer of another large project, and one of his assistants became his successor.

About 80 percent of our engineering staff were engineering-school graduates, but the three highest-paid members of the staff were not college or technical-school graduates. The man who was paid more than three times as much as any other had had only two years of formal schooling. As chief engineer, I had less than three years of high school. The third-highest-paid engineer had gone only partway through Massachusetts Institute of Technology. One department head was not even a high-school graduate.

The American Society of Civil Engineers held one of its annual meetings at the site of the Miami Conservancy District during its construction, and half a century later, in March 1972, designated the system as a national historic engineering monument. Besides innovating the use of flood-control reservoirs, the Miami Conservancy District was the first project in America to work out a complete classification system for national records of flood rainfall and runoff. In this work it preceded the United States Weather Bureau, the Army Corps of Engineers, and the Reclamation Service. It also pioneered in the design of spillways and in the understanding of their limitations.

Its construction camps set a precedent by providing homes and modern school facilities for the families of many of its employees. Labor policies were devised that supplemented union rules and made some of them unnecessary. In adopting most of those innovations, the TVA was a direct successor of the Miami Conservancy District.

As the person responsible for flood-control plans for the Miami Valley, I drafted legislation that became the Conservancy Law of Ohio. Naturally, I used the services of an attorney in the selection of legal language for the law, but the policy and the methods with which it dealt were my own and to a considerable extent created new methods for such work.

My firm, the Morgan Engineering Company, also acted as chief engineer of the Muskingum Conservancy District in eastern Ohio, a project costing fifty million dollars and including six reservoirs. Although I left this and other work of the Morgan Engineering Company to become chairman of the TVA, the overall policy and design, including provisions for recreational use of the project, were decided upon before I left, and one of my engineers succeeded me as chief engineer.

Later, I became chief engineer of other large flood-control projects. My company or I engineered large works in Arkansas, Mississippi, Colorado, and New Mexico. In carrying out each of these projects, I attempted to live and work by the principles I had adopted.

Chapter Six

Vagaries

As President Roosevelt recognized so clearly, the principle of a full and varied culture is not just a casual notion but the criterion of a good society. We should each develop knowledge of those aspects of life necessary to full personal and social development. A person who is unaware of the importance of nutrition may be sentencing himself to a shortened span of life. An individual who has not acquired competence in managing his personal affairs may go through life financially handicapped. And one who lacks a knowledge of the elements of good government is contributing to a weakened society.

A society that does not encourage vital elements of culture results in a less rich way of life for its people. A community that has only one type of culture, a farming community or mill town, for example, probably will be a poor place to develop a full personhood. A society should offer many different outlooks, which will present the opportunity for the development of varied interests, open to a wide range of people, with both the freedom and incentive for many kinds of expression. Further, this should be as true of making a living as of cultural development. Because I had grown up and lived in towns with limited cultural and economic resources, I was determined to try to encourage fuller concepts of living conditions.

I lived for some time in the village of Yellow Springs, Ohio, which once had a strong and active cultural life centered around Antioch College under Horace Mann. But it had little else. After Mann died, the college, and community with it, declined. Upon graduation, young people did not find an adequate variety of activities calling for able men and women, and they left for larger communities. As a result, Yellow Springs lost many of its most able men and women.

I assumed the presidency of Antioch with the aim of educating students in a wide range of important fields through a work-study program. The students spent part of their time at school and part at work, with many choices. No one studied only mathematics or literature or biology or government; each student was introduced to many fields, including some, like the management of personal finances or diet, that are usually thought to require only general human experience. Antioch College was the first liberal-arts college in America to adopt such a program. Over one hundred colleges have since followed its example.

The town sprouted widely varied industrial and cultural enterprises. Many young people were attracted to the college because they desired a wide choice of activities. Upon graduation they had developed a broad range of capabilities and were prepared to explore and contribute to areas of life that much of society leaves undeveloped.

As I discussed the TVA with President Roosevelt, it seemed to me that for twelve years in Yellow Springs I had been actively engaged in an undertaking that was almost identical in spirit to the one he outlined. The TVA seemed to offer a chance to create a new cultural environment, where almost no field would be closed to a competent, able person. I was surprised and pleased to find that Roosevelt had much the same outlook: he wanted the country to loosen up and become conscious of a wide variety of economic and cultural interests. He wanted a new breath of life.

It was common for public works to be undertaken on limited projects of definite scope, such as highways, water control, electric power, and building construction, and the TVA legislation included such programs. However, the President had a more inclusive vision in mind for the Tennessee Valley. To his mind, it should be concerned with every aspect of the region's well-being. There were few areas in America with such a poor and narrowly based agriculture and economy as the mountainous parts of the Tennessee Valley, but he believed in the possibility of its rebirth and larger life. President Roosevelt talked to me about his early experiences as a traveler in the undeveloped parts of Georgia and South Carolina, Tennessee and Virginia. He told of his long-standing hope that he might help to give a new life and culture to the long-neglected descendants of those indentured servants who had, before the days of slavery, largely made up the working class of southern agriculture. The principle of the all-round development of life is only gradually emerging to consciousness. Because of FDR's vision it became a major consideration in the TVA.

My primary hope for the TVA when it was set up in 1933 was that it might create a new spirit and attitude in a public service. I believed that fresh ideas and undertakings in better living might be as important a service as the control of rivers and the production of power, and I felt free to explore them in any way that seemed to carry out the spirit of the TVA and the President's objectives.

To the other two directors, the prospect was different. Harcourt Morgan's dominant concern was the need for a revolution in the technique of using fertilizers. To David Lilienthal, on the other hand, the faulty and wasteful process by which electrical energy was generated and distributed appeared to be a major condition inhibiting the development of the country, and he saw that issue as the dominant one for the TVA.

On October 30, 1933, after the TVA had been in existence for about five months, the other board members summoned me to a meeting and strongly condemned the range of variety in my undertakings, which were later referred to as "vagaries" in the congressional hearings of 1938. They considered many of my ideas—those not directly related to the fertilizer program or to the production and sale of electric power—eccentric and of little practical importance, and told me I must stop those activities and limit myself to the specific provisions of the TVA Act. On the following day, their protest was published as a front-page story in a special midday edition of the *Chattanooga News*.

When Harcourt Morgan took issue with my undertakings, I told him that President Roosevelt, when he asked me to be chairman of the TVA, had spent very little time discussing dams, power plants, power distribution, or fertilizer, but had talked primarily about the general advancement of the Tennessee Valley region. I suggested that he visit the President and clarify his own ideas on that point. To this Dr. Morgan, his mind evidently on the issue between nitrate and phosphate fertilizer (the TVA Act had stipulated nitrate fertilizer, while the

The Making of the TVA

region's need was for phosphate fertilizer), replied vigorously, "I know what I want and I do not intend to see the President!"

Mr. Lilienthal was also scornful of my activities, particularly of the training program for the TVA labor force. He seemed to class my efforts with basket-making and other home handicrafts, and with a few exceptions, such as the elimination of malaria, looked upon them as trivial. In fact, the other two directors, in outlining their own fields of activity and in undertaking to circumscribe mine, gave me the distinct impression that it was not my overall view of the TVA that they opposed but rather Roosevelt's new approach to government, which was perhaps his main contribution as president. Their opposition to my wider interests was in effect striking at the President through me. Harcourt Morgan's reply to me expressed such an attitude. The following conversation between Lilienthal and the President, recorded in Lilienthal's *Journals*, illustrates the differences between us.

> [The President:]... "[Arthur Morgan] is a human engineer—he likes the idea of getting people out of the coves and onto a better way of living. You aren't a human engineer."...
>
> (I didn't say so, of course, but as I said later to Bob La Follette, I don't believe that that is the way to get a better living for people, by human engineering them—and Bob nodded. Welfare work and economic revision are two different things—I don't have much confidence in the first.)*

The other directors stopped entirely all of my work in land development for economic and recreational use, in forestry and forest genetics, in the prevention of soil erosion, and—with a vehemence that was only temporarily successful—in the establishment of a fine-porcelain industry. The other directors sought to confine my efforts to the building of dams, power plants, reservoirs, and locks for navigation. They held that no type of work that was not specifically mentioned in the TVA Act was legal (even though Harcourt Morgan was greatly altering the Act by substituting phosphate for nitrate fertilizer).

During my administration, I sought widely and carefully for people with vision to serve in the TVA. In various cases these individuals took a deep interest in their projects, and when the opposition within the board was no longer present, they were able to take direct action.

As the new spirit began to assert itself, these values began to be recognized to such an extent that the following statement occurs in the TVA's expression of its

---

*Lilienthal, p. 66.

aims and principles in the Thirty-Eighth Annual TVA Report to the President and Congress, reported in the "TVA News," January 1971.

> The Tennessee Valley today is ahead of most other areas of the nation in the quality of its environment, but the region must answer the critical national need for broad perspectives in developing and conserving resources if it is to capitalize on this opportunity, the TVA told the President and Congress today in its 38th annual report.
>
> "Industrial growth is helping to disperse population in the Valley region, countering the national trend toward the creation of giant metropolitan clusters with all of their myriad ills," the TVA Board of Directors reported. "The people who are filling these new jobs still have access to the essential ingredients for a satisfying living and working environment."
>
> The TVA Board outlined the need for a variety of programs aimed at improving the quality of life in the Valley as part of a new pattern of living geared to the needs of a people who for the most part will depend for their existence on the industrial society we have become.
>
> "It is in reaching this goal that TVA continues to offer its greatest opportunity to contribute to regional and national progress," the Board declared.

If I had remained in charge of the TVA, it is doubtful whether I could have given its purpose a better definition.

As I continued to express myself on various issues, those who disapproved developed the habit of charging me with being an impractical "idealist." Mr. Lilienthal referred over and over again to my nonengineering activities by names implying that they were busywork, but for many persons they made the difference between a good and a poor quality of life, and the cultural carry-over from such work made a marked difference in the life of many TVA families. A large engineering project may be looked upon narrowly as a purely economic process, or it can be seen in terms of its widest possible effects on the lives of the people concerned. Mr. Lilienthal contrasted engineering in a business sense with what he termed "welfare work." But large-scale civil-engineering projects, unless they are guided by a quality of human intelligence and overall concern, may prove to be somewhat hollow.

From the vantage point of the years that have passed, I have reassessed some of these proposals of mine. I believe that many of them pointed the way to a fuller and richer design for living that would have stood the test of time. I find that some of those I was able to implement have set up successful patterns of action and cooperation, not only in the Tennessee Valley, but also in other areas of the country.

The Making of the TVA

What follows is a discussion of several of my ventures and their outcomes. While some of them were stopped altogether and others met with derision, some received a grudging tolerance that in several instances later became full acceptance and admiration.

A LOCAL ECONOMY FOR THE TENNESSEE VALLEY

The most severe criticism of my TVA career concerns a mistaken report of a talk that I gave at a regional meeting of the University of Tennessee in November 1933. Harcourt Morgan, a former president of the University of Tennessee, was one of those present. He did not hear all of the talk and did not discuss it with me, but made a public statement about it in Washington that received nationwide publicity. He reported that I had proposed a separate money system for the Tennessee Valley. Today, after nearly forty years, that statement is still presumed to be historically correct in published studies concerning my activities.

At that time, in the midst of the Great Depression, legal tender in rural Tennessee Valley areas was exceedingly scarce. A survey of one mountain county reported, as I recall, that the average cash income per family was about fifty dollars per year. A large part of the economic life of many Tennessee Valley communities was stopped because the local inhabitants did not have the legal tender to pay each other for services, and the tradition of barter had disappeared. The farmer could not go to the dentist because he could not pay his bill. The dentist could not have leaky plumbing repaired because he had no money with which to pay his bill. The plumber could not buy fruit and vegetables, the farmer could not hire labor, and so forth. Much of the local productive capacity was idle.

I suggested that individual small communities, or a few working together, set up a local credit exchange, with exchange credit coupons, to relieve this terrible economic paralysis. Just before the TVA was organized, I had initiated such an exchange in Yellow Springs, where it was serving usefully.

The small amounts of federal currency earned by sales or services outside the community could be used for paying taxes, buying refrigerators and other necessities not produced locally, or for sending the young people to college. The gist of Gresham's Law in economics is that money having less intrinsic value tends to remain in circulation, while that having greater value tends to be hoarded or exported. In other words, the "cheap money" would stay at home to do the local economic chores, and the "dear money" (federal) would be free to go outside the area. Such a program might stimulate the general economy by allowing legal tender to move more easily where only it would serve, and a local and limited medium of exchange might stimulate local employment and sales of local commodities.

This proposal, which was reported as advocating a separate coinage for the TVA area, received national criticism because it was not understood. My suggestion was directed to abnormal circumstances existing in particular areas. I believe that, with certain amplifications and with the omission of some parts that related particularly to the extreme depression at that time, this talk would serve as a fundamentally sound and important statement of a feasible and effective way to greatly reduce the present tendency for half a million persons to leave small communities each year for metropolitan centers, creating our massive urban problems.

The other members of the board opposed my suggestion and it was not initiated.

FOREST USE AND LAND MISUSE

Many of the early fortunes in the United States were acquired by clever manipulation (stealing would be a bad word) of the public domain under the homestead laws. Under those laws a man could acquire ownership of a tract of the unoccupied public domain by living on it for five years. It was assumed that by that time he would be a permanent settler.

In many instances, however, the homestead laws did not work as intended, but provided instead several means by which speculators and business enterprises could acquire great wealth. The laws did not, for example, distinguish between types of land. Some, like that in northern Minnesota and Wisconsin, was covered by dense forest. There was, however, little market for timber near the land covered by the law, and the average man who settled the land could not afford to process his timber and transport it to distant markets. As a result, speculators and lumber companies reaped most of the profits from timber sales. Many men occupied forest tracts intermittently, enough to meet the requirements of the law, and then sold them for one or two dollars an acre to lumber companies. The companies would then cut the timber and sell it many miles away from where it grew, floating it down a river made navigable at government expense. Many lumber speculators hired men at low wages to live on a tract until they received title to it, and then they would sell it to the lumber company.

Gas and oil rights could be acquired by companies in the same way. Since the

The Making of the TVA

average settler did not have enough money to drill for gas and market it, the temptation existed for him to sell his homestead for as much as he could get for it. Property owners who sold the mineral rights to their land discovered later that "mineral rights" were held to include not only underground minerals to be reached by deep mines but also the land just beneath the surface, which would be strip-mined.

In the East, including the land that was in the Tennessee Valley area, the pattern was somewhat different. Homesteads were not acquired under the homestead laws but rather by occupation of land according to ancient rules governing settlement of unoccupied land. Thousands of poor settlers established ownership of tracts in this way. For lumber companies to acquire the timber, they need only pay the price for which the landowner, who lacked the resources, experience, or skill to make use of the timber himself, would sell his land, since it was common in this area to sell the land as well as the timber. There had been so little demand for land that it commonly sold, with timber, gas, and oil, for fifty cents to two dollars an acre. When this small amount had been spent, the former landowner was penniless and dependent on whatever work he could get. Many of these people used the money they got for their land to pay their way to Chicago, Detroit, or some other large northern city, and when the depression of the thirties came, they found themselves out of work and in desperate straits. Their parents back in the mountains often used the few dollars they had to pay their children's way home, where poverty in the midst of natural wealth was already very severe.

When I began working for the TVA, I hoped to develop small businesses for the owners of timberland and to try to keep ownership in the hands of the local people until that could be done. I planned to assemble the timberlands under groups of owners into tracts of about five thousand acres and to help the present owners to start small garden tracts and to use their timber to start small industries. Perhaps financial help could be obtained from the government until they could get on their feet. I believed that with such help timber could become a permanent resource for them and their communities, as is the case in many of the better-managed areas of Europe. It was after the board of directors placed me in charge of the forest program that I first became acquainted with the European system, which works as follows:

> Just recently I was talking with the forester of the TVA about a recent trip he had made to Europe. He was telling of a little community in Switzerland and was showing me pictures of it. Over seven hundred years ago somebody gave that com-

munity a few hundred acres of woodland. Instead of cutting it as quickly as possible, that community began to care for its forest. Every year they would cut only the timber that was ripe and save the rest. And on through the centuries, for seven hundred years, that forest has been a permanent resource to the community. They take care of the wild game and get considerable income from hunting. They care for the fish and get income from fishing. And that entire area of forest has been paying them five or six dollars an acre through all those years. Additional tracts have been bought until now there are two or three thousand acres. That town pays all of its taxes out of the income from its forests.

That is a picture of what might happen in a well-managed community. I have traveled through parts of Europe—Austria, Hungary, Romania, Italy, Germany, Switzerland, and France. I have seen these little town forests. I have seen them cared for so that they are not a burden but a source of wealth.*

I located a creative and energetic young forester, Ned Richards, and we began to work out a somewhat unconventional forest policy. A large part of the Tennessee Valley region is mountain land on which the forest dominates. Much of this land had been badly managed for generations and was yielding much less than its potential. Considerable portions of it were burned over each year in order to increase the yield of grass for cattle, a process that killed many of the young trees and marred others. As useful trees were cut for lumber, deformed trees and the least useful species often were left to grow, so that in many areas the yield was considerably less than half that of a well-tended forest. Much of the land was owned in small tracts of a few hundred acres or less, and the owners of land along the small-stream valleys, which was cleared and planted with corn and tobacco, made a meager living.

Through the years, large lumber companies bought up the land at low prices and let the forest grow. As a result, large areas came under single ownership and thus became unusable for normal community development. Ned Richards worked out a radically new forest policy that had promise. He planned to develop forest districts of a few thousand to several thousand acres, depending on circumstances. Many forest areas were large enough to support a small community by forest work, with the help of the small valley gardens that could be developed along brooks and rivers.

Mr. Richards marked the boundaries of one or two such forest districts and began to train a group of foresters to manage such tracts. He also planned to employ and train local residents for this purpose. Besides preventing forest fires, they would cut out trees and species unsuitable for lumber and sell that part for

---

*From my speech to the Lower Tennessee Valley Association, Murray, Ky., May 16, 1934.

The Making of the TVA

firewood or use the best of it for cabinetwork. The several lumber centers would develop varied technical uses for wood products. In some cases, the local timber industry would produce special woods, such as walnut, cherry, white pine, or the rare bird's-eye maple. Some of the tracts would be large enough to support schools for training cabinetmakers, breeders of fruit trees, and dairy farmers. People could raise their food in the little mountain valleys or become members of bean and tomato cooperatives (like those being developed in another of my projects). Here and there a tract would be specially equipped for training people in forestry or in crafts related to forestry. The people who worked each forest tract would have the opportunity to build a community center if the tract was not located close to a town or village.

This program would make possible varied industrial development, very different from the vast individual timber holdings that leave the little mountain valleys uncultivated, with few or no woodwork craftsmen and most of the local people working as hired laborers. While extensive tracts owned by large companies might be left intact for purposes such as papermaking, it seemed more socially desirable to have a variety of local industrial centers, each with its population center. The extent to which development of special-wood industries was feasible could not be determined quickly, but one such unit had been organized and was at work; it included small-scale farming and a residence center.

> With a hundred species of hardwood, studies are being made for small cooperative industries based on special uses for particular woods. A forest policy is evolving. Abandoned lands are being acquired, several million trees are being raised for reforesting, and a training program for practical foresters is being prepared. A trained man will be provided with a cottage and some farm and garden land. He can pay his rent by working in the forest and can raise the food he needs in his garden. He can get a cash income by making wood products with a cooperative, by working an orchard, raising nut crops, chicken and egg farming, by raising wild game or fur animals, or by some one of various other small industries being planned. As forests mature, cutting, sawing, and manufacturing timber products will support a considerable population. A training course is being developed for forest work.
>
> The raising of tree crops to supply food for hogs, and tree products for sale, is being promoted, and large research and breeding nurseries are already planted. Hickories, pecans, walnuts, Japanese and Chinese chestnuts, Japanese and Chinese persimmons, mulberries, paw-paws and other tree crops are being developed for land too hilly for plow crops.*

---

*From my speech to the Engineering Club and other groups, Madison, Wis., Oct. 1, 1934.

Vagaries

In the field of forestry the same policies should hold. We are endeavoring to cooperate with the foresters of this region and with the foresters of the United States government. We find a large number of possible associations, some of them purely governmental, some of them partly so, and some of them private. We are finding a good many organizations through the country ready and anxious to cooperate with us, such as the American Forestry Association, the National Parks Organization, organizations for social relief and for social development. We are finding it possible to help in the coordination of many agencies.*

A program like the one my assistant and I were trying to develop would have substantially modified the culture of the area. Instead of vast forest areas owned and administered by outside corporations, there could have been locally owned and cooperatively managed forest industries that would strengthen the local culture by giving more people an active concern for the interests and development of the area. Many elements of the timber industry might have developed as varied phases of a "forest culture," sharing in a widely distributed administration and technology, and not have been confined to subordinate functions in great industries.

Instead, the program was stopped by the other two members of the board voting as a majority, and the men who were working in the program were summarily discharged. Much of the land was then made available, at fifty cents to two dollars an acre, to lumber companies and others, who then stripped it of its forests. The former owners were left in poverty. Every year that such practices continued made still more difficult the task of correcting the conditions on which I had been working. This instance was one of the most serious interferences by the other directors with work that had been assigned to me.

In the early days of the TVA, I repeatedly discussed land use and misuse. On several occasions I expressed my views before civic groups and other organizations.

> I was traveling through parts of Europe a few years ago. In the southern part of Greece I saw a region that once was one of the garden spots of the world. It had raised a hardy breed of men who had lived largely by agriculture. The greatest civilization of the world existed there. But they did not take good care of the soil and there is nothing left of it today. The soil has washed away to clay or rock, and agriculture has shrunk and the population has shrunk. What was once fertile land is now barren hillside with little herds of goats picking bits of grass from among

---

*From my speech to the Central States Forestry Congress, Knoxville, Tenn., May 30, 1934.

the rocks and with poverty-stricken peasants watching the goats. The whole civilization was destroyed through lack of care of the soil.

A few centuries ago the population of Spain was about forty million people. The Inquisition drove away or put to death the abler leaders of the country. About two hundred thousand men were killed, and many more were driven away. That masterful leadership was to some extent destroyed, and then nature took its course. The hillsides washed and fertility disappeared. Today the population of Spain is less than half what it was five or six hundred years ago. I have been through Portugal where the same process has taken place until what was once a rich land is now barren rocky hillside. There is one little area of a few square miles that through the centuries has been kept as a natural forest—a sort of king's preserve. There are great trees, over one hundred feet high, wonderful fertility, a vegetation almost tropical in its luxuriance. But you can go a mile away and find barren hillsides, denuded of fertility.

A great part of China is desert. I am told that those parts of China were in forest when America was discovered and that the whole process of cutting and cultivation and destruction has taken place during the time that our country has been settled; it does not take many centuries.*

The President is aware of that great waste. It comes slowly, insidiously, unnoticed. But unless it is stopped, in large areas of the South—I speak very plainly—civilization is going to slip back. When half the land is washed away and the rest is poor, the ambitious man, the man of energy and initiative, will not stay. There will be no schools in the region, no roads. He will go where there are better conditions, and by and by the leadership goes and there is left an inferior population. That is lack of planning. It is not the lack of planning of any industrial magnate but of the average American. So when our President is trying to impress upon the people of the country that planlessness is expensive for today and for the future, he is not pointing the finger at any one man or any one case, but is saying to all of us: "We have been careless. Let us wake up and take hold of our resources before it is too late."

How are we going to do it? There are many ways to begin. The President has asked us of the Tennessee Valley Authority repeatedly to begin a land use survey to determine the best use of the land. To the northwest of us, one or two hundred miles from here, you will find an example of the wrong use of land. The soil has washed away so badly that people have been crowded back into the hills and are farming on hillsides steeper than the roofs of your houses here in town. And because the people have no resources and are starving, they clear off these steep hillsides to grow a few crops of corn; before long this land also washes away and has to be abandoned. Then they move on to the next patch, and so the destruction creeps along the hills. The President would like to have land classified, with land that cannot be used for agriculture without being destroyed required to be used for forest. Even though the big timber has been cut off and only second growth remains,

---

*The People's Republic of China has now undertaken to change the economy and the social attitudes of a nation of eight hundred million people to bring about such changes as I have described.

if it is taken care of it will be good timber and a permanent resource in a few years.

In one of the hardest stricken counties of the region, where all the good timber has been taken off and people are desperate, I estimated that under good forestry conditions almost the entire population of that county could be employed in taking care of the timber—thinning it out, using it properly. If this were handled as a permanent industry and not as loot, it might insure almost enough work in the woods alone to keep the population living decently with an income ten times what they are getting today. So the land-use planning is one of the President's hopes.*

In no area were my proposals and plans more abruptly interfered with and stopped short than in land-use planning. The rest of the board, Harcourt Morgan in particular, held that land-use planning is an individual matter, that a man can do whatever he pleases with his land and no outsider has the right to interfere. In this field my plans never got into full operation. I doubt whether the TVA region has even as yet fully recovered from this setback. In parts of Mississippi and Alabama, for instance, there are large areas that have been destroyed because land use has been so unskilled. With the timber cut off, the loess soil (an unstratified deposit of yellowish brown loam) has eroded so badly that in some places a two-story building would be swallowed up by the deep gullies. Years before the TVA was organized, in my work in Mississippi, I was laboring with the problem of land use, but I had no legal support. I hoped for such support in the TVA but did not receive it. "Practical minds" were turned in other directions.

FOREST GENETICS

Why should not forest growth and forest quality be improved by genetics, just as the production and quality of apples, pears, plums, pecans, and black walnuts are vastly improved by genetic research and experiment? When I was president of Antioch College, I had our able biologist, Dr. Ondess Inman, investigate what was being done in the field of forest genetics. This inquiry indicated that, aside from genetic experiments with a few fruit and nut crops and a very limited study of the development of aspen trees for pulpwood, almost no forest-genetic work had been done in America. Our own vast National Forest Service seemed to be entirely unconcerned with that field. We made some initial plantings at Antioch, and the project continues there on a small scale; it includes, among other trees, some chestnuts that are not subject to the chestnut blight.

After my appointment to the TVA, I located a man, John Hershey, who was

*From my speech to the Civic Clubs, Huntsville, Ala., May 18, 1934.

The Making of the TVA

doing practical work in forest genetics, and persuaded him to join the staff. His work was only reluctantly tolerated by the rest of the board, and continued only on a very small scale. When I left the TVA, John Hershey, not seeing any remaining interest in the program, also left. The program was later prohibited altogether. When the prohibition disappeared under a later administration, the project was revived and has thrived. As sometimes happens in human affairs, small-scale ideas and efforts persist over all obstacles. When Hershey left the TVA, he left behind a young man whom he had interested in forest genetics. This young man, L. V. Kline, continued his study of forest genetics until his untimely death in 1950, and today in the TVA Kline's influence is still felt.

It is now generally understood that certain trees and subspecies are of greater breeding value than others and should be preserved for that purpose, whereas ordinary lumbering removes the best varieties first, leaving the inferior strains to reproduce. The TVA forestry staff now searches throughout the TVA area and beyond for trees that appear to be of rare genetic quality. In the forty thousand square miles in the TVA region, 167 exceptional hardwood trees, representing six species, have been found and are being perserved. An attempt is also being made to interest schoolchildren in the region in receiving seeds from genetically superior trees and carrying out their own small forestry projects under the direction of their schools and the TVA Forestry Agency. Thus, not only is the importance of forest genetics being recognized, but new generations of children are taking an active interest in forest development.

The following excerpts from a letter that I received September 16, 1971, from Thomas H. Ripley, director of the Division of Forestry, Fisheries, and Wildlife Development for the Tennessee Valley Authority, indicate the current status of the genetics program.

> As I'm sure you are aware, early efforts to improve tree crops have evolved into pine and hardwood tree improvement programs. Loblolly, shortleaf, Virginia, and white pines as well as black walnut, black cherry, yellow poplar, white oak, chestnut oak, and northern red oak are included in this program. The genetic improvement of timber and fiber producing trees is our goal and the characteristics of straightness, fast growth, pruning ability, and others mentioned in your letter are traits we are looking for.
>
> We need to always keep in mind the total TVA goal—a better Tennessee Valley. That is why we have chosen the above species. They comprise most of the forests in the Valley.
>
> Breeding these trees, although not too difficult, is very time consuming in terms of growing the end product to see what you've developed. Right now we are selecting outstanding individual trees. These are being grafted and the grafts of all se-

lections of a given species are planted together in a seed orchard. As they develop and begin to produce flowers, we hope they will cross-pollinate within the orchard, thus accomplishing your suggestion of crossing superior selections by Mother Nature's method. At the same time, we control-pollinate in species where this is feasible and observe the progenies for superior characteristics.

We feel we are starting things—being pioneers, so to speak. The real payoff will begin in 10 to 15 years when the developed trees are large enough to evaluate.

Seed of these trees may produce offspring of rare value. However, that promise is greatest if both parents are of superior quality, or where branches of such trees are used for grafts. These rare excellent specimens are the Shakespeares and the Leonardo da Vincis of the forest world.

Forest genetics in the TVA is well begun, and the spirit of inquiry lives vigorously; given time and good management, forest production in the TVA may increase greatly in quantity and quality. As to the long-range effects of forest genetics and forest culture, it does not seem impossible that large forest areas of the TVA may someday produce five or more times as great a value of timber as was being produced in 1933, when the TVA was organized. Our country needs those products.

FINE PORCELAIN

The Appalachian region was often exploited as a source of raw materials to be taken elsewhere for processing and manufacture. One of Franklin Roosevelt's objectives was to increase employment and economic well-being through the TVA by having the people of the region process and manufacture finished products from the area's raw materials. The importance of this is demonstrated by the fact that the industrialized economy of Switzerland supports a far larger population on a small fraction of the area and resources of the Tennessee Valley. I was, therefore, on the lookout for such possibilities, which the TVA could help to develop.

It came to my attention through the late S. T. Henry of Spruce Pine, North Carolina, that in the mountains of that state there were large deposits of an especially fine quality of kaolin, or disintegrated feldspar, as natural dikes, or strata, in the mountains. Most kaolins have been deposited under water, and in the process they become slightly mixed with some other mineral, which makes them unfit for the better tableware products, such as fine porcelain.

I located an especially capable ceramics engineer, Robert Gould, who wanted to return home from Poland, where he had been developing a fine-porcelain industry. He was well informed and an inventive genius. After only a few years he developed very fine porcelain products in a pilot plant at Norris, Tennessee, by methods that greatly reduced the labor cost. His aim was to put a good quality of porcelain into the five-and-ten-cent stores. It seemed to me that here was an especially promising field for an industry, using the fine, undiluted raw material found in this area.

This project was disapproved and stopped in the TVA area by the other members of the board, but was later renewed by the Bureau of Mines. Mr. Gould left and set up a prosperous porcelain industry near Niagara Falls, New York.

Today, with the rebirth of varied interests, the rural population in the TVA area is not flocking to the cities, as in so much of the United States, but is finding productive activities near home.

A memo from the TVA Technical Library in Knoxville, Tennessee, dated October 11, 1973, tells briefly the story of the Ceramics Research Laboratory at Norris.

> TVA's Ceramics Research Laboratory was established in April, 1934. In July F. W. Weigel, of TVA's Industry Division, submitted a report which concluded that the ceramics industry in the South would have advantages in low-cost labor and availability of raw materials. In December 1934 R. E. Gould, Chief Ceramics Engineer, was sent to Europe to inspect successful ceramics plants which used electric kilns. He concluded that the electric process could be competitive where power was cheap.
>
> Laboratory work was started in a building located at Norris in March 1935, the work being directed toward three ends: development of raw materials, development of electric kilns, and development of processes for the production of a truly American vitreous dinnerware which would be competitive with foreign brands. Due to the activities of the Laboratory, a supply of satisfactory primary kaolin was located in Western North Carolina. This kaolin is of good plasticity, of fairly high and uniform dry strength, excellent firing color, and quite long firing range. It was determined that this material must be handled in ways somewhat different from the English materials. Considerable work was also done on the technique of electric firing.
>
> The Laboratory turned out a final product that combined the thinness, translucency, and beauty of fine china with the durability and strength of hotel ware. One of the Laboratory's special achievements was the development of new techniques which permitted workmen of only average skill to produce fine products.
>
> In 1935, under a cooperative agreement between TVA and the Harris Clay Company, research work was begun on the improvement of both the methods of mining kaolin and the refining process. Contributions were made to every step in both processes.

The Laboratory was transferred to the Bureau of Mines in 1938, apparently because the primary objectives were approaching completion, and further operation of the Laboratory by TVA was unwarranted.

Under the administration of the Bureau of Mines the program was made considerably broader. The Laboratory continued under the administration of the Bureau of Mines until October 1965, when it was closed down.

The most obvious development from the work of the Laboratory is the Pigeon Forge Pottery at Pigeon Forge, Tennessee. This was started by Douglas Fergusson, a former TVA employee, in 1946 and has been highly successful.

There has been considerable development of the ceramics industry in the Tennessee Valley. It is difficult to say how much of this development has been due to the work of the Laboratory, but there is obviously some connection. The National Ceramics Society is constructing a building for their national headquarters at Cosby, Tennessee, perhaps attracted by the local development of the ceramics industry.

RECREATION THROUGH CONSERVATION

Recreation is not a casual thing: it is an essential for a well-balanced life. On the other hand, it should be part of a well-balanced life and not the main issue.*

I saw recreation as having an important future in the TVA area. As far as I was able, I kept title to marginal forest land acquired in the process of purchasing reservoir right-of-way and to a strip of land a quarter of a mile wide around each reservoir. The purpose was to control the development of the area, especially of its recreation facilities. After I left the Authority that policy was largely discontinued and only that land that would be actually submerged by construction of the reservoirs was bought. The board gave away or sold one hundred thousand acres of land that were reserved for recreation. But the concept continued to live and the program has since been reactivated. The TVA is now actively concerned with recreation and has retained ownership of sizable areas for that purpose.

The policy of buying only that land that was to be flooded by construction of the reservoirs disregarded human interests: a farmer who sold that part of his land that would be submerged might be left with only several acres, too small a tract to continue as a workable farm. In short, a farmer might not be paid for his entire tract and be left too little land to sell or work effectively. Because of his limited acquaintance with business affairs and the smallness of the tract, he could not turn his remaining land into a recreation area. But if many such farms

*From my remarks to the National Recreation Congress, Washington, D.C., Nov. 1934.

were purchased as wholes, the combined fragments remaining above water could be turned by the TVA into a valuable recreation area.

In its project "The Land Between the Lakes" the TVA is creating one of the outstanding large-scale outdoor-recreation and environmental-education areas in the nation, in a location where it can be reached in a day's drive by perhaps a third of the American population. A considerable area of land between two reservoirs has been developed, with wildlife and forests and undergrowth that have few equals. For instance, a fine buffalo herd is being developed there, and the area is visited by more than two million people a year.

These excerpts from a report by J. Porter Taylor, who is in charge of TVA shoreland purchase and use, show a continued awareness of the public need for managed recreation areas.

> Several years ago concentrated public use of underdeveloped TVA shoreland reached proportions which were creating undesirable conditions for the users and potential abuse of the land. That people were using this unimproved land to reach and enjoy TVA lakes pointed up the inadequacy of suitable access to the lakes.
>
> Public funds built these lakes and TVA has an obligation to the general public to assure their right of free access to the lakes. In recognition of this obligation, TVA has acquired land for the purpose of access even at its earliest projects. Most of this land has been placed under the administration of state and local agencies which have provided improvements for public use but have been unable to keep pace with the demand.
>
> In 1969 TVA began to improve selected areas on its reservoir shorelines and dam reservations to the minimum extent necessary to help assure safe and sanitary access for the users and to protect the land.*

The following quotation from the Thirty-Ninth Annual TVA Report (1972) tells of the continued expansion of recreational opportunities.

> Scenic rivers, lakes, historic trails, parks, and other attractive public areas figured prominently in efforts to expand recreational opportunities in the region during the past year.
>
> A canoe shuttle service on the rugged Hiwassee River in east Tennessee received widespread attention and continued to attract large numbers of users. The service provides rafts, assorted equipment, and transportation to put-in and take-out points on the scenic Hiwassee and Ocoee Rivers. The success of the river-oriented service since its beginning in 1970 has stimulated interest in the future establishment of similar services on both the Obed and Elk Rivers in Tennessee. TVA is

---

*From a mimeographed report by J. Porter Taylor, "Land Use in the TVA, 1973" (Knoxville, Tenn.)

currently exploring the recreation possibilities and float-stream potential of the two rivers with local citizens' associations. A study of the Obed by the Bureau of Outdoor Recreation is nearing completion at year's end. The study is being made in preparation for possible inclusion of the stream in the National Scenic Rivers system.

In middle Tennessee, a task force of area citizens examined the possibilities for recreational development of a 44-mile reach of the Elk River from Tims Ford Dam to Fayetteville. The proposed development, called the "Elk Recreation Riverway," emphasizes protection of scenic quality. Proposed improvements will be rustic or primitive and all activities will be planned around the stream's natural setting.

Lakeside recreational development along the shorelines of nearby Tims Ford Lake in middle Tennessee continued during the year. One marina is now in operation and a 500-site campground is being developed. Future additions being considered include overnight lodging facilities, additional marinas, shops, restaurants, public golf courses, parks, beaches, and hiking and riding trails.

The Tennessee Elk River Development Agency is in charge of overall shoreline development on Tims Ford, which focuses on residential and recreational uses. In addition to carrying out comprehensive land-use planning on the TVA-built lake, the agency has provided public access and boat launching areas.

A new water system, constructed through the cooperation of the Bear Creek Development Authority, state and local health authorities, and TVA, helped stimulate development of the Horseshoe Bend Recreation Area in North Alabama. Improvements continued to be made at the Goat Island camping and recreation area in northeastern Mississippi during the past year. Additional picnic tables, litter barrels, and electrical outlets were added and area roads and water supply facilities were upgraded. The Yellow Creek Watershed Authority, long active in making Goat Island Recreation Area into a major public-use facility, continued working with state officials and TVA representatives concerning future recreational development opportunities in the area.

Parks, scenic hiking trails, and open-space areas in wide variety are urgently needed in the rapidly urbanizing Valley of today. Such developments under way or completed through TVA's tributary-area development program during the year included: parks to serve the citizens of Highlands community, Bryson City, and Macon County in N.C.; parks in Pikeville and Whitewell, Tenn.; a joint park development for the community of Trenton and Dade County, Ga.; and a historical trail and related public recreation area on the Red Clay Council Grounds, once the tribal capital of the Cherokee Nation, in lower east Tennessee.

Development also continued on the Chatuge Shores Recreation Area in western North Carolina, and on the "Trail of Tears" [so named for the many deaths which occurred on this route taken by the Indians when they were driven from their homes to Indian Territory in Oklahoma—AEM] and the Arrowhead Trail in Tennessee. During recent years both trails have attracted a growing amount of attention for their scenic beauty and historical interest.

The creation of open space for public use in downtown areas of Valley communities is the focus of a new TVA program. In one beginning effort, for example,

TVA worked with the Walker and Dade County Development Association and the local Chamber of Commerce in LaFayette, Ga., to landscape grounds around a historic public building. Planning in other areas has been directed toward creating mini-parks in central business areas.*

A brief statement in the fortieth anniversary newsletter of the TVA is evidence that the early and complete suppression of the recreation policy was contrary to the real spirit of the President's original message to Congress. The fortieth anniversary letter notes the following with regard to recreation: "More than 900 recreation facilities have been established on TVA lakes, ranging from state and local parks and access areas to group camps and commercial docks and marinas. TVA has made land available and in many cases provided technical help in getting these facilities established."

During the latter part of my service with the TVA, I was planning a recreation area around Norris Lake. One of the tracts bordering the lake included most of the forested land within a mile or two of the town of Norris and seemed to me exceptionally well suited for development as a wild woodland playground and vacation area. That plan faltered with my departure but has since been revived and vigorously pursued. The TVA area is fortunate in having considerable land that is too rough for agriculture but suitable for camping and playgrounds. It is likewise fortunate that the present administration of the Authority is alert to these values. Each reservoir and lake now has a number of recreation areas, a situation that is a far cry from the absolute and peremptory condemnation by my colleagues on the TVA board of any interest in providing for recreation.

BEANS IN THE MOUNTAINS

Sometimes I did have "permission" for my "vagaries." In the early days of the TVA I talked with Harry Hopkins, who was the President's preferred agent for spending relief money, and he gave me three hundred thousand dollars to spend as I saw fit for relief in the TVA area. I thought such funds could be better used in ways other than direct giveaways to people in need, so I decided to finance the raising of beans in the mountains.

In the mountains of the Tennessee Valley, where people lived in deep poverty, there were many small valleys with fertile tracts too small for modern large-scale corn or wheat culture but large enough for truck farming. The high mountain

---

Thirty-Ninth Annual TVA Report (Knoxville, Tenn.: TVA, 1972), pp. 89-90.

valleys were good for growing beans. I organized the Tennessee Valley Associated Cooperative for vegetable canning and found an experienced manager and canner, John E. Barr. He encouraged the ventures in mountain bean growing and canning, canvassing the mountains, meeting the farmers, and teaching them how to raise beans. Then he built a small cannery. In only a few years there were many mountain bean growers and we had built three canneries. I asked David Lilienthal and Harcourt Morgan to be co-directors of the project with me and they agreed, though shortly afterward Mr. Lilienthal insisted that they withdraw on the grounds that the project was not an appropriate TVA activity. I found others to take their places.

After I left the TVA, I followed the progress of this cooperative project with interest, but because of the press of other commitments, I had little contact with it. It seemed to prosper under Mr. Barr until the end of World War II, when it came to grief. Shortly before the canning season, army supply agents had come to Mr. Barr and pleaded for a large planting. When he asked about a contract, he was told that the red tape would take months, which would be too late for planting, but that if planting was begun at once, a contract would follow. As an incentive for a large planting, the military purchasing officials offered an unusually high price, and Mr. Barr in turn made agreements with the growers on the basis of that price. When he pressed the army to sign the contract, he found that the agent had been moved to another territory and that no other government agent would assume responsibility for it.

After the war ended, the army did not want beans, and it was impossible to get the contract signed. Other growers were in similar straits, and canned beans were a glut on the market. It took the whole accumulated capital of the cooperative to pay the growers the contract price for their beans, which left Mr. Barr no capital to refinance the cooperative.

Before the Tennessee Valley Associated Cooperative folded as the result of the failure of the government to carry through on its agent's agreement, the amount of the original three-hundred-thousand-dollar grant had been realized two or three times over. I should have liked to have returned to the Tennessee Valley as a private citizen to reestablish the cooperative, but during this later period I was continuously engaged in other projects.

RACE RELATIONS

We also confronted the race issue in the TVA work. Through the initiative of our personnel director, Floyd Reeves, we established a three-man commission on race problems. One of the men we chose was Will Alexander, a white southerner known throughout the South for his active interest but somewhat moderate views on improving race relations. Another was the president of Fisk University, a well-known and highly respected black leader. I believed that we needed such counsel for dealing with thorny questions of race that would inevitably arise in an active public-works program in the South, but the board would have no part of it.

There were some things I could do on my own authority as the head of the construction program, like paying equal wages regardless of race. We were able to convince old-line southern union men to respect the terms of our labor policy and to work along with blacks. We had some black foremen supervising work crews that included whites. In meetings with workmen, we broke precedent by having blacks and whites meet together.

In housing I gave some ground. While we provided identical housing with equal facilities, we maintained separate housing areas. A representative of the NAACP said that he would give me no credit whatever if any trace of discrimination was left. Separate housing was certainly more than a trace, but had I tried to impose integrated housing—this was the early 1930s in the Solid South—I probably would have been out of the TVA. Another concession was made on the construction of Norris Dam, where we did not employ blacks. The following speech from 1934 describes my overall commitment.

> We hope that the Tennessee Valley Authority may bring opportunity to the people of this region and, through them, to all Americans. We hope that the black people of this region may have their fair share of this opportunity. There has, I think, been a deep sense of disappointment among black people that the Tennessee Valley Authority has not led to greater opportunity for them. They are not alone in that disappointment. For every white person who has been employed, a score must be left unemployed. We are trying to employ black people in about the same proportion that they bear to the population. In the territory from which men are employed for the Norris Dam, about 6 percent of the population is black. We are endeavoring to employ about the same percentage of black labor. In the territory from which men are employed for the Wheeler Dam, about 20 percent of the population is black. As fast as living arrangements and other conditions permit, we are increasing the employment of black men to equal their proportion of the population. Black and white workers are paid the same wages for the same work.
>
> In ways such as these, we are trying to give a fair deal to both white and black workmen. Through meetings with the Interracial Council we have tried to understand the problem. We do not claim to have done a perfect job as yet, but we do claim that we are making an honest effort.
>
> Nevertheless, with the vast unemployment, work provided by the Tennessee

Valley Authority cannot bring prosperity to this country by supplying jobs on government work. Of greater importance is the help that can be given to people, by encouragement and advice, to enable them to work out their own salvation.*

While the results were not fully satisfactory, I was striving to improve conditions. I recently received a letter from Harry Wiersema, the assistant chief engineer on dam and power-plant construction. The following comments indicate his opinion of the shortcomings of our race policy. Although I faced difficulties in maintaining suitable racial conditions, I think I might have done better in some respects noted by Mr. Wiersema.

> Personally I think this [race relations] is one of the greatest failures of the TVA. We even put in separate toilet and drinking facilities on all our dams—we certainly could have pioneered on that point.
>
> I also blame Dr. Reeves and Clapp for their timid personnel policy. Black college graduates were kept at mail carrying or other manual occupations for years and years, and only now are being used in positions of their competence. I feel somewhat to blame myself, although I tried very hard and succeeded in employing a few Howard University engineers.**

LAND ACQUISITION

The policy of land acquisition was not actually a "vagary," but I mention it here because it is a common occurrence that should involve human understanding. Since I was the chief engineer of the TVA and because I alone of the board members of the TVA had experience in purchasing land for reservoirs, it was natural that the acquisition of land for the TVA reservoirs would be primarily my responsibility.

In my extensive experience with building reservoirs, including purchasing the necessary land, I had become aware of a serious and sad deficiency in the policies of public land purchase. At that time the land-purchase policies of the government gave little consideration to human welfare. Land purchase was looked upon, by both the Army Corps of Engineers and the Forest Service, two of the largest purchasers of land for public purposes, as a routine, almost solely fiscal operation. It was my intention to give careful consideration to land purchase. However, when the other directors decided to ignore me and make ma-

---

*From my speech at Knoxville College, Knoxville, Tenn., June 12, 1934.
**Letter from Harry Wiersema to Arthur E. Morgan, Aug. 1969.

The Making of the TVA

jority decisions of the board without consulting me, one of their first acts was to take the responsibility for land acquisition from me. They appointed in my place a local man who was completely lacking in the knowledge and competence necessary for the job. I talked with him and told the other directors that he was not qualified. Shortly thereafter they were compelled to replace him because of his incompetence. (Harcourt Morgan asked me at the time the man was discharged how I could, simply by talking to a man, know that he was not competent for a job.) The man they chose as his replacement said that his predecessor's incompetence was so total that it would have been better had nothing whatever been done. The new appointee, under the dictatorial policy of the two members who constituted a quorum and acted independently of me, had the rough competence commonly associated with government land purchase. He was proceeding in the arbitrary and inconsiderate way that at the time characterized land purchase by federal agencies.

A group of women who observed some of the tragedies that were resulting from this manner of land purchase came to me and told me of this. I thereupon interfered vigorously and was able to a significant degree to bring about fair and reasonable consideration in land purchase, especially for persons with small holdings, who naturally received meager payments for the deteriorating little cabins that were the homes they had to sell. In the case of one elderly woman, whose family had kept a fire burning perpetually in their cabin for a hundred years and who refused to move unless it was kept burning, the TVA was able to move her and her still-burning fire to a new location.

There had been almost no recognition of the fact that tens of thousands of cases of land sales to the government involved an important and often tragic human experience. Of the many tracts of land purchased by these agencies, most concerned the purchase of the homes of persons who were required to sell. Most of these homeowners, usually with families and small resources, had little or no experience in the selling and relocating of their homes. In the Forest Service, for instance, purchasing agents dealt with families whose homes had been almost their only real property. The owners of the small cottage homes, especially those in the rough hill land, had become adjusted to life in small quarters and had little idea of what to do next when parted from their land. Their old houses had little monetary value, and new small homes built under modern construction conditions might cost several times as much. Government agents purchased the land, paid with a check, and said "good-bye." The man, often with a family, who sold his land had to live while finding a new home. He was hunting for a new tract when numerous persons whose homes had also been

Vagaries

bought were also looking for land, so that vacant homes were not abundant. The small amount he had received for his land was soon used up and the family was broke. Having paid the price, the government considered the transaction finished.

An example of what goes on routinely, even in more prosperous parts of America, will illustrate the need for radical change in the process of acquiring public land. A former secretary of mine grew up on a Kansas farm. Her brother had a large stock farm that was to be taken by the Corps of Engineers for a water-control project. For a considerable period he was aware that the land would be taken, but he could get no definite date. He would have to move his herd of cattle and could not find an alternative tract on the spur of the moment. Finally, a tentative date was set and he went about finding another tract for his livestock. But there was a delay in the final commitment and payment. He could not get the new farm until he could pay for it, and payment could not be made until the sale of his own farm was completed. Eventually the option on the new farm expired and he had to give it up. Then suddenly, the sale of his land was completed and he was paid, but immediate surrender of the land was demanded. To buy a farm in a well-settled community is no simple matter. On such short notice, he was not able to find another location and was compelled to sell his stock and give up cattle raising. When they finally took his land, the Corps did not share with him the risk involved in finding another farm.

I had acted as chief engineer of more than twenty water-control districts and had been involved in the acquisition of many thousands of acres of land from thousands of residents. Usually the purchases were made not by the chief engineer but by purchasing officials, who were often amateurs at such work. Frequently I would train the purchasing officials at their work and accompany them to see that they understood their responsibilities. Along with the officials whom I had trained to oversee the acquisition of land, I found that human concern and reasonable care could greatly reduce the tragic element in that process. There were several steps that one could take. First, the land to be bought should be visited personally so that one could learn the status, desires, and necessities of the family. The owners might, for example, be an elderly couple whose children had migrated to the North and who wished to use the money from the sale of their land to retire to a small community, buy a modest home, and live on the balance. Or the owner might be a young man, with a family of boys, who needed land to work, perhaps a fairly large tract that needed much developmental work that would increase its value. By assisting families in finding another location, the possible tragedy of transition might be alleviated. The purchasing organiza-

The Making of the TVA

tion might acquire a number of tracts fitting a variety of needs, among which a family that was required to sell its home could find improved circumstances.

The purchasing agent who, under Harcourt Morgan's direction, acted for the board in such cases believed that when a purchase was made the person selling the land should be located on a similar tract, which might sometimes be, for instance, a primitive mountain cabin not at all suited to the age and condition of the person making the sale.

The following quote describes my hope that the TVA might initiate a new custom in the acquisition of property.

> There are other opportunities to work out programs. We are going to have to move about three thousand families out of the reservoir area. It is customary to pay the people their money and take no more interest in them, but we are spending a lot of money and have quite a large force of people at work trying to find suitable homes for these people, so that they can move into a situation where the roads are well laid out and the land is fertile; where they will have a water supply and decent houses and electricity and some guidance as to farming. We hope the money will put them in a better situation in a new home. We do not have to do this, but we are taking the job that is given to us and trying to do it decently. In many cases, we do not know how to do it. This particular job has never been done. Suppose we do buy a tract of land and build houses with water and electricity and good facilities and, possibly, with a central creamery. Will the people accept it or will they want something else? Nobody knows the way. We are exploring. That is one of the characteristics of a job like this.*

In developing a purchasing organization for the TVA, we made mistakes that could have been avoided, but perhaps we also made some history in land acquisition. Even with the improvement of conditions when a new director of purchases was hired and installed, it was not possible to do as good a job as I had hoped and planned for. But we were able to make a marked improvement.

The effort to acquire land for reservoirs in a humane manner and the time spent in speaking to groups concerned with developing particular aspects of culture did not interrupt progress in construction of the great dams. Before the end of October 1934, it was announced that Norris Dam and Wheeler Dam were each one-third completed. Only by intense application could such all-round progress be maintained.

TVA land-acquisition practices since that time have continued to reflect a

---

*From my speech to the Summer Student Group, Norris, Tenn., Aug. 3, 1934.

Vagaries

philosophy of human concern. Charles J. McCarthy has summarized TVA policy thusly:

> The importance of conducting the land acquisition program in such a way as to insure the retention of the good will of the people directly affected was recognized by TVA from the outset and two major objectives were established for this program: first, to obtain the lands needed at a cost which is fair to the government; and second, to leave the area in which a reservoir is built and the people who lived in the reservoir area at least as well off as they were before the TVA entered the picture. Experience has shown that there is no inconsistency between these two objectives.*

In public-works administration, it is possible to be human as well as competent.

THE BERRY MARBLE CASE

Much publicity has been given to the "Berry Marble Case" and my part in it. When I became chairman of the TVA and began to make the acquaintance of people in the district, one man who came to my attention was George Berry. According to the information given to me, he had served as president of the International Pressmen's Union for six or seven years. I learned that during that period he had never called for an election and had seldom, if ever, arranged for a meeting of the union. He had assumed that he would continue as president, and any disagreement with a union employer would be settled personally by Mr. Berry and the employer. An industrialist whom I met on a train and who gave me some information about personalities in the area had told me: "It would be well for you to become acquainted with George Berry. He is a man that you can deal with." Berry had political influence. According to Thomas McCraw, "In 1935, Roosevelt appointed [Berry] Coordinator for Industrial Cooperation, to preside over what was left of the NRA [National Recovery Administration]. The following year Berry helped to form Labor's Non-Partisan League, a political organization which spent nearly a million dollars in the Roosevelt campaign."**

I had met Mr. Berry casually, but while he sought to establish relationships with the members of the board and praised me highly in newspaper items, I chose not to become involved with him. He seemed to be on quite intimate

---

*"Land Acquisition Policies and Procedures in TVA," *Ohio State Law Journal* (Winter 1949).
**McCraw, p. 91.

The Making of the TVA

terms with Harcourt Morgan and Lilienthal, though as they never asked me to join them when he came to see them, I judged their relationship only by the attitude of friendship that was apparent when they met. The status of the situation is indicated by the following quotation from McCraw.

> In the fall of 1934, TVA's chief geologist, Edwin Eckel, had discovered that Berry and two associates had leased mineral rights to land that would be covered with water when Norris Dam was finished. The group had already quarried a small amount of marble, and some of it had been used in a new federal building in Washington. In Eckel's view, commercial operation of the quarries could not possibly be profitable for a variety of reasons, chiefly a difficulty of transportation. Putting two and two together, Eckel discovered what appeared to him to be a very neat plan to defraud the government: the marble taken out was sold not for profit, but to establish that a market existed; once the land was flooded and the evidence safely underwater the Berry group could submit a huge claim for damages against the TVA. Eckel reported his findings to his immediate superior, with a recommendation that the matter be thoroughly investigated.
>
> In 1935 Eckel repeated his warning, and the TVA hired several outside geologists to inspect the lands. All found them commercially worthless. In 1936 Eckel told Arthur Morgan about the affair, and when the chairman departed on his long vacation he took along the geologists' reports. After reading them, he wrote the other members of the board that in view of Berry's connection with the administration, the President should be informed, "so that he may take action or make any investigation necessary to assure him of the facts."
>
> Instead the other directors met with Berry, and entered into a conciliation agreement. As Lilienthal and H. A. Morgan viewed the matter, there might well be bad faith on Berry's part, but no definite evidence had yet been uncovered. The usual procedure in cases of this kind was to enter proceedings for condemnation, but the other two directors felt that this method was hazardous. The condemnation commissioners, who would not be experts on the geological and commercial technicalities of the case, might make a compromise award to Berry. He had consultants of his own who claimed value for the properties running into millions of dollars, and TVA might find itself obliged to pay an enormous sum. According to Lilienthal, the question in his mind was simply how to get TVA out with the least loss, and the conciliation agreement seemed the best method. As the power director said later, "I believe that Major Berry would have dropped the whole thing, and settled for a small sum, say maybe twenty or twenty-five thousand. . . ."
>
> Acting as the board, Lilienthal and H. A. Morgan met with Berry on June 10, 1936, about three weeks after Lilienthal's reappointment. Their agreement stated that the conciliator would "act as a medium between the parties and use his best efforts to assist" in possible legal action, and his recommendation would not bind either party.
>
> When Arthur Morgan returned, he protested violently against the agreement.

Vagaries

> To him, "the immediate question was not the value of these claims but was a question of what seemed to me a clear effort to 'hold up' the United States Government." In addition, Morgan contended that a phrase in the preamble to the agreement, which spoke of "the amount to be paid by the Authority to Major Berry and his associates" acknowledged that the claims had some value. The inference of this passage, said the chairman, might prejudice any claim of worthlessness the TVA made later in court. He therefore delayed appointment of the conciliator, and wrote Berry asking him to state details of his interest in the properties. Morgan told Berry that in his opinion "the primary and most important consideration" was not the value of the claims, but the propriety of the matter, since "a claim is being made by one (federal) official for the payment to himself and his associates of public money, a claim which must be considered by a board of public officials."*

I had looked into the situation thoroughly, and it seemed to me there was no possible question of the facts. Limestone (no sharp distinction was being made between limestone and marble) was common to that part of Tennessee and in many places outcropped on poor farmland of low price. Berry had leased the land in question after plans for Norris Dam had been completed and made public—when it was evident that the land would be submerged by the creation of the reservoir. His mining of a little of the limestone on the land for use in a public building in Washington was obviously only a tactic designed to strengthen his case for a claim against the government.

When I first became aware of the total situation, I informed the President. He requested that I ask the governor of Tennessee to get Berry off his hands. I preferred not to see the governor personally on this matter and asked my intimate personal assistant, Walter Kahoe, to deliver President Roosevelt's message. He was accompanied by a man who had been brought into the TVA by Mr. Lilienthal.

According to Mr. Kahoe, there was a brief but animated period of conversation between the governor and himself. The governor commented, in effect: "The President wants me to get him out of trouble again. I have already relieved him of the services of Cordell Hull [who had been the secretary of state]. I cannot serve him in this instance. The President will have to do his own dirty work."

Berry had filed a claim for five million dollars. If a settlement were made for one million dollars, the public would undoubtedly think of it as favorable to the government. After protesting the conciliatory course of the other two directors, I considered that it would be a public service to enable the people to understand

---

**Ibid.*, pp. 91-93.

The Making of the TVA

the character of the action that Berry had undertaken. Mr. Lilienthal and others sharply criticized my action in testifying at a public hearing on the case. I had in mind not only my position as chairman of the TVA but my responsibility as an American citizen possessing information of public import. Berry had been appointed an interim senator and was planning to seek the nomination for a full term. He did run for nomination for senator but was defeated. A friendly conciliation such as the other directors preferred might have left him in the clear and ready to participate in other political manipulations. The Berry Condemnation Commission, which investigated the claims, decided that they were worthless. That ended the Berry case, though not the references to it.

Lilienthal's attitude in the matter is illustrated by his testimony at the congressional hearings on the TVA. He understood the issue and stated it well, but said that he disregarded ethical questions in dealing with Major Berry.

> *Mr. Lilienthal:* I had considerable difficulty in understanding the position [of Arthur Morgan], but it seemed to be an insistence that good citizenship required that these questions [about Major Berry's claims] be answered, that we could take no step whatever, condemnation or any other step, that would in any way imply that we were approving this matter of low ethics in dealings with the Government, as Arthur Morgan described it.
>
> I tried to make the point, and apparently was unsuccessful, that all we could be concerned with were legal rights, that the question of morals and ethics had not been conferred upon us by law, and that as administrators we were concerned only with legal rights.
>
> *Mr. Biddle:* You mean you were not concerned with Major Berry's ethics and morals, is that your point?
>
> *Mr. Lilienthal*: Yes.*

OTHER SIGNIFICANT PROGRAMS

Not all of my "vagaries"—most notably the initiation of a program to rid the region of malaria—were disapproved by the other directors. Also, Mr. Lilienthal came to oppose patronage after he fell out with a congressman from Memphis whom he had previously supported. The program of housing at Norris was opposed but not prohibited by the board, and my actions relating to housing standards did not come to their attention. These programs are discussed below.

*Hearings Before the Joint Committee on the Investigation of the Tennessee Valley Authority, 75th Congress, 3rd Sess., Part 6 (Washington, D.C.: Government Printing Office, 1939), pp. 2462-3.

Vagaries

NO PATRONAGE

As a boy I had seen a congressman whom I considered markedly unfit appointed to a federal judgeship on being defeated for reelection to Congress. Here, it seemed to me, the very heart of government was being corrupted. Through the years I saw case after case where political patronage sacrificed character in government, and I came to oppose it as a source of deep harm to good government. When President Roosevelt asked me to serve as chairman of the TVA, I urged as a condition that the TVA be free from political patronage. He pounded his fist on the table and said, "There is to be no politics in this!" Just down Pennsylvania Avenue from the White House was the post office department, with its arrangements for appointing thousands of politically selected officeholders. To that massive political institution, the refusal to make patronage appointments in a government agency soon to be set up would be seen as too big a break with established practice and would undoubtedly be bitterly opposed.

Senator Norris of Nebraska had included in the TVA Act a provision prohibiting political appointments and requiring the removal of any TVA officer practicing such appointments. When he visited me at Norris Camp shortly after the TVA was under way, he reminded me of that provision and told me that he would uphold me in maintaining it. Without my requesting it, Gordon Clapp, who was in charge of the TVA appointments program, submitted a formal statement to me in which he told of two cases where David Lilienthal had employed men—one the cousin of a congressman—who had previously been found unqualified. Mr. Lilienthal had been informed in writing about the decision of the personnel department regarding these men, yet he appointed them to important positions in the TVA, without informing me that he had done so.

After a time I took Gordon Clapp's statement to Senator Norris. The Senator declined to receive it and began to tell me how essential the President was. He spoke to me as though he were speaking to an enemy of the President who needed to be reproved and corrected. He then retired to his office. When I came back later in the day, his son-in-law, who was also his personal secretary, told me that he was very much concerned about the Senator, who had appeared greatly agitated as he left, and that he feared he might have done damage to himself.

Late that afternoon the Senator returned. He said he had been walking up and down the riverbank all afternoon. He kept repeating, "We need the President. We cannot get along without him." He did not ask for the statement by

The Making of the TVA

Mr. Clapp, and from this time on he tended to treat me as an enemy. It was not until Lilienthal's correspondence with Senator Norris and the President became available in public records that I learned that Lilienthal had repeatedly charged me with undermining the President and acting on behalf of the private-power companies. These charges were entirely contrary to fact, but Senator Norris apparently had believed them and had decided that making patronage appointments was the lesser of two evils.

I did not make public Mr. Clapp's charges because he, as head of the appointments office, had been the chief supporter of the no-politics provision of the law. Had I made them public, I think Mr. Clapp would have been immediately dismissed, as others of the staff who seemed to favor my policies had been. He had looked on me as safely established as chairman, which was the general opinion at the time.

Desirable principles of action do not appear full-grown but are worked for and fought for and under favorable circumstances emerge little by little. A large part of the values of human culture come into being through that process. The high quality of the TVA staff is due to the large extent to which the Authority has kept itself free from patronage appointments and to the exceptional care in selecting the original staff. In public statements I had made the issue clear.

> Political parties have come to have very practical use. If your candidate is elected, you get a job—if mine gets in, I get one. To some extent, where people are isolated, they think more about politics; it comes to be the chief employment, and then politics means patronage. I wish that I had brought along a set of resolutions by a political party organization. It was substantially this: "We are proud of our party—the party of Andrew Jackson. Andrew Jackson said, 'To the victors belong the spoils.' Our own representatives in Congress are becoming remiss. They are not turning men of the opposite party out of office. They must become more active in finding public offices for their constituents, and in removing others."
>
> I think "social and economic planning," not only locally but over the country as a whole, means a revolution in that regard. I think the institution of patronage must be eliminated or it will destroy our government, locally and nationally. The situation may seem hopeless. I think there is just one alternative. We must find ways of handling our affairs without patronage, or else democratic government will sag and sag until some form of dictatorship takes it over.*
>
> In the Tennessee Valley Authority, we are trying to do our work in the spirit of each working for the general good. As we build dams, sell power, do our business, we are trying to avoid patronage and to employ people to do the work who are

*From my speech to the Ohio Society, New York, N.Y., Nov. 13, 1933.

best qualified for the job, regardless of friendship or of influence. We are trying to make it characteristic of the Tennessee Valley Authority that the best man available for each job shall do the work. I hope the people of the region as a whole can realize that what gets a man his job with us is his ability and not his influence.*

Through Mr. Clapp's opposition to patronage while he worked for Lilienthal, and Lilienthal's subsequent change of attitude, a permanent policy of "no patronage" was established for the TVA.

MALARIA MUST GO!

One of my undertakings that seemed consistent with the President's hopes and which was actively approved by the other directors was the effort to eliminate malaria. Many streams, marshes, and ponds in the TVA area were breeders of anopheles mosquitoes, a genus that carries malaria, and the building of the TVA dams would greatly increase the area of marshy margins. Norris Reservoir alone, I believe, has a longer shoreline than Lake Superior.

Twenty-five years before, as the supervising drainage engineer in Louisiana and Arkansas for the U.S. Office of Experiment Stations, I became acquainted with the dangers of malaria. I saw malarial conditions and contracted a severe case myself. I had also made an extensive study of malaria and its causes and of possible ways to combat it.

I was naturally concerned about the problem of malaria in the Tennessee Valley region, particularly with regard to the great increase in water margins that construction of the reservoirs would introduce. I searched for someone to direct an antimalaria program. I decided upon Dr. E. L. Bishop, chief health officer of the state of Tennessee, who seemed very promising. I mentioned him to Harcourt Morgan, who said he knew Dr. Bishop well and fully approved of my choice.

Dr. Bishop was ideal for the job. He took the whole broad subject of malaria for his field, studied its every aspect, and assembled an excellent staff, which he seemed to inspire. He made very extensive studies of widely differing conditions, worked out experimental methods that he compared in practice, and established sound and effective working programs.

The course followed by Dr. Bishop typifies what is fundamentally important in responsible engineering—persistence in exploring, discovering, appraising,

---

*From my speech to the Lower Tennessee Valley Association, Murray, Ky., May 16, 1934.

The Making of the TVA

and comparing all possible solutions to an important problem, including solutions that have been generally dismissed or gone unproven and also solutions that seem so improbable as to merit no consideration. This policy may break through many established dogmas, sometimes into fertile territory.

Dr. Bishop certainly did one of the best jobs anywhere in the TVA. Not only did he work out methods for reducing the probability of contagion, but he undertook to eliminate existing cases of malaria, and so to remove the possibility of the infection being passed back to mosquitoes. The fantastic and seemingly impossible job of wholly eliminating this most common disease in the TVA area took courage, initiative, and persistence. Without striking improvements in the methods of control, the more than twenty TVA reservoirs, the many thousands of miles of shoreline, and a population not informed or trained in medical care would have made malaria a much more serious health hazard in the region.

I shall not undertake to describe the many elements of the methods that Dr. Bishop developed, but one single item is of special interest. A malarial mosquito in its larval stage lives for about ten days as a small creature in the water. In open water the fish can devour the larvae. But along the lake margins the larvae are protected by plants growing in the shallow water and are comparatively free from attack by fish.

A program was worked out for periodically fluctuating the depth of the water in the reservoirs. The reservoirs are fluctuated about a foot a week, and are gradually lowered during the mosquito breeding season. Due to this fluctuation, food supply for larvae is poor and they are exposed to natural enemies (fish and other predators), to wave action, to sunlight and drying, and to other disturbances. A TVA newsletter, dated June 19, 1972, notes the beginning of the annual fluctuation of the water levels in seven Tennessee River mainstream lakes. "The fluctuation is part of a yearly cycle of TVA water level management to control mosquitoes, particularly the malaria-carrying species. This disease was once common along parts of the Tennessee River, but there has not been a confirmed case of locally-contracted malaria in the region since 1950."

A battery of other devices helps. Many little pools and marshes are provided with adequate outlet channels into the reservoirs. Insecticide power-spray dusters travel by power boat along the margins of reservoirs, and airplane dusters are also used.

Before the TVA was organized, it was estimated that in many villages along the streams more than half the inhabitants suffered from endemic malaria. It is doubtful whether in the entire world there is a finer example of malarial-mosquito control. Fortunately, this particular initiative on my part had the full approval of the board.

HOUSING STANDARDS

One of my small undertakings had its origin in what was the nearest I came to making a political appointment while I was at the TVA. Eleanor Roosevelt asked me to give a job to a young Yale graduate who was at the Roosevelt Sanatorium in Warm Springs, Georgia, recovering from a severe attack of polio. He could move about only on crutches. I took him on. (This young man, on completing his work for the TVA, joined one of the housing authorities in Washington, and before long he was head of the organization.)

We were building many house at the damsites. We built enough permanent housing to accommodate the operating staff of the dam, reservoir, locks, power plants, and the necessary community services. In the interim before construction of the dam was completed, those facilities were used to house some of the work crew on the dam. The rest of the workmen lived in temporary dormitories.

I wanted the houses for our workers and operating staff at the damsites to be suitable, but not by uneconomical standards. In carrying out our housing program, I thought we might be able to determine how expensive a house would be socially justified for a competent workman. One way of arriving at an estimate was by asking, "What part of a man's working life would be used in building an adequate house?" The young polio victim went to work answering this question.

We were building the houses with our own labor supply and keeping our own records. Under the direction of this young man, we carefully determined the actual working time for building a house of a given type. We avoided rows or groups of identical houses, though at the several damsites we might build twenty identical houses. In measuring the cost of ten or twenty houses of one type, we could arrive at a reasonably close limit of error in the cost of construction. Also, we undertook to determine what part of the cost of the lumber we used represented actual human labor, and we made similar estimates of the labor cost of the equipment used in producing the lumber. We did the same for the other materials used in building the houses. Then we tried to make estimates of any other costs, including taxes for general government, schools, highways, sanitation, and so forth. (We found that these costs were commonly about as much as the actual cost of the house.) In this way we got a roughly accurate estimate of the cost of a man's house in terms of the part of his working time it represented.

The Making of the TVA

Many economists had estimated the part of the total family budget that goes into housing. Taking the most frequently used figure of 20 to 25 percent, we could get a close approximation of the range of a competent workman's expenditure for housing and we could check our own housing standards by that data. We found that, for the types of housing provided at the damsites—at the village of Norris, for instance—our modest but respectable and comfortable houses were in fact being constructed at 20 to 25 percent of the workmen's wages. This indicated that the type of housing at Norris and other towns cost no more than workmen's houses would generally, even though they were markedly superior to the dwellings commonly built for workmen and though we made no allowances for contractors' profits beyond a reasonable wage for supervision. In other words, TVA workmen were not being subsidized by the government to any noticeable extent. Naturally, this finding pleased us.

Although this study was made on my own initiative, I cannot recall being criticized for it by the other directors.

HOUSES AT NORRIS

Some of the difficulties confronting TVA projects were created within our own organization. The plans for houses and dormitories for the workmen at Norris were delayed for six months or more by the opposition of one of the directors to the construction of workmen's housing. Until the building of those facilities was finally permitted by the board, both the men working on construction of the housing and those working on the dam had to travel long distances. Some workmen drove fifty miles each way to work, for lack of facilities nearby.

The building of decent houses for workmen was not in the director's experience and seemed to him a waste of public resources. But, in fact, adequate housing made it possible for able men to bring their families and thus was a large factor in getting economical labor and in lowering other construction costs. It was highly productive economically as well as socially and was partly responsible for the TVA's low labor turnover. Speaking to the Central Labor Union at Knoxville, Tennessee, in 1933, I stressed the importance of this factor.

> There was some talk of building temporary quarters to be used for three years and then thrown away—just torn down and done away with. It seemed to me that that was a waste, that we would be better off to spend some more money and build permanent houses that people could live in, such houses as most people ought to live in—not expensive, but good substantial houses. It has not been easy to get that across. I have been blocked here and there in trying to get the right to build that

Vagaries

town. For one thing timber has gone up and our architects tell us that it will cost about 40 percent more to build the town than it would have last June when we got our appropriation. What are we going to do about it? Are we going to have to throw up our hands and say we can't build the town? I have been advised, "Just give up that town. Build cheap houses and tear them down afterward." I would like to put in the extra money and get the town built. It was a narrow squeeze to get it authorized. I have been turned down, and I have gone back, and back, and back. It has not been easy to get the Authority to authorize its construction but if we do build it, the building trades of Knoxville will get the work. I am going to be told, "This is not what you said the town was going to cost." But wages have gone up, materials have gone up. I need cooperation there; I need some friends; I need some help in getting the town actually built. Now here is where I think the building trades of Knoxville can help us. The houses will be frame or brick. Brick houses add substantially to the cost of the town. We can save twelve to fifty thousand dollars by not using brick, but we are going to use it. That will mean work for brickmasons. I hope that in that work we can get a hearty support. We hope that you will try not to make these houses too expensive. I have met much opposition and I am not out of the woods yet, but I think I have won. I have gone the very limit in trying to get substantial houses built. We are arranging to have a couple of acres within reach of every house in the town, so that a man can have his small garden farm, and we can have a prosperous little community, something like a suburb of Knoxville.*

In providing family residences for men constructing the dams, to be used by the operations staff after the dam was finished, the TVA made a considerable advance over the conditions that too frequently existed on outdoor construction jobs. Besides the family dwellings we also built a schoolhouse and a community recreation building, a large barn-like structure where training and recreational facilities were provided. Since we had reduced the working day to only five and one-half hours to spread the labor opportunities, there was much time for social and training activities. We built a combined store and post office and also a gas station. Since the members of the construction force for building a dam were of many different religious denominations, which might not be the same as those of the later, permanent residents, we built a single structure to serve as a nondenominational community church.** We prevented saloons, gambling houses, and houses of prostitution from springing up, as they frequently did at other outdoor construction jobs. With these favorable living conditions, we were able to secure higher-caliber employees.

*From my speech to the Central Labor Union, Knoxville, Tenn., Oct. 21, 1933.
** Forty years later (June 1973) a religious association open to all denominations continues its vigorous life and contributes to the cultural harmony of the community.

The Making of the TVA

Mr. Lilienthal was one of those who, late in 1934, chose one of the houses for his residence.

Somewhat similar communities were built at some of the other dams. In several speeches that I made, I attempted to describe life in these communities.

> We are building about three hundred and fifty houses at Norris, and we have there a young woman who conducts classes in homemaking and in work that a woman can do to earn money at home. We are trying to teach the women to do housework, to cook, and to care for children in the best and the most up-to-date ways.
>
> The courses are voluntary. We post a notice at Norris, stating that a certain course will be given and asking all those who want to take it to sign their names. Applicants swamp us with their requests. We put up a notice that a course in mathematics would be given and two hundred men signed up for it. They are there for business. There is no regimentation, only an offering of opportunity.
>
> It is sometimes asked how much cooperation we are getting from the people of the region. We are finding an ambition, an energy, a patience, a willingness to work, an industry, an eagerness to learn that is surprising.
>
> You may ask, "Isn't this adding to the cost of the project? Will not the training program increase the expense?" I think not. We are far enough along now to measure expenses. For instance, we are finishing up the rock excavations in the riverbeds. The government made an estimate, before the organization of the Authority, of the cost of the rock excavations at the Norris damsite. Their estimate was four dollars per cubic yard. It has cost us $1.65. Our workers are on the job. They are not drunk or sick.
>
> Once in a while a different kind of workman comes in. Perhaps he has been thrown out of some labor union. I was told of such a man who was working on one of the small houses at Norris, laying brick. He talked to the other workmen, urging them not to lay so many brick, telling them it would do them no good to work so hard. The men ran him out of camp. They understand that no one is making any profit on these houses, that no one receives anything from them but the men who live in them. The workmen realize they are taking part in a great undertaking and they do not want anyone to obstruct their efforts. They know they are helping the New Deal. The training program costs perhaps 2 percent of the estimated cost of the dam, but it is adding a life and ambition and a spirit of goodwill that makes up for the cost.*
>
> We have tried to consider the welfare of the men working here. What living conditions have men on construction jobs a right to expect? Many of these workers spend their lives going from one job to another, living always in temporary quarters. We feel that a man is entitled to decent living conditions during all jobs. In the TVA cafeteria we feed the men at cost. We have a recreation building, with

---

*From my speech to the Lower Tennessee Valley Association, Paducah, Ky., May 17, 1934.

movies and games. The dormitories, or bunkhouses, are clean, well ventilated, and have good bathing and sanitary facilities. They are simple and plain, but they are decent and wholesome quarters where self-respecting people can live. After the dam is finished, we plan for this to be a permanent town with its own industries and means of subsistence.*

CONCLUSION

After I left the TVA my "vagaries" spread over a wider range. In Mexico in 1939 I tried unsuccessfully to work out colonizing possibilities for Jewish refugees from Germany. In 1947 in Finland I tried to make a contribution to the revival of industry after the Finnish-Russian War. I studied Indian education, as a member of the National Universities Commission, and found that 80 percent of the Indian population, who lived in villages, had almost no share in the benefits of higher education. I proposed the creation of "rural universities" as "rural institutes" to help remake the culture of the countryside. Of the ten members of the commission, all but one opposed my proposal. That one member, Zakir Hussain, the only Moslem on the commission, later became the president of Hindu India. Slowly over the course of a year attitudes changed and the proposal was approved. The Indian government has since established between fifteen and twenty of these rural institutes. In addition to general education, some of them are making marked contributions to increasing the food supply, while at the same time being active in family planning.

In India I also made it possible for an unusually gifted young Indian to develop a social-educational project in southern India that unites academic education with work in economic life and production centers, in community and other social organizations, and in health and family planning. This project, Mitraniketan, was started in 1955 and has been growing vigorously.

In another "vagary," as consultant in 1953 to the government of Ghana, West Africa, on the Volta River reservoir and power project, I was concerned with the policy followed in removing the native population in the process of creating what was then the world's largest reservoir.

Not all of my post-TVA "vagaries" have been overseas. I was chairman of a committee appointed by the Ohio Legislature to reorganize and consolidate the several state agencies dealing with ecology, including forests, parks, rivers, solid-waste disposal, and strip mining. Before assembling this committee, made up of legislators and other public men, I first made a survey of related policies in

---

*From my speech to the Southern Tuberculosis Association, Norris, Tenn., Oct. 10, 1934.

many other states and drafted suggested legislation for the initiation of a Department of Natural Resources. I had the very effective help of an attorney friend, Victor Jacobs, who was not then a committee member. I then called the committee and gave them the draft to work on. They held sessions for the better part of a year, during which time I made trips to Finland and India. Various drafts were prepared during my absence, and then my draft was adopted, substantially as I had written it with Mr. Jacobs' cooperation. A provision concerning strip mining of coal was added. The Department of Natural Resources is now in operation as part of the legal structure of the state government.

In another "vagary," I served for a time as "impartial chairman" of negotiations between the steelworkers union and the United States Steel Corporation, during which period the employment of blacks was approved by a branch of U.S. Steel.

Along the way there have been other "vagaries," such as initiating a program for suitable housing, a social organization, and organized activity for the older people in my own community. For many years, until 1968, I was the president of a small organization, Community Service, Inc., concerned with the organization of the small community and the improvement of social life.

Chapter Seven

Multipurpose Engineering

My major responsibility in the TVA was the planning and construction of the dams, power plants, reservoirs, and navigation locks, which involved about 70 percent of the total cost of the TVA program.

The quality of the technical work was not a matter of chance or routine. Two elements entered into it, the first being my own earlier experience. Twenty years before the beginning of the New Deal and the TVA, the first flood-control reservoirs in the United States were created after the great Dayton flood in 1913 by the Miami Conservancy District in Ohio, of which I was chief engineer. The Army Corps of Engineers had condemned flood-control reservoirs for half a century and had never built any. Their nearest approach was the construction of broad, shallow storage areas in the vast swamps of northern Minnesota, built to make it possible to raise low water levels in the upper Mississippi and some of its branches enough to enable logs to float from the forest down to the sawmills.

The Making of the TVA

Thus, in flood-control reservoirs, which would be necessary for the TVA, the Corps had no experience. Since the Corps was the principal agency in America for controlling rivers and the issue seldom arose in other cases, engineers rarely had to deal with it. Therefore the question of flood-control reservoirs was generally taken as settled in American engineering.

The Mississippi was the first large river system in America where an effort was made to treat it as a unit with respect to its various elements. But the conditions for that effort were not favorable since the science of hydraulics was in its infancy. Moreover, the Corps of Engineers, which had the habit of writing very authoritatively, presumed to give faultless direction before the work was begun. A former chief of engineers, Captain A. A. Humphreys, assigned supposedly faultless accuracy to his overall analysis with these words: "Thus every important fact connected with the various physical conditions of the river and the laws uniting them being ascertained, the great problem of protection against inundation was solved."*

For approximately a century the Corps of Engineers treated Humphreys' work as a bible to be followed literally. As a matter of fact, however, in nearly every respect the elaborate instructions in this ponderous volume were highly inaccurate, as, for example, in repudiating the use of the hydraulic laboratory, cutoffs on the Mississippi River, jetties at its outlet, and flood-control reservoirs. It was not until President Hoover set aside ten consecutive nominations for the office of chief of engineers and then appointed to that position a scientifically minded and creative engineer that the program of Mississippi River control was revolutionized.

As soon as the TVA Act was passed and I had been appointed as chairman and chief engineer, I sent Sherman Woodward, the ablest engineer I knew, to examine the work of the Corps at their St. Louis office, where most of their work was done, and to look into the quality of their water-control designs. He reported to me that the plans of the Corps with regard to the Tennessee River were "rather naive" and advised us not to depend on them. We were anxious to get a dam under construction to aid in relieving the depression and decided to have plans for the first two dams, Norris and Wheeler, prepared by the Reclamation Service, which had extensive experience in building dams for irrigation storage. That would give us time to assemble an engineering staff.

The second element that added quality to the technical work was the use of a method, which I dubbed "dynamic design," that consisted of never finally fixing

---

*From a letter of transmittal, Aug. 8, 1861, in A. A. Humphreys and H. L. Abbot, *The Physics and Hydraulics of the Mississippi River* (Washington, D.C.: Govt. Printing Office, 1867), p. 11.

and completing the design but of keeping it open to take full account of any special advantage or disadvantage that appeared in the course of construction. Whereas in some cases, especially with the Army Corps of Engineers, it was customary for the actual building of a large structure to follow the preliminary plans almost exactly, I had found that in large outdoor constructions there would almost certainly be actual conditions that could not be anticipated at the start. By keeping the plans flexible such unanticipated conditions can be worked into the plans as they are discovered, often resulting in large economies or improvements in the design. Some of the engineers we recruited from government agencies or from conservative engineering firms were not accustomed to dynamic design and were in the habit of working by fixed plans sent from home-office designing engineers that were to be used, unchanged, at a distant work site; they would almost tear their hair because of the lack of finality in our plans.

Yet, the dynamic-design approach worked. The hurried designs by the Reclamation Service were well done, but by continued study at the site and by keeping our minds and our plans open, we were able to increase the density of the dam structure at Norris, thereby making it safe against a 10 percent greater head of water while at the same time reducing the cost by about four million dollars. By building as we planned and planning as we built, we put unemployed men to work far sooner, yet with high labor productivity. With the resulting economy we could undertake additional construction work and thus turn what would otherwise have been unemployed time into enduring values.

It was decided to construct the dams, locks, and power plants with our own labor force and equipment rather than have the work done by contract, as was the nearly universal custom on large public-works projects. The idea to take this course was mine. The decision was justified by the urgent necessity for putting men to work in a period of unprecedented depression. Work would have been delayed six months to a year if plans and estimates were prepared with the completeness and detail required to let major contracts.

In searching for staff members for the TVA, I looked for people of character and ability and tried not to ignore men or women because they lacked conventional preparation. In many fields, including some not usually associated with advanced training, I sought men of more than usual capacity. The general ability that emerged in many of the various fields of the TVA helped to make the dynamic-design approach a success. In several instances we were able to improve upon the original design materially. The notable excellence in the construction program of dams, power plants, and navigation locks bears evidence to the generally high level of this work on the part of a staff selected without regard to political affiliation.

When I went to the TVA, I took with me a considerable staff of engineers who had been trained in "conclusive engineering analysis." This was not a hastily assembled group. Although some members of the staff were new, others had been my associates for five to twenty years and came with me to the TVA as members of a group well adjusted to each other and familiar with a wide range of problems. Several had reached high rank in their fields through their work with other engineering firms and had advanced the science of water control in many ways. They had produced some of the ranking literature in the field and had applied some of its findings.

The first task of the staff was to work out a design for the TVA system as a whole. The leader and creative genius of the group was Sherman M. Woodward, an engineer of exceptional technical knowledge who had previously done an outstanding job on the Miami Conservancy District project. He was a very modest man and reached key positions because others recognized the high caliber of his work and placed him there. He was the ablest man in applied engineering theory that I have ever known.

Woodward's work was supported and supplemented by several other engineers, each a master in his field. Of equal rank in a different field was Charles Locher. Although he had only about two years of formal schooling, he was a disciplined wizard in the skillful use and placing of wood forms and concrete and the handling of earth. He had performed the seemingly impossible task of unscrambling the hopeless confusion of sewer lines, water lines, power lines, gas, electricity, and building foundations that had developed under New York City, to permit the construction of subways. With the TVA he acted as a consultant in difficult situations.

Carl Bock served as the assistant chief engineer, and I delegated many of my functions to him. He carried out these responsibilities with exceptional competence. In both the general management of the engineering program and as coordinator of the staff in general, Mr. Bock was my efficient and dependable general assistant, helping me not only on major issues but on the whole program of my office.

There were also Barton Jones in design and construction; Albert Fry, in charge of the pioneering hydraulic laboratory; Harry Wiersema, general office engineer and assistant to the chief engineer; Ross White, superintendent of construction of Norris Dam; and numerous others.

This range of skill and experience was substantially enlarged and refined by

Multipurpose Engineering

the contribution of other able men in various fields who brought their own special abilities to the TVA. Their services were utilized on specific problems such as railroad relocation and crushing rock. On the whole these highly qualified men made up a TVA team that had few equals anywhere in the world. A spirit of tried fellowship and experience grew among the members of the staff. Throughout the selection of this able group, there was no political patronage, despite a few instances of intense congressional pressure. For example, had we followed uninformed political recommendations without thorough investigation, we would have employed, to manage construction of a 150-million-dollar dam, an engineer who was later discovered to be in the employ of a group of mineowners bent on the destruction of the TVA. In addition to the men who joined the TVA staff as full-time members, there were others from my earlier staff whose paths had taken them into other fields, but who were available for consultation.

Whatever controversy existed with regard to other aspects of TVA administration, there was never serious question concerning the quality of its engineering. Given the fact that the engineering involved over two-thirds of the total expenditures of the TVA, this is a significant record. It is more significant when we recognize that the soil and rock conditions posed major difficulties. Because of underground limestone cavities, Tennessee River damsites were very uncertain. The Tennessee Power Company had built the first dam on the Tennessee River under these conditions and had advertised it widely as a "properly constructed dam." Yet, it had underground leaks and in later years was wholly abandoned by the TVA and replaced by another dam downstream. The eight large dams on the lower Tennessee River were built where there were similar subsurface conditions but have functioned with complete effectiveness. The dams required careful design to meet these difficult conditions. It was not just a matter of chance that they have been uniformly successful. All of the eight TVA dams on the Tennessee River below Knoxville were built closely within the TVA's preliminary estimates of cost and constitute a notable record, not of a single person's skill, but of the teamwork of able men who were not hampered by routine bureaucratic procedures or political loyalties.

The construction program proceeded not only with careful design but with marked speed. Within a year and a half of the organization of the TVA, Norris Dam, one of the largest dams in the United States, and Wheeler Dam, three-fourths as large as Norris, were both one-third finished.

Concerning one of the TVA dams, I have considerable personal pride. It was desirable to locate the lowest dam on the Tennessee River, the Kentucky Dam,

The Making of the TVA

near where the Tennessee empties into the Ohio River. This site would provide water-storage capacity far beyond that at any other. Altogether, a larger reservoir on the lower part of the river would be worth one hundred million dollars more in storage space and other possibilities than one located farther up the river. When the Corps of Engineers tried to find a site for this dam, they were not able to find a downstream location and established one at a point twenty miles upstream. The Corps' design would limit the navigation channel to an enlargement of the river channel in an area where the river bottom was mud or quicksand, and flotillas of barges would have to travel in single file instead of being towed together in large groups. The Corps of Engineers' faulty plans for control of the Tennessee River, which were part of their faulty overall plan for the Mississippi River system, were characteristic of their ineptitude.

I was determined if possible to find a location that would provide a larger storage area and provide other services. To find whether it would be possible to build a dam near the mouth of the Tennessee River, we established a research team. After three months' study, the research team returned with the word that the downriver site where we had hoped to locate the dam was under ninety feet of quicksand and mud and that safe construction could not be assured. The costly loss of storage and navigation values was hard to take. In this case I took an unaccustomed action and decided to go beyond my engineers and to make another investigation. The engineering staff supported this decision wholeheartedly. They took exceptional care in selecting a staff of men and picked Eugene Prokop, an exceptionally creative and vigorous man, as chief of the party. I was thankful for such full cooperation because without it my decision might have been useless. In the course of the research Mr. Prokop used a daring and novel device. He surrounded an area of the proposed site with refrigeration pipes that penetrated the ninety feet of quicksand and mud and then excavated the mud and quicksand inside this frozen wall. He was thereby enabled to examine the underlying rock foundation, which proved to be excellent. This method provided information that ordinary drill holes down to rock could not supply. It was similar to the method used by James Eads sixty years earlier in ensuring a safe foundation for his bridge at St. Louis. Eads broke all records for depth of foundation.

This decision of mine worked because I had such wholehearted cooperation, and major credit for the result belongs to the man who undertook this unusual method of exploration. But if I had not personally decided not to give up after "final inquiry" had shown the downstream damsite impractical, the further effort, which took another six months while Kentucky congressmen were urging me to hurry and build a dam, would not have been undertaken and the TVA would not have gained the additional storage space and navigation facilities. That persistent thoroughness paid off well. Throughout the TVA construction staff there was an attitude of stubborn competence.

I mention this instance to indicate that, while I seldom disagreed with my excellent staff, I could and did sometimes take action when they did not feel justified in undergoing the necessary extra expense. It was fortunate that the mutual confidence existed that made such action possible.

Except for the years during World War I when power and explosives were produced, the traditional purposes of river improvement on the branches of the Ohio River were flood control and improvement of navigation. But with the establishment of the TVA, those aims were changed. The issue of electric power had begun to attract a larger interest, and expansion of fertilizer production was planned. As a result, electric power and fertilizer production took prominence in the active interests of the TVA, and the construction of dams tended to be of interest primarily for those purposes.

However, flood control and navigation continued to loom large, though they had no major departments assigned to them. The needs of power development largely coincided with those of flood control and navigation, so that additional and separate action for flood control and navigation was seldom a controlling issue.

The issue of TVA navigation policy had no such clearly defined commitment on the part of any member of the board, but I had major responsibility for it. The existing policy, which was continued by the interests that promoted the TVA, was to develop water transportation at public expense. The character of TVA improvements lent themselves strikingly to such a policy on the Tennessee River. This had formerly been largely ignored, and large-scale, practical navigation had ended near the mouth of the Ohio River. In planning the overall design of TVA improvements, I assumed that the dominant national policy concerning water navigation would be continued, and I strove to make TVA policy conform to that pattern.

Not only was the additional water-storage capacity of the Kentucky Dam reservoir highly useful, but the use of the reservoir for navigation was also a major asset. It was equal to the best of deep-water navigation. In addition, it was possible by digging a short canal through glacial drift to unite this reservoir with one we were almost sure would be built on the Cumberland River, which has since been built. Thus, compensation for uneven rainfall on the two reservoirs can be made, with maximum benefit to each. As far as Mississippi Valley flood protection was concerned, this system would catch the water from all the branches of the Tennessee River.

The needs of navigation were largely met by the building of wharves on the river and, in a few cases, excavating for additional channel depth. Substantial dockage sufficient to meet the full needs of navigation, but without excessive cost, was secured in this way. To handle the navigation problem by building low dams, as had been planned by the Corps of Engineers, would have cost 225 million dollars. But through the construction of nine high dams, the needs of navigation were largely provided for at a cost of just 155 million dollars. Thus, in this case the need for storage and high water fitted in perfectly with the requirements for navigation. All the elements of river control were considered in the process of inclusive analysis.

In another related issue during the early period of the TVA, David Lilienthal expressed great concern about the possibility of the Tennessee River dams creating an oversupply of power. Yet when he learned of the search of Richard S. Reynolds for power to build an aluminum plant that would be a competitor of the Aluminum Company of America, Mr. Lilienthal abruptly terminated the inquiry as entirely beyond consideration, although at that time the TVA had a large amount of unused power on hand. He also strenuously opposed the construction of the Chickamauga Dam. He urgently said to me, "What will we do with all that power?" I held that power was only one of the purposes of the TVA, that navigation and flood control were equally as important issues, and that the Chickamauga Dam should be built to meet navigational needs as well as to supply power. In this case, my insistence prevailed and the dam was built.

The Chickamauga Dam was a striking example of the fact that TVA dams were not the routine achievements they were sometimes represented to be. There were underground water passages up and down the Tennessee watershed that demanded the utmost care to master. By careful research and able construction, however, the Dam was made one of the permanent improvements of the Valley. No critical issues have emerged to seriously complicate that part of the TVA program, which was nevertheless of large consequence since navigation of the Tennessee was made feasible.

CEMENT SALES

In the building of reservoirs, power plants, and other structures for the purposes of the TVA, the material that called for the greatest expenditure was cement. Altogether, expenditures for cement amounted to many millions of dollars. In our attempt to acquire supplies of cement, we came upon perhaps the most rigid organization for the manipulation of prices that occurred in the whole TVA program. Cement manufacturers had united to control prices, which were uniform throughout the country. Some cement plants were not more than twenty-five miles from where their product would be used. However, bids were received from cement companies as much as one thousand miles away. In such cases, a large part of the cost went for transportation. It was evident that the basic cost of cement from the factory to its place of use would differ greatly between a five-hundred-mile and a fifty-mile haul. The fact that distant plants found it profitable to ship the material a long distance and still sell it at the uniform price determined by the cement combine made it evident that the close-by factories were making an undue profit.

I brought this fact to the attention of the cement organization but was completely rebuffed. They indicated that they were the sources of supply and that if we wanted cement it would be necessary to meet their condition of uniform price regardless of the distance of shipment. They were so sure that we could not find cement outside of their combine that they were completely inflexible.

What were we to do about it? One way out would be to build our own cement plant. With my many varied responsibilities as chief engineer, I did not welcome the prospect of having to take on another taxing job. In addition, cement manufacture was not a simple process. There were different types of cement for different uses. For instance, in building a power plant, special types of cement would be needed for different parts of the plant, and inaccurately made or proportioned cement might leave marked deficiencies in the resulting structures. In short, the manufacture of cement was more than a single bulk process.

The cement organization seemed to rely on such difficulties to protect them from competition. Further, individual engineers who worked for the cement companies and were knowledgeable in cement production were afraid to offer their services to the TVA because that would make them enemies of this tightly controlled organization. There was also a considerable element of controlled service by the firms supplying equipment for cement-manufacturing plants, and if such a firm supplied equipment for a TVA cement industry, it would at once have the enmity of the cement organization as a whole and would have trouble selling its equipment to members of the organization.

Thus the problem of becoming free from the clutches of this organization was no simple matter. Government organizations in general had accepted this powerful control and had bought cement at the controlled prices set by the organization. In some cases where particular values were required, cement was

The Making of the TVA

being imported from as far away as England.

We went over this problem backward and forward to find ways to avoid this extra expense, which might run to several million dollars. We finally concluded that the proper course for the TVA was to build its own cement plant so that the element of transportation cost would be as low as possible. We would explore the Tennessee Valley region for natural materials suitable for making cement in accessible locations.

We had a well-qualified geologist who was interested in the undertaking, and I secured an especially capable mechanical engineer. They found one location on the banks of the Tennessee River where there were cliffs about one hundred feet high of unusually good limestone that was suited to our purpose. Moreover, a few miles away there were adequate deposits of other minerals necessary for making cement.

There were other favorable factors in the situation. At the foot of the limestone cliff, there was a flat area ideally suited for a manufacturing plant. A railroad passed through the area, which would make loading and transportation convenient. Not only that, the site was also on the shore of the Tennessee River, which made it ideally located for shipping cement by water.

The cement industry began to take note of these conditions. The engineer who was in charge of the project was frequently visited and consulted by members of the cement industry, and I learned that he was giving them inaccurate information that exaggerated the favorable aspects of our situation. I criticized this practice and told him I did not want any false information disseminated to our opponents. His reply, in essence, was that deceit was necessary, that you could not do business without it. He had been employed by a major locomotive factory for twenty years and had come to feel that convenient deceit was an elementary business practice. As a Quaker, he had been strongly committed to personal integrity, and in an effort to escape the practice of deceit, he told me that he had observed the methods of competing industries. Yet, there too he had found that dishonesty seemed to be an inevitable element of big industry in its important dealings. This engineer had thought of changing his job to another organization, but came to the conclusion that he would only have been up against the same necessity elsewhere.

I told him that we were not in conventional industry and that I wanted our word to be dependable to friends and enemies alike. This was a new concept to him and he welcomed it as though he had just been let out of jail. He dropped his practice of saying things that would be of particular disadvantage to his competition and reverted to his youthful habit of uniform honesty.

It was evident to the cement industry that we had an excellent location and could supply our cement more cheaply than they could. Since we had a considerable number of dams to build and the companies did not want to lose that business, they gave up their policy of a single price to all customers. We worked out with them a reasonable price for a short haul and made a contract with them on that basis.

There was much turmoil in the cement industry over having made this concession, and wild stories were told of how I had departed from industrial propriety. I had a friend in California, John Trainor, a civic leader who was prominent in the cement industry, whose character I greatly respected and admired. He wrote me repeatedly about the evil stories he had heard concerning me and wanted to know what truth there was in them. He was satisfied from my replies that my negotiations had been wholly honorable and wrote some letters to the cement industry criticizing their action in making false statements. The Federal Trade Commission, in looking into the records of the cement industry, came across his criticism of his own industry and made utmost use of it.

We had almost completed our own plans for a cement plant when we negotiated the agreement with the cement industry, but I was very relieved to be free from the necessity of trying to become a master of cement production or of securing such mastery in our organization. There remained some criticism within the industry of its change of policy, but after my departure from the TVA, they respected our conclusion enough to continue with fairly appraised prices. I considered this a real victory, one that with the help of my friend John Trainor, who had high standing in the industry because of his creative contributions to it, may have affected the entire cement industry. I do not hesitate now to mention the role played by my friend. He died several years ago, and I do not think that the rules of the cement industry are operative on the other side of the River Styx. And being myself ninety-six years old, I do not anticipate the purchase of cement to build a dam across that river.

Chapter Eight

The Fontana Dam

When the bill to create and establish the TVA was in the process of legislative development, neither the President nor members of Congress nor the Army Corps of Engineers nor any other government official was fully aware of the complex problems involved in establishing unified control of the Tennessee River system to improve navigation, control destructive floodwaters, and generate hydroelectric power. In the course of my department's early studies of the Tennessee River and its tributaries, I found it mandatory that the Little Tennessee River be integrated into the control system of the main Tennessee River. However, there was one obstacle to such integration: the Aluminum Company of America (Alcoa) had staked out the Little Tennessee River system as its private property and source of hydroelectric power.

An adequate supply of electric power is a primary need in the production of aluminum. Alcoa had made careful and wise provision in this respect by planning for the total development of the Little Tennessee River. Considering the conditions of power supply at that time, it is doubtful that there was a better area for aluminum production east of the Rocky Mountains. By way of contrast, the great demand for the electric power generated at Niagara Falls, near the center of industrial America, made it relatively expensive there. Another advantage of the Little Tennessee plant sites was that, since they were outside centers of industry, there was little competition for the abundant local labor supply.

With remarkable foresight Alcoa had purchased the major reservoir sites in the high mountains on the Little Tennessee River so that it could use the heavy winter rainfall of the region. The company built its first plants at sites that provided only moderate-size reservoirs for power plants, but the resulting power supply was adequate for production needs at that time. There was also a much larger potential source of power on the Little Tennessee River. This was the exceedingly valuable dam and reservoir site at Fontana, in western North Carolina. The Fontana area had perhaps the highest annual rainfall in the eastern United States—a rainfall so great that all the reservoirs on the Little Tennessee could not hold the total winter water flow. Under existing circumstances, it was wise for Alcoa to take steps to assure that this exceptionally valuable power site would be available if production grew to such an extent that more power was needed.

Before 1933 Alcoa and its Little Tennessee hydroelectric system existed more or less in isolation. The water that rushed over or through Alcoa's dams was of no further use to the company and flowed down the Little Tennessee into the Tennessee River below, contributing to flood conditions on the Tennessee, Ohio, and Mississippi Rivers in flood season.

With the creation of the Tennessee Valley Authority the whole situation changed. The eight large dams planned for the Tennessee River could produce in the aggregate many times as much power as a dam at the great Fontana site owned by Alcoa. But this important opportunity for power development had a limiting condition: the heavy winter rains were followed by inadequate summer rainfall. The proposed damsites would not have enough water during the six months of the dry season. If water could be stored during the rainy season in the high headwater reservoirs then owned by Alcoa and released during the dry season to generate power at the eight TVA dams downstream, the river system could yield a much more even supply of power all the year round and at the same time improve navigation and flood control. The additional power thus created would be only slightly less than eight times as great as that yielded by a dam at the Fontana site. Alcoa's very large reservoir site was the only one in the whole upland area with enough storage potential to hold a substantial part of the

The Making of the TVA

water flow resulting from the winter rainfall.

When Alcoa had the Fontana area to itself, its course was clear. It would use water at the Fontana site to create, insofar as its storage capacity made possible, a year-round flow. This meant that the reservoir would not be fully emptied before the dry season. The winter rainfall, beyond what could be used or stored, would flow downstream and be lost for power generation because the downstream dams could not hold it. It would also overrun the dams, adding to flood damage along the Tennessee, the Ohio, and the Mississippi Rivers. During the summer the river system would be left without sufficient water for navigation and power generation.

In an integrated system of the type that the TVA was developing, the most important use of the Fontana damsite would be not for wet-season power supply but for storage and flood control during the months of heavy rainfall and high water and for power generation and navigation along the entire river during the summer months. With the Fontana reservoir able to store a large part (but still not all) of the upland rainfall, its capacity, used in conjunction with that of the eight dams and reservoirs below it on the main river, would produce several times as much power as when operated in accordance with Alcoa's private plan. The need to achieve the unified control implicit in the TVA program caused me, as chief engineer of the water-control system, to feel a great responsibility for the use made of the Fontana site.

There was a related issue that surpassed in importance even that of Alcoa's power-supply possibilities: what was the extent of property rights accruing to private ownership of land? Did Alcoa become the private owner of the vast electric-power potential of the upland area because it had the foresight to acquire the major dam and reservoir sites and had title to the power generated at those dams it had built? Pursuing the thought further, would Alcoa have title to and retain control of the heavy rains that fell on its extensive landholdings, drained into the Little Tennessee River, flowed into its reservoirs and through its dams, and then moved downstream to the Tennessee River, where it flowed into TVA reservoirs and through TVA dams? If Alcoa did retain title to and control of the water, did it thereby acquire title to some of the electric power produced at TVA dams and become entitled to share in TVA revenue from the sale of such power? Obviously, the issue was of national importance.

In our culture the earth has been regarded as a surface to provide living space for the population on the basis of private ownership. Private ownership of the land has been assumed to include resources above and below the surface, even though other standards have developed which limit the rights of private property,

Fontana Dam

such as highway rights-of-way, zoning ordinances, navigable-water laws, and the like.

On the basis of the principle of private-property rights, Alcoa officials had been striving for recognition of their ownership of the water *after* it had gone through their property and was on its way to the Ohio and Mississippi Rivers. This seemed to me a new and exaggerated claim for ownership that seldom, if ever, had been recognized in legislation. If the Fontana reservoir was built by Alcoa, then the company might claim ownership of that water flow well past the Little Tennessee area, down the main Tennessee River to the Ohio. There was a prospect that the large winter water flow out of the Little Tennessee River would be included with land and water adjoining the river as Alcoa's property. I felt the claim was socially unwise and should be protested. I considered it my responsibility to bring this unique combination of factors to public attention and, if possible, to prevent the Little Tennessee waters from being appropriated as a source of private gain.

This issue of water ownership was but one example of a vital issue that had only barely begun to enter the public consciousness. There have been many other instances. For example, wealthy and clever lumber companies acquired title to vast territories of forest at a nominal cost by exploiting the homestead laws, and have taken the full profit from this great forest wealth. Should persons or firms who own the land take precedence over the population as a whole? Are they justified in taking permanent possession, or should the country's great resources be considered public wealth, for which those who use them would be required to pay the public for such use? Should not the vast natural wealth of the country remain an asset of the whole people, to be thriftily and carefully used in the development of public riches subject to public ownership?

What could be done to save the high water of winter floods for use at the dams farther down the river? If Alcoa should dam the Fontana site, it might agree to share the high winter water only on the condition that the TVA pay a high price for the resulting power made available to the eight lower dams. This might amount to many millions of dollars a year more than the value of the power generated solely by the Fontana dam. (Such exploitive demands were in fact made by Alcoa in subsequent negotiations.)

I suggested a plan that would guarantee Alcoa the amount of power that would be yielded by the proposed Fontana dam and the dams they had already built on the Little Tennessee River but that would leave the TVA in possession of all additional power created by the integrated control of Fontana's reservoir and the seasonal needs of the eight TVA dams proposed for the Tennessee

River. The TVA would take possession of the Fontana site and would supply to Alcoa as much power from other sources as the Fontana dam would yield.

To include the Fontana site and existing Alcoa dams in the integrated management of the Tennessee River system under the TVA would require congressional authorization. It was achieved in 1935 by a bill that I was instrumental in preparing and that was guided through Congress by Representative Lister Hill of Alabama. While the bill was being considered by Congress, I waited in the TVA's Washington office to learn the outcome. David Lilienthal came in. He had the manner of a defeated and discouraged man, his feet dragging across the floor, his arms hanging down. He said in a tone of despair, "We are licked; we are licked. I have counted the votes in the House and we are licked." After a few more such remarks, he was gone.

I was surprised at this display because I knew he wanted the bill defeated. His course throughout had been to protect the interests of Alcoa, with whom he had a long-established, intimate personal relationship and whom he had made the largest customer for TVA power sales. I was also reminded of the fact that Lilienthal's chief recreation was dramatics—he was head of the drama group at Norris—and I suspected that he was exercising his theatrical bent on this occasion.

When Mr. Lilienthal had left the room, I immediately went to Congressman Hill's office in the House Office Building. As I approached his open door, Mr. Hill called out, "Mr. Morgan, I am so glad to see you come. Mr. Lilienthal has just been here, and he tells me that your legislation is a mistake and that it should be withdrawn from the calendar." I explained the situation and the reasons for Mr. Lilienthal's opposition. Mr. Hill was convinced and pushed the legislation through the House, which passed it without much trouble.

That, however, was not the close of the incident. Alcoa continued to voice vigorously its objection to the bill. Lister Hill's actions to protect the bill after it had been passed by Congress and Alcoa's attempts to amend it are described in the following letter to me dated June 19, 1973, from Aubrey Wagner, chairman of the TVA. Mr. Wagner had looked up the detailed record of the incident.

> You asked in your letter of June 4, 1973, about the subsequent history of section 26a [which required that any project affecting the Tennessee River system be approved by the TVA Board of Directors*] of the TVA Act, which was added by amendment in 1935.

*The unified development and regulation of the Tennessee River system requires that no dam, appurtenant works, or other obstruction affecting navigation, flood control, or public lands or

Fontana Dam

The second paragraph of the section, dealing with structures on the Little Tennessee River, was added in Congress in the interest of the Aluminum Company of America and its subsidiaries. The companion bills introduced in March of 1935 by Senator Norris and Representative McSwain provided for review by the TVA Board of all plans for construction anywhere in the Tennessee River system and did not include this special provision relating to the Little Tennessee. The Norris bill passed the Senate unamended and went to the House. There it was referred to the Committee on Military Affairs, among many of whose members there was substantial opposition to the entire TVA program. The committee held hearings, at which Arthur V. Davis, Chairman of the Board of the Aluminum Company, testified and objected to the proposed amendment providing for TVA review of the company's plans for development of the Little Tennessee. (*Hearings Before the House Committee on Military Affairs*, Tennessee Valley Authority, 74th Cong., 1st Sess., vol. 2 at 664, 1935) The committee eventually reported out a new bill, H. R. 8632, generally much less desirable from TVA's standpoint. It deleted altogether any provision for TVA review of construction plans anywhere in the entire Tennessee River system. On the floor of the House, Representative Lister Hill of Alabama obtained an amendment to the bill restoring the entire section but adding the second paragraph on the Little Tennessee, explaining that the paragraph had been added to meet the objections of the Aluminum Company and "avoid any possible adverse effect which the Aluminum Company might claim by giving it a right to appeal to the Federal Power Commission from any requirements of the Authority." (79th Cong. Rec. 10794, 1935) The bill was finally approved with section 26a in this form except that in the course of the debates the Secretary of War (now Secretary of the Army) was substituted for the Federal Power Commission as the final arbiter on the Little Tennessee.

The Aluminum Company and its subsidiaries have added several dams to the Alcoa system on the Little Tennessee since the enactment of section 26a. However, there has been no significant disagreement between Alcoa and TVA over these structures, and most of them are operated as parts of the TVA system under the Fontana agreement... Under that agreement, the power generated at these dams is delivered to the TVA system, and TVA controls the storage and release of water. In return, TVA delivers a relatively firm and uniform supply of power to production plants and other installations of the Company and its subsidiaries....

It has never been necessary for TVA to go to the point of actually filing suit for an injunction prohibiting a structure in the Tennessee River system on the ground that it was being constructed or maintained in violation of section 26a. However,

reservations shall be constructed, and thereafter operated or maintained across, along, or in the said river or any of its tributaries until plans for such construction, operation, and maintenance shall have been submitted to and approved by the board; and the contruction, commencement of construction, operation, or maintenance of such structures without such approval is hereby prohibited. When such plans shall have been approved, deviation therefrom either before or after completion of such structures is prohibited unless the modification of such plans has previously been submitted to and approved by the board. (Amended TVA Act, Sec. 26a, HR 5081, 74th Congress, 1935, pp. 19-20.)

we know that in at least two or three cases the express statement in the statute of TVA's power to do so was persuasive in getting certain industrial plans altered so as to be consistent with TVA development plans and water quality standards.

Under the National Environmental Policy Act of 1969 and recent amendments of the Federal Water Pollution Control Act, TVA is now both authorized and required to take cognizance of the water quality and other environmental impacts of facilities for which approval is sought under section 26a. The section as a whole has been extremely useful throughout its history in providing the necessary authority for a reasonable general surveillance of structures of all kinds in the Tennessee River system.

In a statement on May 22, 1935, to the House Committee on Military Affairs, which was considering the proposed amendment to the TVA Act, I had said:

> Whoever controls the Little Tennessee River to a very considerable degree will dominate the TVA as to its power policy and as to its navigation policy and as to its flood-control policy.... If the Little Tennessee is administered independently of the rest of the system, whoever so administers it will have a coercive power over the administration of the river system as a whole.
>
> Word has come to us privately that [Alcoa was] endeavoring to buy up all of the land in an area so that [it] could go ahead independently of the TVA. It seemed to us that the issues were so great that the control of the Little Tennessee River [by Alcoa] would mean a damage to the TVA (of perhaps ten or twenty million dollars a year—or more)...*

It is no wonder that Alcoa was unwilling to give up one of the best dam and reservoir sites in the eastern United States. The company had at stake not only its own power-supply source but also a strategic bargaining position from which it could force the TVA to pay dearly for Alcoa's cooperation. In the 1935 hearings held on the amendment to the TVA Act that would place the Little Tennessee under TVA control over the protests of Alcoa, Arthur V. Davis, chairman of Alcoa, told the House Committee on Military Affairs:

> We... engineered out 104 miles of this [Little Tennessee River]... We have had for twenty-five years, from ten to seventy-five engineers, all the time working on this engineering development and we have plans which comprise developments which completely and absolutely utilize the entire flow of the stream. There is no possible conservation plan which could be devised which would be superior to

---

*Hearings Before the Committee on Military Affairs, House of Representatives, 74th Congress, 1st Sess. (Washington, D.C.: Govt. Printing Office, 1935), vol. 2, pp. 703, 705.

ours... And whatever development could be made or ever would be made on this river would be exactly the same as ours.*

With all this money spent, with twenty-five years of record behind us, with all this engineering data, with our plans so completely laid out for the future, we submit that we are entitled to proceed with our development, which we bought with our own money... That is our only objection to the bill as it now stands. I refer now to that section of the bill which is known, I believe, as 26a.**

In effect, the Aluminum Company of America was claiming that, since it had discovered the possibilities of the Little Tennessee River, it should become the sole arbiter of this great natural resource.

When Alcoa fought to avoid integrated control, President Roosevelt and Senator Norris personally gave me strong support. My position was that this resource was still a part of the domain of the United States and should not be subject to uncoordinated and independent private control, even at the wish of a powerful corporation like Alcoa. Here was a great issue of government that, so far as I know, had never been adjudicated. The notion that "we acquired title, so the property is ours to do with as we see fit" did not seem to me valid when great natural resources were involved. The President desired to create in the entire Tennessee River system a program that took national responsibility for flood control, navigation, and the development of electrical power. An important principle of public control was at stake.

Mr. Davis' indignant complaint that Alcoa's engineers and surveyors had spent thousands of dollars and years of time in surveying and planning development of the river and had thereby established rights to "their property" is typical of the attitude of autocrats toward property they wish to dominate. Mr. Davis said: "It is just simply a question of whether we as a private corporation ... should be legislated out of the jurisdiction of our own property."†

Throughout the Fontana issue, during my service with the TVA, Mr. Lilienthal largely aligned himself with the position of the Aluminum Company of America. However, in his journal for 1941 he expressed a critical attitude toward Alcoa.††

Mr. Lilienthal expressed his earlier attitude in many ways over the years: in his dramatic objection to the Section 26a legislation; in his and Harcourt Mor-

*Ibid., p. 662.
**Ibid., p. 664.
†Ibid., p. 665.
††Lilienthal, p. 350.

gan's decision, acting as a majority of the board, not to seek from Congress authorization to construct Fontana Dam and to discontinue negotiations with Alcoa for acquisition of the dam and reservoir site; and in his firm refusal to make TVA power available to a prospect who wanted to compete with Alcoa in the production and sale of aluminum.

Mr. Lilienthal's relationship with the executives of Alcoa led him to take the secretary of an Alcoa executive to be his own secretary. This young woman confided to my secretary a difficult situation that she found herself in. She said that her former employer had asked her to extract confidential information from TVA files and give it to him.

Another incident pointed to the same conclusion concerning Lilienthal's alignments. William B. Mayo, who was chief engineer of Ford Motor Company, dealt with Ford's many varied interests and proposals aside from the manufacture of automobiles. As he was also a trustee of Antioch College, I had occasional meetings with him. At one of our meetings he said he wanted to talk with me about aluminum. He told me that the American automobile industry was concerned with the availability of aluminum. They wanted very much to consider the use of aluminum for parts and accessories for automobiles, but thought it unwise to do so as long as aluminum production was almost a monopoly. (Alcoa was the only large producer.)

Mr. Mayo explained further that Richard S. Reynolds wanted to establish an aluminum industry that would compete with the Aluminum Company of America. Reynolds had adequate financial resources and was looking for a source of electrical power, the major factor in aluminum production. He asked if the TVA, with a large power supply for which it wanted a market, would be interested. I told him that responsibility for electric-power sales was in Mr. Lilienthal's hands and that I would inquire of him at the next TVA board meeting. When I asked Mr. Lilienthal about power for this purpose, he replied forcefully that such a supply would not be available. And then he dropped the subject as a closed issue.*

---

*When the proposal for construction of the Chickamauga Dam was before Congress, Mr. Lilienthal argued vigorously with me that the dam should not be built because it would result in a power supply far in excess of the demand. The feasibility of providing large amounts of power was as clear when Mr. Reynolds was searching for a source as it was later. The inquiry concerning a source of power for Mr. Reynolds preceded the construction of additional dams, but it seems that an adequate supply of power might have been provided by the time it would have been needed for additional aluminum production, and that the needs of the automobile and other industries would have supplied an adequate market for the aluminum produced. Also, the existing power plants at Muscle Shoals generated power for which an adequate market had not yet been found.

Fontana Dam

This sampling of my extensive experiences with Mr. Lilienthal's opposition to TVA development of Fontana Dam serves as necessary background for an account of how my effort to include Fontana in the TVA system was finally blocked. This was by far the most important single project on which I came into conflict with the other members of the board.

Following the passage of legislation I had introduced giving the TVA the right to obtain unified control over the Little Tennessee River watershed (including Alcoa's Fontana site), I had responsibility for negotiating the purchase of Fontana. The negotiations had been promising.

On May 19, 1936, the day after he was reappointed to the TVA board, David Lilienthal brought Dr. Harcourt Morgan to my office and told me that we would have a business meeting. He then announced that the purpose of the meeting was to take construction of Fontana Dam out of my hands and put it in his. (During the year that I was responsible for the negotiations, Mr. Lilienthal had insisted that he have a representative present because of their importance. When they were no longer my responsibility, however, I was excluded from them.)

There was no engineering or administrative justification for my removal from the Fontana project, which naturally fell under my duties as chief engineer of the TVA. To look at a particular case, before large structures such as dams were built, an estimate of cost was submitted to the appropriate authorities in Congress. Technical Monograph 55, Vol. I, published by the TVA in August 1954, when neither Lilienthal nor I was on the staff of the TVA, records significant data. The estimated cost is given along with the actual cost of dams and reservoirs as follows:

	Estimate	Cost
Norris	$ 36,025,230	$ 30,508,024
Wheeler	32,116,537	29,294,720
Pickwick	32,529,685	29,701,267
Hiwassee	15,250,000	15,922,637
Guntersville	29,500,000	31,098,760
Chickamauga	31,650,000	33,730,996
Total	$177,071,452	$170,256,404
Fontana	$ 48,000,000	$ 69,043,688

The first six dams, constructed under my direction, were built at a cost that was within 2 percent of the estimate.

113

The Making of the TVA

TVA construction of the Fontana Dam, finally approved in 1941, was under Mr. Lilienthal's direction. Construction-cost records were so inadequately kept that a detailed breakdown was not available, but the total cost was $69,043,688, or approximately 44 percent above the estimate of the Aluminum Company of America.

The Tennessee Valley Authority's negotiations for the purchase of the Fontana site were formally ended at a board of directors meeting on June 2, 1936. I had been given no notice of this meeting; it was held when I was away from my office overnight visiting dams under construction. The minutes of the meeting read as follows:

> As a result of its lengthy discussion concerning the proposed Fontana Dam construction project, the Board arrived at the following conclusions:
> 1. No further communication is to be had with Congress concerning authorization to construct the Fontana Dam.
> 2. All negotiations with the Aluminum Company of America involving acquisition of the Fontana Dam site are to be immediately discontinued.
> 3. The conclusions of the Board with regard to the acquisition of the Fontana Dam site are not to preclude further negotiations with the Aluminum Company of America relating to the interchange of energy.*

But the third item in the minutes was vitally related to the first two, as I explained to the congressional committee investigating charges that Lilienthal and Harcourt Morgan made against me. I asserted that in negotiating with Alcoa for the purchase of Fontana "we had one bargaining point, and that was that the Aluminum Company needed power. They owned the Fontana damsite, which we very much needed. They needed power so much at that time that they had indicated their willingness to sell us the Fontana damsite and to take their pay in secondary power, and let us operate . . . the rest of their plants. . . . Now, if we sold them power and met their other needs for power without getting control of the Fontana site, we were giving away all of our bargaining power, our power to get control of that very critical damsite."** The minutes of the meeting of June 2 recorded the surrender of the TVA's exercise of its bargaining power to obtain Fontana. Until about this time the TVA had been authorized to exchange power for damsites.

Mr. Lilienthal had to justify two serious departures from propriety. Why did

---

*Senate Document 155: Removal of a Member of the TVA, 75th Congress (Washington, D.C.: Govt. Printing Office, March 1938), p. 49.
**Hearings Before the Joint Committee on the Investigation of the Tennessee Valley Authority, 75th Congress, Part 1, July 19, 1938, p. 372.

he scuttle TVA's negotiations with Alcoa, which had been originated with the full backing of the President and Senator Norris? And why had he called a meeting without notifying me and decided so crucial an issue in my absence, since as chairman and chief engineer I was responsible for the selection and purchase of damsites and for the unified control of the river system? He excused the second impropriety by saying that I was away on an extended vacation. He had told the President that my absence was the beginning of an extended absence of some six weeks. In fact, the meeting was held *before* my vacation.

The reasons Mr. Lilienthal gave the President and the congressional investigating committee for ending the negotiations were various and only superficially valid. His *Journals* entry of June 30, 1941, gives a completely misleading excuse.

> The crux of the aircraft program now is additional power supply. And the center of that problem is a water-power site up in the mountains of North Carolina on the Little Tennessee River—the Fontana site. The dam to be built on this site, which the Aluminum Company has owned for many years, would be the highest dam east of the Rocky Mountains, and the most favorable, economically favorable, water-power site remaining in the Eastern United States.
>
> The fact that the Aluminum Company failed to build a dam on this site, although there has been a great need for the additional power supply, was the occasion for a violent attack upon it by the Truman Committee of the Senate just the other day. Six years ago the Tennessee Valley Authority began negotiations to buy that site from the Aluminum Company. Those negotiations were conducted for the TVA by Dr. A. E. Morgan and an engineer by the name of Ackerman. The majority of the board rejected the basis of the negotiations because, as I discovered to my horror, underneath engineering computations that I didn't understand at all was the proposition that the Aluminum Company would receive a share of the benefits that the building of that dam would produce in TVA dams downstream all along the river. And so the negotiations were terminated six years ago.*

It was precisely this eventuality of the Aluminum Company's demanding benefits downstream from Fontana that I had sought to prevent by setting up legislative and bargaining conditions for the TVA to obtain Fontana. In 1935 I had stated to a congressional committee that control of the Little Tennessee by the Aluminum Company of America would mean a damage to the TVA of perhaps ten or twenty million dollars a year.

Mr. Lilienthal's expression of ignorance of the engineering computation seems strange because these were the very problems repeatedly discussed with

---

*Lilienthal, p. 350.

him in the congressional committee and discussed by Alcoa in trying to make their wishes prevail. Therefore, his ignorance as to what was at stake and his indignation at the position of the Aluminum Company, seems to be subterfuge, an effort to cover up the facts.

After the majority of the TVA board in my absence discontinued negotiations for Fontana, I visited Mr. Davis to see if there might be grounds for reviving the negotiations. I wrote a memorandum to the board about this visit on August 15, 1936, from which the following material is taken.

> I told him [Davis] that inasmuch as I considered the matter to be vital to the unified control of the Tennessee River, it was my intention to ask for renegotiation of their action. . . . [Then I pointed out that the Aluminum Company engineer, James P. Growden] . . . has a theory concerning the additional power which will result from unified operations with which our engineers cannot agree. Mr. Growden, in their opinion, assumes that of the additional power which would result from integrated control a very large part should go to the Aluminum Company. Our engineers do not agree with this suggested apportionment. It seems that perhaps the next step would be for the Aluminum Company to bring some disinterested outside engineer, who is not committed to any theory about the matter, to make a review of the situation with our engineers to discover if the Aluminum Company would find a more moderate position acceptable. Unless that result can be achieved it would seem an almost impossible gap between the engineers of the Aluminum Company and those of the TVA. Mr. Davis indicated that he would not be adverse to such an appraisal. I reiterated to him, however, that the Board had taken official action discontinuing negotiation.*

This memorandum was used as evidence of my failure to accept and abide by decisions of the board majority and as grounds for my discharge from the chairmanship of the TVA.

According to Mr. Lilienthal's own statement, he was responsible for ending the negotiations over Fontana on issues that *were* negotiable and thus for five years leaving the site in the hands of the Aluminum Company. This left an impaired bargaining position that would be yet more difficult were the Aluminum Company to build the Fontana dam independently of the TVA.

The Fontana issue was a major subject of my testimony to the congressional committee investigating differences within the TVA board, but it was not then nor has it since been reported to the public, either in newspapers or books. Immediately after the hearings my son Griscom asked a newspaper publisher

---

*Senate Document 155, p. 49.

why my testimony was not reported in the press. The publisher, who had followed the issue closely, answered that the extensive advertising Alcoa placed in the newspapers and magazines was such a significant source of income to the publishers that they did not want to risk losing it by reporting this aspect of the TVA controversy. Moreover, the company had political, as well as journalistic, influence. Its founder, Andrew Mellon, had been a Republican secretary of the treasury, so it is evident that both political parties had an interest in keeping the Aluminum Company issue from public view.

In the spring of 1941 America's growing involvement in the Second World War brought about a severe aluminum shortage, accentuated by Alcoa's monopoly of aluminum production. Harry Truman, who then headed a Senate committee investigating the defense program, was giving particular attention to the aluminum shortage because of its crucial role in aircraft production. As Mr. Lilienthal's statements show, it was discovered that the Aluminum Company had left this most important of the remaining hydroelectric-power sites in the eastern United States undeveloped and that *it was asking the government to finance the building of this dam,* which was common practice among defense industries. Mr. Truman asked why, if the dam were going to be built at government expense, it should not be built by the TVA.

An urgent national defense need, and a general outcry about the monopoly that restricted aluminum production, created pressure for Alcoa to negotiate with the TVA. Again the Aluminum Company sought to exact a heavy price for the benefits of unified control of the river. Mr. Lilienthal tells in his *Journals* how he finally saw through and avoided the company's endeavor to keep much of the benefits to itself and how the TVA at long last worked out with Alcoa the unified control of the watershed, thereby achieving, to the benefit of both parties, the objectives that I had sought in 1935 and 1936.

Chapter Nine

The Personnel and Training Program

Up to and including the first third of the present century, most large construction works in this country, especially in the central and western states, were built without much regard for the living and working conditions of the workers. Recognizing this deficiency, I had endeavored to establish new standards for labor relations in the Miami Conservancy District, and I felt that I had achieved considerable success. The TVA, with its prospect of even more extensive work, seemed to me to call for even greater improvements in the planning of general working conditions. Therefore, starting from the standards that had been established for the Miami Conservancy District, I undertook to set still higher standards for the TVA.

The man most intimately involved with me on this phase of the TVA undertaking was J. Dudley Dawson. My association with Mr. Dawson began at Antioch College in 1924, when he became head of the Department of Mathematics.

Later, he was in charge of the work-study program for Antioch students for a number of years. He also served as vice-president and dean of students for fourteen years, prior to his retirement in 1967. His work at Antioch had given me confidence in his judgment and effectiveness.

I recently discussed the TVA training program, for which he was so largely responsible under my direction, with Mr. Dawson. Because of his intimate knowledge of the details of the program, I shall include our discussion here.

DUDLEY DAWSON: In July 1933 I was about to take a leave of absence for a year from Antioch to resume graduate studies. But at that time you became chairman of the Tennessee Valley Authority, and at your request I joined the TVA to help develop a training program you had outlined. I started work as an assistant to Dr. Floyd Reeves, who was the director of personnel. I devoted the first few weeks to getting acquainted with civic and educational leaders in the Tennessee Valley and to exploring personnel possibilities for the TVA. Then I took on a special job dealing with the recruitment of workmen for employment and training. After a more formal organization was established, I became the director of training for the Personnel Division, a position I held for the rest of my two years with the TVA. Initially I also had some responsibility for development and management of the town of Norris, although as my training responsibilities grew, it became necessary to establish a separate town management. When work began on Wheeler Dam and then on Pickwick Dam, we established phases of our training program at those places. The headquarters of the training section remained at Norris, with subdivisions at Wheeler and Pickwick.

ARTHUR MORGAN: I had relations with the TVA that you did not, and you had some that I did not. When I was on the Miami Conservancy job, I felt that the working conditions in outdoor construction in America were at such a low level that I undertook to improve them.

When I was a boy I wanted to get a construction job. The boss where I had applied told me, "All right, get you a blanket and a woman and come along." Often a construction site was surrounded by saloons and gambling houses and houses of prostitution and so forth. I thought that working conditions should be such that a man could bring his family to the job with pride. Before I came to the TVA, I had tried to create such conditions on jobs where I was in charge.

There was an additional reason that made such improvements seem more necessary in the TVA's case. The Authority had very strong enemies, especially among private-power companies and, at that time, in the coal-mining industry. When you become part of a big complex like that, you discover interrelationships that you did not know existed. I found, for example, in my first months at Knoxville that there were elements within organized labor that aimed to do the TVA as much harm as possible. The president of the Trades and Labor Council in Knoxville evidently had some schemes. At a time when he was praising me highly in public, a letter he had written to his people happened to fall into my hands. It indicated an explicit aim to "do in" the TVA. Such developments in the labor field were not accidental.* We had to select men carefully or we might have found ourselves in a nasty position. Later, the Army Corps of Engineers encountered in St. Louis a very bad situation of deceit and conspiracy, where the Mafia was involved in a so-called labor organization.

It seemed wise to be careful. Within fifty miles of a construction area there were communities of several thousand people. Many really good men were out of work. We thought we could find in those communities men who would be free from the crosscurrents I have referred to.

Dudley, you can correct me on this, because you were the man who did a good deal of the work, you and the employment department working together. With the manpower needs of the TVA and the prospects for providing some training for employees in mind, we developed a register of the best workers we could find in the Tennessee Valley. We set up simple tests for employment that could be adapted for those who could not read or write, as a means of securing capable workmen who could profit from the training opportunities. We finally had between forty and fifty thousand prospective employees.

DAWSON: This employee register grew and was used for four or five years. Many more people took the tests and applied for employment than we had reason to anticipate—in fact, there were many more qualified persons than could be hired in the first year or two of the TVA.

The TVA region included nearly all of the state of Tennessee, a small part of western North Carolina, a bit of northern Georgia, a considerable portion of Alabama, and parts of Mississippi and Kentucky. The parts of these six states drained by the Tennessee River constituted the area from which workmen on TVA projects were drawn.

It was your idea, Mr. Morgan, that in addition to locating and employing high-quality workmen from the region, the TVA would provide supplementary training for its unsalaried employees. This would serve several purposes: upgrading employees in their work with the TVA, giving many an opportunity to develop the skills and knowledge to enter new occupations, and laying the foun-

*"TVA News," May 1972.

dation for improving their standards of living when they returned to their homes after TVA employment. This made the process of selecting workmen doubly important. We wanted to recruit not only good workers but also persons who could profit from the training opportunities and through whom the whole region would benefit.

At the beginning of the TVA program it was assumed that most of the workmen would return to their homes when Norris Dam was finished. But as highly qualified and trained construction workers went on to other sites at Wheeler, Pickwick, and Hiwassee, the training many had received at Norris (and later at other dams) was valuable to them in their future work with the TVA and in their everyday living.

MORGAN: In order to provide more jobs in a period of severe depression, the working day was reduced to five-and-one-half-hour shifts, with two shifts for each part of the work. Thus there was time to train people in many forms of household skills and activities. Such training was made more desirable by the manner of settlement of the mountain areas. Parents and growing children moved from their early cabin homes, where few skills were known, to their new cottage homes, where they needed to learn the arts of living. There had also been few cultural relationships in most mountain homes. A four- or five-hour period of social life with various arts and activities helped to enlarge and enrich the lives of formerly isolated people. Learning to make gardens, to raise poultry, to make furniture and clothing, and to take part in social activities enlarged the lives of those involved and was greatly appreciated by them. Whole families made it a practice to work and learn together. The contempt some people higher up in the TVA expressed for such activities was misplaced.

When President Roosevelt had told me of the changes he hoped to bring about in the lives of the mountain people, including those parts of their day that otherwise would have been largely idle, I felt that he was thinking and speaking intelligently. For parents and children to live and work or play together—sharing household interests and recreation and making household belongings—was better than being in a camp surrounded by gambling houses. It was well to meet the needs and wishes of workers for both work and leisure and not to assume that the TVA was interested in providing only work and wages.

DAWSON: To return to the recruiting process. Because the TVA was a semi-independent government agency, it was not technically under civil service, so we had a great advantage in flexibility of employee selection. But that also opened the door to strong political pressures. You were determined to keep employment free from political influence, but it was far from easy. I think it is fair to say that one of the great and notable accomplishments of the TVA in the personnel area was its almost complete success in keeping politics out of employment.

It seemed desirable to have some kind of objective test for applicants, to find out something about their aptitudes, skills, and mental equipment, but no suitable ones existed. Dr. Reeves arranged for Dr. L. G. O'Rourke, who had long experience in test preparation with the Civil Service Commission and elsewhere, to develop a fairly simple aptitude test for skilled and unskilled workers who applied for employment.

The recruiting plan we developed was concerned first with making large numbers of qualified persons in the Tennessee Valley (especially in the rural areas) acquainted with the opportunities for employment and training with the TVA and then with getting them to file applications and take the qualifying test.

With these concerns in mind, I assigned ten able young men, mostly from nearby colleges and universities, to secure capable assistants, who would select and train men. We organized in teams of two to visit every county seat in the six states of the TVA region. Letters were sent asking the county agent or the county superintendent of schools to bring together a group of leading citizens in the county—ministers, doctors, mayors, teachers, county agents, lawyers, and so forth—for a meeting with the two TVA representatives. At these meetings we explained the general purposes of the TVA and described employment and training opportunities. Detailed instructions were given about procedures for filing applications and taking the employment tests, which were handled through the post office in each county seat. Arrangements were made to give assistance to those who needed help in filling out application forms or in understanding the test questions. The main appeal directed at county leaders was for their active assistance in informing capable and reliable workers of the employment and training opportunities and in urging them to apply.

The interest and cooperation of these local leaders was most friendly and useful. The fact that many able-bodied men needed work so badly naturally led community leaders to help the TVA locate responsible applicants. The thousands of men, many of whom had been solicited, arriving at the county seats to take the test and apply for employment, far exceeded our most optimistic expectations. Applications, test results, and references were later checked and rated in the Knoxville office to establish a roster of qualified personnel for employment in the skilled and unskilled labor force of the TVA, and, as we have said, workmen were hired from these lists over a period of years.

MORGAN: I think you will find that this is the first instance in the history of major outdoor construction work in the United States where such a high degree

The Personnel and Training Program

of selection in hiring a work force was used.

DAWSON: I wonder if it has been done since.

MORGAN: It is significant that there were good minds and good personalities available. We got such people and they developed. In the years since then, the TVA, in no small degree, has been living off of that selection. The work that TVA has gotten done has been exceptional.

DAWSON: We operated in an unprecedented way, but it worked. It was the only way, as I think back, that we could have accomplished our purpose. When people came to visit the TVA, they often said, "Where did you get such a fine-looking group of workers?" The character and quality of the employees were obvious even to those who came into only casual contact with them.*

MORGAN: What about the training program?

DAWSON: First, a little more on its design, part of which has already been indicated. In addition to the construction of several large dams for the purpose of flood control, improved navigation, and electric power, the TVA was also concerned with the improvement of agricultural practices. This included questions relating to soil erosion, land use, forestry, and other related economic developments. Attention was also given to stimulating small industries appropriate to the Tennessee Valley. The TVA was concerned with many phases of economic and social development designed to raise the standard of living of the people of the Valley; these were directly and indirectly related to the broad purpose and specific technical aspects of the TVA Act.

The training program was conceived and carried out with two main objectives: (1) to upgrade the workmanship of TVA employees on their jobs, and (2) to assist employees in their personal and occupational development beyond their immediate work. To spread employment during the depression, the construction work ran continuously in shifts of five-and-a-half hours each. When workmen came on the job we noted the training they would like to undertake—things they would like to learn and prepare themselves to do. We then tried to work out with each interested employee a suitable plan of education or training for his off-duty shifts.

MORGAN: President Roosevelt's statement of his expectations for the TVA, as well as our conversation when he asked me to be chairman, disclosed his very definite interest in raising the economic and cultural level of the entire Tennessee Valley.

---

*In Chapter Twelve I have given a sketch of the later evidence of personal development that helped bring about group projects for improving life in the Tennessee Valley.

DAWSON: The TVA built the town of Norris with a construction camp, a cafeteria, and a community center for recreation and community activities. It was a demonstration town, with low- and medium-cost housing for a number of families of workmen and staff.

Large barnlike trade shops were built in Norris for conducting training in the electrical, mechanical, and woodworking trades. Training classes at these shops were very popular with the workers, who saw them as a way of developing useful trade skills for future employment. To head this training program we employed Howard Briggs, who had been in charge of industrial-trades training in the Cleveland, Ohio, school system.

At the trades-training center there were classes in machine-shop practice, welding, wrought-iron blacksmithing, electrical work, carpentry, and other kinds of woodworking. There was a lot of interest in craftwork. We employed as teachers master craftsmen—one from a High Point, North Carolina, furniture factory and a couple of teachers from the Berea, Kentucky, craft shops.

MORGAN: Highly developed skills in many trades were necessary for the complex design and construction of dams and power plants, and the training program upgraded our employees' skills for this very demanding work.

DAWSON: We carried on a very interesting and successful form of training in woodworking. For one phase of it, our training staff explored locally in the Valley for samples of Early American furniture that were good-looking, of good quality, and useful in the household. They made large-scale drawings of these samples, broken down in sectional models that could be duplicated and constructed by an amateur using power tools. On the outskirts of Norris we built a demonstration dairy farm stocked with a herd of highbred cattle. This farm became a training center for growing cover legume crops for cattle feed, for soil terracing and erosion control, for animal breeding, and for the economics and practice of dairy production. Adjoining the farm was a modern creamery operated for demonstration and training, as well as to serve the community. To reduce the cost of the training program, dairy products from the farm were processed by the creamery, which in turn furnished the workers' cafeteria at Norris with milk and ice cream. Close by was a demonstration poultry farm that provided training for those interested in poultry raising. All of these training activities in agriculture, as well as training in forestry, were also demonstrations of the possibilities of economic and social development in the Tennessee Valley. Such demonstrations reached well beyond those enrolled in formal classes.

MORGAN: Agricultural activities, though provided for construction crews and their families, were properly the field of Harcourt Morgan, who took an interest in them. Much of the training had a social effect. In the crafts work, for example, a man and his wife could do something together. The children also joined in. They might work in one part of the shop and the father and mother in another. They had something to talk to each other about. It was a family-building place as well as a product-building place. I know of no other construction job on which such an opportunity was offered. There is nothing like participation in interesting and productive activities to reduce the occurrence of undesirable types of action. An excerpt from a 1934 speech I made speaks to this theme.

> We hold that we ought not to draw a line and say that no young man without special privilege or a crafts-union membership will have a chance, because if we find a young man especially able in any field, he ought to have a chance in that field. You know some of the types of labor that drift into a construction job. You know how poorly the hiring system works at times. We have a body of young men today that is heart and soul interested in the work, a clean-cut lot of fellows, who are anxious to do the job. They have been told—and they believe it—that they are part of the New Deal. If they can produce electric power cheaper, they can have it in their houses cheaper; if they can build homes for workingmen cheaper, more workingmen can have homes. And nobody is making anything out of it; the people are getting the benefits of it. If they can do a good job, they are supporting the President in his policies and making it possible for the average man to get his share out of life.*

DAWSON: We did considerable training related to dam construction, and I'll get to that later. Right now I would like to speak of other aspects of the training offered at Norris that relate to what you have been saying.

As I indicated earlier, a number of workers' families lived at Norris. We used one of the family-type houses as a home-demonstration center, with a number of training classes for women—cooking, child care, home furnishings, and family budgeting. We employed the highly respected former director of the Home Extension Service for the state of Tennessee, Marie White, who left her post in home economics with the Extension Service in Washington, D.C., to join our staff. Miss White's demonstration house had a broadening educational effect on the many who came to see it. She got women volunteers from the community to assist in the training projects.

There were other significant results of the training program and the activities and life at Norris. For example, we operated a fairly well-stocked commissary in the community building. We were advised to limit the selection of reading

---

*From my speech to the Central States Forestry Congress, Knoxville, Tenn., May 30, 1934.

materials largely to comics, westerns, and cheap literature, as it was believed that these were the only things that people from the mountains and rural areas would read. Instead we stocked the shelves with *Time, National Geographic, Scientific American, Harper's,* and other magazines, and a reasonably good range of fiction, science, and biography, some on a very elementary level. The men and their families devoured this type of reading and did not press for the cheaper stuff, which they could buy outside Norris if they wished. This was a revealing experience.

There was also an interesting experience with the food served in the cafeteria. To manage the cafeteria we brought in a woman well trained in dietetics, who was also well acquainted with the region. Our cafeteria manager was advised by some that the men would eat only things they were used to. But it did not turn out that way. They thoroughly enjoyed the salads, vegetables, milk, and other foods that we served. Many workmen got the first balanced diet they had ever had. Our feeling was that these men would never be satisfied to go back to their homes and live on the monotonous and inadequate local diet, which resulted in strikingly poor physical development in so many cases.

We had bunkhouses somewhat like dormitories, though much simpler in layout and less costly. In fact, the construction camp resembled a simple college campus. There was also a dormitory in the construction camp for women workers in the cafeteria and bakery.

At the center of the camp was a community building that housed recreation and reading rooms, the commissary, and a large auditorium. The director of recreation was Scotty Forbes, a jolly Scotsman, who had a knack for working with the men and women in the camp and the families in the village. He worked out a motion-picture booking plan, so that a continuous flow of high-quality movies could be secured without having to take a block of indiscriminately selected ones. He also developed a series of dramatic productions, using local talent. There was a lot of interest in play productions.

The training section developed an adult-education program that ran concurrently with the specialized training classes. It was headed by a liberal and broadly educated minister, who also led religious services each Sunday that appealed to a wide range of differing beliefs. The community center was open day and night, and something interesting was always going on during each of the eight-hour leisure shifts.

MORGAN: Will you discuss the training of foremen?

DAWSON: Yes. This was part of the training related to the upgrading of men on their jobs. For example, we trained many of the construction foremen rather than import them. The construction superintendent at Norris Dam, Ross White, was interested in a program to train additional foremen. As workmen came on the job, those who appeared interested and capable were invited to enroll in foreman training. Their training included engineering technology, health and safety practices, human relations, and supervisory management. This was highly successful, not only as to personal development of the workmen, but also as to the quality of construction, supervision, and economy of the TVA operation. It also contributed to an accident rate that was notably low as compared to other such projects.

MORGAN: By picking out the best foremen while they were being trained, we got a "new breed," you might say, of foremen. Some of those young fellows came to hold quite responsible positions. They made a fine body of workmen for the TVA for the next twenty or thirty years, and contributed enormously to the quality of our job.

At the outset we estimated the cost of and asked for an appropriation to cover construction of twenty dams. Those twenty dams were built at a cost of eight hundred million dollars, which overran our original estimates by less than 1 percent.

DAWSON: This sets a standard not common today.

MORGAN: And it doesn't happen by accident.

DAWSON: In fact, there is another interesting example of the type of thing that you were referring to regarding training people that has some application to the present talk about law and order and training people in police administration. I think of this now because I have been doing some consulting work recently with community colleges in developing courses in police administration. In this connection I recalled what we did at Norris, which was not a city but *was* a sizable town of about fifteen hundred people. In addition to its size and the mobility of its population, there were hundreds of visitors who came to Norris from all over the country to see what was often referred to as a model town. There were problems of guiding visitors, safety, and—occasionally—policing. Instead of employing the usual trained guides and police officers, we selected a group of qualified young men, mostly young college graduates with the potential for being broadly trained for these jobs. We then hired an able young man who had been educated in safety and police administration to manage training and operation of the information and guide service and the police department of the town of Norris.

MORGAN: He had been trained at the University of California, Berkeley, the top place in the United States for that training. This man, by working with these young people, brought about an excellence in performance that could not have been achieved by just going out and hiring policemen.

DAWSON: So we selected and trained a dozen young fellows with good personalities who appeared to have the necessary qualities for dealing with people in both pleasant and unpleasant situations. Because of their character and the quality of their training, these young men served the town of Norris, the TVA, and the general public admirably. They were regarded as friends by those they met and we had little rowdyism and crime. When any trouble was brewing, they seemed to be able to get on top of it quietly and at the same time to maintain the goodwill and respect of the entire community.

MORGAN: Have you covered the major elements in the training program?

DAWSON: There is another aspect I want to mention, although it was not a part of our program at Norris. This was the excellent program for secretaries and clerical workers in the TVA office at Knoxville. Nellie Upton, whom we had known through her superior work as college manager at Antioch, was employed to coordinate this type of training. Although scores of young women were available and needed employment, few were very skilled in secretarial work. The only solution, using the local personnel market, was to hire those with adequate personal qualifications, although they had only minimum skills, and then to train them on the job. Miss Upton provided the leadership for setting high standards of training and workmanship for service personnel, most of whom were women. Many of them were able to advance within the Authority or elsewhere.

I should like to bring one thing in here, because it's timely and significant: the employment and training of blacks, which Mr. Reeves was most interested in. Until that time, in the South blacks were not employed to a degree nearly commensurate with their ratio to the population. The TVA established at the outset a policy of hiring approximately the same percentage of blacks from a given district as their percentage in the population of that district, which was not easy to do in the six southern states of the TVA. Most of them were placed in some type of training program and upgraded on their job. We employed a black sociologist to develop and manage this training. The employment and training of black people above a menial level, at that stage of American race relations, was truly a pioneering undertaking in public service.

MORGAN: The unions in the South were generally exclusively white, which added complexity in working things out. We decided that blacks and whites would work on the same jobs and that if the union was going to work with us, they would have to adjust to that.

The Personnel and Training Program

DAWSON: Something should be said regarding the attitude of the TVA Board of Directors toward the training program. I'm not sure the board ever took a formal position on the matter, but there was a good deal of opposition within the board to the whole training concept. The legal counsel, Mr. Lilienthal, contended that personnel training was not justifiable under the TVA Act. I think this is an accurate and fair statement of the opposition within the board, which had a somewhat dampening effect on the fulfillment of the training possibilities. Our aim was not only to get more efficient work but also to develop the human resources of the region. These purposes were interrelated. I think that had our only objective been to train and develop personnel without reference to the immediate tasks, it probably would not have been in the spirit of the TVA Act. But I think our men did a better job because of the fact that they had the opportunity for training. And as we have indicated, large numbers were upgraded for continued TVA employment.

MORGAN: The Army Corps of Engineers had already estimated the cost of building Norris Dam. I wondered how far I could trust that estimate so I looked up the record of their estimates for Congress and the actual cost of the dams they had built on the Ohio River during the previous ten years. Costs averaged about 50 percent more than the estimates they gave the government. Their estimate for Norris Dam was forty-two million dollars and their actual cost for building it would probably have been 50 percent more than their estimate. We did it for somewhat less than thirty-three million dollars, less than 1 percent more than our estimate.

Migrant labor was commonly used for the average large outdoor construction job in the United States. Often men would work a few weeks or a month on a project and then go somewhere else. They would come in hungry and would overeat, and were often laid up for a few days as a result. They would get drunk and mess with women. The whole pattern was not one that encouraged effective work. In the TVA, on the other hand, the men generally liked their jobs and their living and working environment. They liked the self-respect they found in it. The foremen treated the workmen as human beings.

DAWSON: I think, actually, that the labor-selection process plus supplementary training and high-quality supervision were the key factors. We went to the local leaders, who were concerned about their people, and gave them a picture of what the project was about. The result was that they enlisted people of reliability and character, who became the core of the TVA work force.

MORGAN: Now, we were building dam after dam and the Corps was building dam after dam, but with the Corps the contractors were doing it. The Corps had

The Making of the TVA

relatively little to say about them. The contractors and the Corps of Engineers men belonged to the same political organization and acted together as a single political lobby. Both were members of the Water Resources Congress, formerly the Rivers and Harbors Congress, a registered national lobby—and one of the most powerful. With the TVA there was no ulterior purpose. We found the best men that we could, treated them as human beings, and trained them. The results signify the high quality of the labor force.

DAWSON: The selection process was not perfect, of course, but it did produce a tremendously large reservoir of high-caliber workmen. I recall the frequent and favorable comments of Gordon Clapp, who later became chairman of the board of the TVA, and Carl Richey, who, along with Clapp, was involved in the early stages of employee selection. They were impressed with the high quality of the early applications, which provided a continuous source of personnel over a period of years.

A great many organizations fail in their recruitment of personnel. You do not often get the best personnel by just taking the people who happen to apply. You may, of course, get some very good people through conventional employment channels, but you don't build the best organization that way. You have to search for people and you have to build a reservoir of data on good prospects so that when jobs are open you have sources to draw from. Occasionally, when an extremely able prospect appears, you hire him and make a place for him in the organization. Much more attention should be given to the basic character and human qualities of an applicant, as well as to specific skills and training. These latter qualities can often be effectively developed after employment; but the former ones are indispensable and are not easily developed later.

Chapter Ten

The Fertilizer Program

As David Lilienthal and Harcourt Morgan, acting as a majority of the TVA board, had divided the responsibilities among the three directors, Harcourt Morgan was to direct the fertilizer program. Dr. Morgan was an agriculturalist, with a strong interest in fertilizer use. Although he had gone from Canada to Louisiana to study the life history of the boll weevil, he made his reputation chiefly by his work with phosphate fertilizer.

Southern agricultural authorities had become aware that the soils of the southern mountain region were not well balanced. The common practice of using nitrogen fertilizer was suited to cotton and a few other crops, but in general the soil was deficient in phosphates. The exclusive use of nitrate fertilizers, in the very process of stimulating cotton crops, further robbed the soil of its inadequate phosphorus, making it progressively more difficult to successfully grow any crop other than cotton. Harcourt Morgan was aware of this condition,

The Making of the TVA

and through his connections with the work of the land-grant colleges, he had learned of and been greatly impressed by the new theory of using phosphates. He promoted the use of phosphate fertilizer with an almost religious zeal.

The hydroelectric plant at Muscle Shoals seemed an almost heaven-sent provision for supplying the South with fertilizer. The plant dated from World War I, when Wilson Dam was built by the government to furnish electric power for making nitrate munitions. After the war, Congress, who was not aware of the dominant need for phosphates in southern soils, decided that the process and resources the power plant had used to produce nitrate-base ammunition should now be used to produce nitrate fertilizer.

When Harcourt Morgan was made one of the directors of the TVA, it was expected that he would use the Muscle Shoals plant for that purpose. But, without giving notice, he turned his attention to producing phosphate fertilizer. In so doing he rendered a great service to the Tennessee Valley and to the entire South. As president of the University of Tennessee while also a member of the board of the TVA, he was able to use presidents and deans of universities in the TVA states to help in the free distribution of phosphate fertilizer. Through his influence and the use of TVA finances, the land-grant colleges arranged for demonstration farms. These farms were to show the practicability of turning from growing cotton to raising livestock, on soil that produced good grass crops when fertilized with phosphates.

This change would greatly increase income, but it produced its own kind of crisis. Cotton growing required one farm laborer for cultivating and picking each ten to twenty acres of cotton. For grass crops, however, one laborer sufficed for forty to fifty acres. As a result, in large areas of Georgia and some other states, more than half the cotton workers—generally black tenants—became unnecessary and left the farms for the cities. The need for workers to make ammunition and supplies for the Second World War gave work to many of these displaced cotton farmers and lessened a critical unemployment situation.

In securing Harcourt Morgan as one of its directors, the TVA acquired much more than simply the services of one man as an individual. As president of the University of Tennessee and a leading agriculturalist in the South, he had close relations with personnel of the land-grant colleges of the region. They formed a sort of advisory body that he could consult. Through the finances of the TVA, he was able, without further congressional action, to direct substantial funds to the land-grant colleges to finance the distribution of fertilizer and related activities without cost to the colleges or the farmers.

Dr. Morgan was a genius in bringing about this great change in southern

The Fertilizer Program

agriculture. But his mind and interest were so centered on that agricultural revolution that he was relatively impervious to other concerns.

A biologist and an agriculturalist, Dr. Morgan knew little of technical chemistry. Fortunately my search for able staff members in the early days of the TVA helped resolve this dilemma. I had explored the country for men who were knowledgeable in the field of fertilizer chemistry, and through the able help of a leading organic chemist, I located Dr. Harry Curtis, who had a reputation as one of the best chemists in the country in his field. I told Harcourt Morgan about Curtis and Morgan gladly employed him. Dr. Curtis came to dominate the work in fertilizer technology of the TVA. Through him, fertilizer patents acquired by the TVA were freely shared with the fertilizer industry. He took the novel course of helping small firms to become experienced and progressive while remaining of moderate size. This broke with the almost universal American industrial pattern of the increasing growth of Big Business through the consolidation or elimination of small firms. Thus, in this field he helped to check the growth of Big Business, which had tended to destroy widely distributed and highly efficient small industries, and contributed to the development of a wholesome industrial process in this field. His efforts also took him beyond our borders. He cooperated with forty-eight fertilizer firms in nineteen foreign countries to bring them the best in modern technology. How different might American and foreign industry be if his methods were to become standard policy!

Not only was Dr. Curtis a man of unusual ability, but he attracted and employed other men of first-rate ability. Among them was Travis P. Hignett, who had a worldwide reputation for his fundamental contributions to the improvement of fertilizer processes and products. Dr. Curtis was later appointed a director of the TVA, and Hignett was named director of the Chemical Department in 1962.

The aim of Curtis, and later of Hignett, was not to compete with the privately owned fertilizer industry but to cooperate with it in improving technology in the field. This characteristic of their work became an outstanding and continuous feature of the TVA. The following report illustrates TVA's cooperation with various private and public organizations.

> From the beginning of TVA, the main emphasis [in the field of fertilizers] has been on research and development. The new agency moved promptly into pilot-plant work. Plant-scale test work and demonstration projects followed completion of the initial large-scale facilities in 1934. The TVA Muscle Shoals facilities now consti-

The Making of the TVA

tute the Nation's most complete fertilizer research and development center. TVA research has stimulated many new developments in fertilizers and fertilizer technology—developments which have been highly influential in improving and modernizing the fertilizer industry. *Chemical and Engineering News*, August 20, 1962, stated that "TVA generally is acknowledged as a leader in developing fertilizer technology and manufacturing methods, and the industry itself is quick to use TVA developments."

When TVA scientists find a new fertilizer compound which may offer advantages to industry or the farmer, it receives preliminary testing in TVA's greenhouse. If plant response is promising and other factors are favorable, TVA may build a pilot plant to test-produce the material. Pilot-plant output is used for testing by college experiment stations and on a limited number of farms across the country. If the product passes these tests and seems commercially feasible, TVA may build a demonstration plant to work out processing techniques and determine production costs. The larger plant will furnish valuable information for industry and provide the material for widespread introduction to farmers through educational programs.

The program for improving and cheapening fertilizers for the farm is conducted in cooperation rather than in competition with the fertilizer industry. Information developed in TVA laboratories and demonstration-scale plants is freely available. Some 1,350 industry representatives visited the laboratories and demonstration-scale plants in fiscal year 1963 to consult with TVA technical people. TVA chemical engineers made 82 visits to industry plants to assist in the adoption of new TVA processes and products. Staff members also responded to 3,200 mail and telephone requests for information.

During the same year, TVA staff members helped train a group of Peace Corps members going to Brazil. Two staff members were loaned to the Department of State to assist the Moroccan Government in a review of plans for a fertilizer industry. A three-man team from TVA went to Korea to assist in planning fertilizer plants there.

Adoption of the new developments has been facilitated by technical demonstrations, held every second or third year. At the last demonstration, nearly 500 engineers and technologists gathered at Muscle Shoals. Many of the world's best known chemical firms were represented, as well as numerous small fertilizer manufacturers. They came from 163 organizations in 35 states and from 48 firms in 19 foreign countries.

Reports, publications, and engineering drawings are furnished upon request, and patented TVA processes are licensed without royalty. Through June 30, 1964, 382 such licenses had been granted for use of TVA-patented developments in 370 plants.*

Practically all the concentrated superphosphate produced in the United States—2.2 million tons annually—is made on TVA-type cone mixers, as is much of the

---

*General Outline of Chemical Engineering Activities, Chemical Engineering Report No. 1 (1965), pp. 8-10.

ordinary 20 percent material. *

Nitrogen and phosphorus have roles in both fertilizers and munitions, and plants that produce these materials often can be utilized for either purpose. Congress defined TVA's dual responsibility in this respect when it specified that the laboratories and plant should serve both the peacetime needs of agriculture and the wartime needs of the Nation. The chemical research and production facilities of the TVA were quickly mobilized for national defense at the outbreak of World War II.**

In addition to its concentrated national defense efforts during periods of national emergency, TVA makes available the services of its facilities and personnel to the defense agencies in peacetime. TVA's capabilities in the field of research and production are made known to the Armed Services and other defense agencies and services are rendered as requested. Materials furnished under such arrangements are phosphorus and phosphoric acid to the Army, and nitric acid, ammonia, and phosphoric acid to the Atomic Energy Commission. Fundamental research work was done on a chemical compound for the Redstone Arsenal Research Division of Rohm and Haas under contract with the Army Rocket Missile Agency, Huntsville, Alabama. Thermodynamic properties of phosphorus compounds are now being measured to provide information for the Chemical and Radiological Defense Laboratory, Edgewood Arsenal, Maryland. †

Harcourt Morgan's program of distributing fertilizer without charge to representative farmers on the condition that they make the results known to neighboring farmers was highly satisfactory. It is doubtful whether another man who more clearly realized the superiority of phosphate over nitrate fertilizer or one more useful in handling its distribution could have been found. With the technical aspects of fertilizer manufacture ably taken care of by Harry Curtis, the program could scarcely have been better.†† With these two major elements of the fertilizer program taken care of, I did not need to worry about that part of the TVA program.

---

*Ibid., p. 13.
**Ibid., p. 34.
†Ibid., p. 37.
††In the depressed agriculture of the 1930s, the products of a year's work on an average Tennessee Valley farm brought about $300 for the farm family. Many hillside fields, worn out by too many years of corn or cotton or tobacco, were abandoned and eroding. Today's farming brings greater harvests from much less land. Annual sales of Tennessee Valley farm products total about $1 billion, averaging over $6,000 per farm—20 times the level of the mid-1930s. Over the years more than 55,000 Valley farmers have participated in the cooperative [fertilizer] program. ("TVA News," Oct. 19, 1973).

Chapter Eleven

The Political Conditions of Power Negotiations and Sales

Prior to my appointment as chairman and chief engineer of the TVA, I had been actively engaged in promoting municipal generation and distribution of electric power. The private corporation controlling power distribution in the area in which I lived was strongly opposed to power production by municipalities, and its officials widely and violently criticized me for my support of public power. Representatives of the utility company went so far as to insist that neither I, as president, nor members of the Antioch College faculty should make speeches about or otherwise create publicity supporting public power in the area of Ohio served by the utility. Their criticism of me on the public-power issue was so effective that I got a reputation as a political extremist, which lasted for years.

However, I persisted in promoting municipal power generation and distribution. Charles F. Kettering, inventor, General Motors executive, and a major financial supporter of Antioch, was subjected to a barrage of telephone calls, telegrams, letters, and personal pressure on the power issue. He suggested that I try to avoid criticism by asking my staff at the college to refrain from discussing public power before citizens' groups. I argued that freedom of expression on this issue was of great social importance. He accepted my argument and afterward substantially increased his contributions to the college.

It was while I was being actively opposed by the private power company, but not because of that opposition, that I was appointed chairman of the TVA.

In my capacity as chairman of the board, I insisted that the TVA's power-program records and associated publicity be complete, accurate, and truthful. President Roosevelt and Senator Norris, who in general were my strongest and most active supporters, were consistently given the impression by David Lilienthal that I was opposed to the power program and was actively conspiring against it. In March 1937, for example, in a letter to the President bearing his signature and that of Dr. Harcourt A. Morgan, Mr. Lilienthal wrote: "We have come to you for counsel. Recent events have made it plain to us that the Chairman of the TVA Board is actively cooperating with Mr. Wendell Willkie in such a manner as to prevent the Board from carrying out its obligations to the President and the Congress."* (Senator Norris received similar misinformation.)

Wendell Willkie was head of the principal electric utility in the Tennessee Valley, the Commonwealth and Southern Corporation, which had recently been formed after bad management caused its predecessor to be separated from the organization that controlled it. The exploitive policies of southern power companies had been established long before Mr. Willkie became an executive in the electric-power industry. Consequently, he had no part in their formulation. His selection as president of the Commonwealth and Southern Corporation did not mean that he condoned the unethical conduct of the Insull companies or the electric-power utilities that operated in Mississippi, Alabama, and Tennessee. Rather, he had helped to completely reorganize the Commonwealth and Southern Corporation and had been instrumental in having a good deal of inflated capitalization eliminated. This corporation was an exception, one whose ethical standards were high enough for him to become associated with it.

Wendell Willkie was not a conservative and certainly not a reactionary. In-

*This letter is only one of a series designed to alienate the warm support the President had given me. Another in this series, dated Jan. 18, 1938, is dealt with at length in Chapter Thirteen. These letters indicate not only an attempt to influence the President behind the scenes but also the existence of a group of persons who were assembled by Mr. Lilienthal for the purpose of giving credit to such statements. The letter is in the Roosevelt Library, Hyde Park, N.Y.

stead, he was the progressive son of a labor lawyer, who on occasion had voted for Socialist candidates; his mother was the first woman lawyer to be admitted to the Indiana bar. Willkie's principal area of political activity had been an intensive campaign on behalf of the League to Enforce Peace, for which he made approximately a thousand addresses advocating the concept of a "league of nations." It took a special brand of courage and firm conviction to campaign as Willkie did for a cause as unpopular as the League of Nations was at that time. He was not serving any political party or special economic interest in fighting for the League; he was serving a great historical cause.

Senator Homer Capehart of Indiana, who was an opponent of Mr. Willkie, once stated that although he disagreed with him about the League he had great respect for Willkie as a straightforward and honest man.

In 1932 Wendell Willkie voted for Franklin Delano Roosevelt, who eventually came to appreciate Willkie's character. In the April 1973 issue of *Vista Magazine*, Donald S. Connery reported the following incident.

> In the White House, when Harry Hopkins made a slurring remark about Willkie, President Roosevelt thundered, "Don't you say anything like that around here again. Don't ever think it. You of all people ought to know that we might not have had Lend-Lease or Selective Service or a lot of other things if it hadn't been for Wendell Willkie. He was a godsend to this country when we needed him most."
>
> By 1944 Roosevelt . . . was seriously considering him as his running mate in the forthcoming election, that the marriage of the leaders of the progressive wings of the Democratic and Republican parties might have a salutary effect.*

Wendell Willkie was not a public enemy nor was he an irresponsible administrator of private power. The engravings on Mr. Willkie's tombstone (d. 1944) indicate his ethical standards.

> Whenever we take away the liberties of those whom we hate, we are opening the way to loss of liberty for those we love.
>
> The moral losses of expediency always far outweigh the temporary gains.
>
> The test of a people is their aim and not their color.

Mr. Lilienthal recorded his thoughts upon learning of Mr. Willkie's death.

---

*Donald Connery, "One World Revisited," *Vista Magazine* (April 1973), p. 24.

I feel deeply that here is a great tragedy of the loss of a terrifically vital personality at a time when we could afford to lose some fox terriers and fatheads....

At the moment I think of the gracious and personable side of him—his letter to me, for instance, after we rowed before the TVA Board at the time the "division of territory" agreement blew up, about 1936, apologizing for losing his temper....

To think that this man who so fully occupied my thoughts and time for so many years, and then who gave me such a bad summer four years ago with his amazing rise to fame, should be the subject of an obituary comment from me.*

It is to Mr. Lilienthal's credit that he came to have a better understanding of Wendell Willkie and developed some appreciation of Mr. Willkie's character and of his value as a public servant.

I talked with Mr. Willkie on only three occasions. The first time was shortly after the TVA was established. On that occasion I told him that I felt the general public interest and the interests of both public and private utilities would be ill served by an unethical, knock-down-and-drag-out fight between public- and private-power advocates and that both should make to the public truthful presentations of their positions. I suggested that a basis of concern for the public interest should be established between us; he thought about my comment for a few moments and then expressed full agreement. I reported this brief discussion to the TVA board.

On the second occasion, I met Mr. Willkie unexpectedly at Princeton University, where I was scheduled to make an address. He said he would like to discuss with me the difficulties he had encountered in dealing with representatives of the TVA's power division. I politely but firmly declined, saying that his contact regarding that matter must be Mr. Lilienthal. Our conversation was very brief, lasting only five to ten minutes, and it did not include any discussion of specific issues.

Mr. Lilienthal and Mr. Willkie conferred at the Grove Park Inn in Asheville, North Carolina, and Mr. Lilienthal reported on their meeting to the TVA board on November 2, 1937. The recording secretary, Carl A. Bock, prepared the following notes, which, after being approved by all of the board members, became a part of the official minutes of the meeting. "David E. Lilienthal reported that, during a recent conference, representatives of the Commonwealth and Southern Corporation stated that, after general problems had been worked out, the utility would enter into an arrangement, without reservation, for the transfer of power facilities from private to public ownership in communities selected by

---

*Lilienthal, pp. 655-656.

the parties and that it would be willing to issue a statement to the public concerning the policy adopted if requested to do so by the Authority."*

Shortly thereafter, Mr. Lilienthal presented to the board members a copy of a personal letter to Mr. Willkie that he had prepared, purporting to summarize the Grove Park Inn conference. A copy of the letter, which is now on file at the Roosevelt Library in Hyde Park, was sent to President Roosevelt and to Senator Norris. The letter depicted Mr. Willkie as intransigently opposed to any tenable basis for cooperation with the TVA. Its conclusion reads:

> Your companies are not willing to contract for the sale and interchange of power from the Tennessee Valley Authority unless that contract bars the TVA from selling power to any other agency in any part of the vast areas in the four states in which your companies carry on operations. In other words, as a condition of the purchase of any power, your position is that the TVA must give you a monopoly which would prevent it from selling power to municipalities, rural cooperatives, or industries in any part of the four states in which you operate.
>
> I am unable to see how the Authority can confer such a monopoly upon the private utilities of the Southeast . . . the whole subject can, of course, be reviewed at your meeting with the Board on Tuesday next. . . .

The content of the letter was so different from Mr. Lilienthal's earlier report on November 2 that I considered it imperative to have Mr. Willkie discuss his corporation's position in person. With the board's approval, I invited him to meet with the board. Later, on the train to Washington after the meeting, Willkie told me that he had received a wire from Mr. Lilienthal telling him that plans had been changed and the proposed meeting would not be held. Since the invitation had come from me as chairman, Mr. Willkie decided to disregard Mr. Lilienthal's wire, visited the board anyway, and discussed his views. This meeting with Mr. Willkie was the third and last time I had any contact with him.

---

*This entry remained a part of the official minutes of the Nov. 2, 1937, meeting of the TVA board until about the time the Eighteen Power Companies suit against the TVA got under way. Then Mr. Lilienthal, realizing that the minutes would probably be impounded and made available for examination by opposing attorneys, ordered the assistant secretary of the TVA to remove the entry from the minutes of the meeting. The page containing that entry was retyped with the entry omitted. Then that set of minutes was resubmitted to the board members for routine signing. I signed the changed minutes without being aware that they had been altered. I have no recollection of Mr. Lilienthal telling me he had ordered the entry deleted. Later I learned that Mr. Lilienthal did not want opposing counsel to note that Mr. Willkie and the Commonwealth and Southern Corporation had shown a willingness to sell to the TVA corporate power facilities in selected areas.

Power Negotiations and Sales

The following is a portion of my statement on May 25, 1938, to the congressional committee investigating the TVA, as to what ensued at the Knoxville meeting between Mr. Willkie and the TVA board.

> At the meeting of the Commonwealth and Southern representatives and the TVA board on February 2, 1937, I read this letter (of Mr. Lilienthal's) to Mr. Willkie and asked whether it correctly represented the position of his company. He replied very positively that it did not. He then proceeded to outline what would be the position of his company. Mr. Willkie's typed statement and the succeeding discussion before the TVA board constituted a statement of the conditions under which, he said, his company would consider the sale of all, or any reasonably separable part of the Commonwealth and Southern properties.
>
> This was the first time I had discussed the attitude of his company with Mr. Willkie, except in June, 1933, immediately on the organization of the TVA board. The conditions he stated were strikingly different from those which had been reported by Mr. Lilienthal.
>
> I did not want any misunderstanding on the matter. Therefore, after the meeting I wrote up the substance of the conditions which Mr. Willkie had stated, and then went to him and checked over the statement with him point by point, to be sure that I fully understood the terms he had stated, and that my notes agreed with his understanding.
>
> Having done this, I sent a copy of my memorandum to the other members of the Board, telling them plainly that I had checked the statement with Mr. Willkie, and that he had approved that statement point by point.
>
> This, gentlemen, was the "impermissible conduct" referred to by Mr. Lilienthal in his charges to the President.*

Mr. Lilienthal sent to the President a copy of my memorandum containing Mr. Willkie's comments and pointed to it as an instance of my conspiring with Mr. Willkie. In fact, this was the only occasion on which I discussed the TVA with Mr. Willkie, except for our first meeting in June 1933, when I emphasized the necessity for both sides of the power issue to deal with complete honesty with each other.

Lilienthal described the February 2 meeting as so damaging that he asked the President for advice, implying that there was a secret conspiracy between Mr. Willkie and me, which was the essence of the offense attributed to me by Mr. Lilienthal. It was not possible for the President to get any meaning out of Lilienthal's message except that Lilienthal wanted his help in relieving the board of my presence.

*Hearings Before the Joint Committee on the Investigation of the Tennessee Valley Authority, 75th Congress, Part 1, July 19, 1938, p. 28.

The Making of the TVA

My only other even remote contact with Mr. Willkie was when I sent a memorandum to all persons invited by the President to a conference on the pooling of power between public and private agencies (such as the Federal Power Commission). Mr. Willkie, as one of the persons invited by the President, received a copy.

Although these were the only contacts I ever had with Mr. Willkie, Mr. Lilienthal used them as grounds for saying that "the chairman of the TVA board is actively cooperating with Mr. Wendell L. Willkie in such a manner as to prevent the board from carrying out its obligations to the President and Congress."*

In the same letter to the President in which Mr. Lilienthal charged me with conspiring against the TVA, he stated that I had also conspired with a former engineer of an Insull company, George Hamilton. "Many incidents of cooperation with the opposition form the background for this latest disclosure. At the time of your Power Pool Conference of September 30, Dr. [Arthur] Morgan privately made available to Mr. Willkie and the opposition press copies of his Memorandum on Pooling which we believe you have seen. That Memorandum was prepared with the aid of the former Chief Engineer of the Insull Middle West Utilities Company."**

In response to the President's request that I be a member of a group he had appointed to consider the possibility of a power pool for Commonwealth and Southern and the TVA, I had looked for a technical adviser on whose objectivity I could depend. I chose Mr. Hamilton from among Mr. Lilienthal's own TVA technical personnel because of his expertise, and I had his assistance for about ten days. Mr. Lilienthal, in vigorously condemning me for conferring with this man, gave no hint that Mr. Hamilton was from his own personal staff, where he had been employed for several months, nor did he mention that in drafting the memorandum I had also had the intimate assistance of three other men whose loyalty to the TVA was well known and beyond question.

Mr. Lilienthal's charges to the President that I had conspired with Willkie and that I had employed an "enemy of public power" were received by President Roosevelt as evidence of prejudice and conspiracy on my part. These cases, in which evidence exists that refutes Mr. Lilienthal's charges, represent unquestionable instances of entirely misleading charges.

As a man sincerely concerned with an overall solution to the relationship be-

---

*Memorandum to the President from Lilienthal and H. A. Morgan, March 5, 1937, Roosevelt Library, Hyde Park, N.Y.
**Ibid.

tween public and private power, Mr. Willkie was an inappropriate antagonist for Mr. Lilienthal's carefully promoted image as a crusader against the private-power monopolists. It appeared that Mr. Lilienthal's plans to put himself at the head of the public-power movement were to be achieved by avoiding any agreement between the public and private organizations concerned. He denied and misstated Mr. Willkie's avowed position, which I shared, that there should be open inquiry and mutual examination of the issues, and thereby created a false issue, which he promoted. Mr. Lilienthal persistently charged Mr. Willkie with being dictatorial. He grossly misstated Willkie's position in making it appear that Commonwealth and Southern was opposed to allowing the TVA to occupy "any of the vast areas tributary to the TVA."* In fact, Willkie had asked only that the transfer from private ownership take place in reasonable units of distribution. In contrast, Lilienthal insisted that the TVA should have the right to occupy any territory in the entire area, regardless of its relationship to distributive systems.** This position was adopted by a majority of the board (Harcourt A. Morgan voted with Lilienthal on practically all issues), while I voted against the motion—one of my very few votes against my fellow directors.

*Letter from Lilienthal to Willkie, Jan. 29, 1937, and quoted in a letter from Arthur Morgan to Lilienthal, Feb. 24, 1937, Roosevelt Library, Hyde Park, N.Y.
**Mr. Lilienthal's heavily propagandized argument to the President and the public that I stood for restricting TVA power sales to a limited territory and that, in contrast, he was following the dictates of the TVA Act in insisting on unrestricted sales of power is reflected in Thomas K. McCraw's carefully documented book *TVA and the Power Fight* (Philadelphia: Lippincott, 1971). There are many references to me and my position on public power in this book. They do not accurately represent my position, but do demonstrate the need to correct the misinformation that has prevailed for so long. For example, Mr. McCraw writes: "Chairman Morgan regarded the power issue as an apolitical problem of economics and engineering . . . He wanted to negotiate the peaceful transfer of a representative rural-urban area from Willkie's companies to the TVA. After this transfer there would be no direct competition for customers and no propaganda by either side . . . Morgan did not want TVA's other missions endangered by political agitation over the explosive public power question." (pp. 54-55)

This is simply not true. With regard to propaganda, I made my position clear during my first months with the TVA and reiterated it throughout my chairmanship. I sought "the process of making propaganda accurate and representative." (Roy Talbert, "Arthur Morgan: The Human Engineer," M.A. dissertation, Vanderbilt University, Nashville, Tenn., 1967, pp. 113-118).

In 1938 I stated to a congressional investigating committee that I was not criticizing campaigns of publicity and promotion for their aggressiveness but only for their failure to make honest statements to the public. Whether the public supplies itself with power or is supplied by private companies is for the public to determine. Further, whether power should be supplied under the jurisdiction of the federal or the state or the local government is again a matter for public decision. But the right of the people to supply themselves with such an essential service as power ought to be fundamental in any power policy, and the public must be given full and accurate information and not be misled by an-

The Making of the TVA

If Mr. Willkie's position had resembled Mr. Lilienthal's statement of it, it would have been wholly untenable. The position Mr. Lilienthal had adopted was, of course, equally untenable, and the TVA in time backed away from it. Lilienthal's unjustified treatment of him made Willkie an enemy, an opponent of public power. Willkie's advisers apparently had given him some good advice on power policy. If Lilienthal had explored the power situation with Willkie, the Commonwealth and Southern head might have arrived at desirable policies earlier than he did, because Willkie was full of ideas and progressive policies. Since I was left uninformed of even the names of most of Mr. Lilienthal's advisers, the misrepresentation in his report of Willkie's position impressed me when I was kept uninformed of other intelligent, competent elements of Lilienthal's program. If he had treated Willkie, the President, Senator Norris, and me differently, the strong points of his arguments might have carried the day.

POWER SALES

The administration of power sales was assigned to Mr. Lilienthal by action of the TVA Board of Directors in July 1933. Mr. Lilienthal did not keep me informed on his development of the TVA power policy; neither did he inform me of his relations with his staff of consultants and assistants. Since I had to rely for my information on Mr. Lilienthal's public statements and on reports of his activities in the press, I was not as well informed about the development of the power policy as I was about other features of the TVA.

A rather complete account is available in *TVA: The First Twenty Years*. At

nouncements that do not disclose all of the truth. For example, open records of costs are imperative.

Mr. Lilienthal finally came to agreement with Commonwealth and Southern for a restriction on TVA's making further intrusions into the private utilities' markets. Mr. McCraw writes: "For Lilienthal, the prohibition on TVA's going outside this area for customers conceded a point not only to Willkie, but to Chairman Morgan. Originally Lilienthal had flatly refused to make such a commitment, which apparently violated the preference clause of the TVA Act." (McCraw, p. 66)

With regard to ending competition between public- and private-power areas and limiting areas of electric service, I had said, "We should not agree to permanently stay out of any areas, but I think that with a reasonable area to serve we should agree to stay out of other areas for a reasonable period." (McCraw, p. 66)

I said further that agreement should be sought with the private utilities as a first effort, but I was deeply aware that careful bargaining and strategy would be necessary. This was the case when my staff and I dealt successfully with the cement companies, and it was what we attempted to do with Alcoa. My concern was that the TVA not insist on raiding and disrupting integrated units of power-distribution systems, leaving uneconomic fragments. Mr. Lilienthal made this appear as meaning that I was opposing an aggressive policy to expand and extend public power to serve larger areas.

Power Negotiations and Sales

the end of his introduction to the book, Dr. Harry Curtis states: "This book, then, is a staff report on the Tennessee Valley Authority for the years 1933-1953. The essays have not been presented to the Board of Directors for approval; hence, they do not constitute an official statement of TVA policy or practice. They are nothing more, and nothing less, than individual statements by men long associated with the TVA. They delineate the TVA as it appears to a group of the agency's chief architects."*

The place of power in the TVA is discussed in "The Power Program" by O. S. Wessel.

> ... the prime purpose of the new agency, as defined by the Act of 1933, was to bring the Tennessee River under control and to put it to work. Flood control and navigation were listed in the Act as primary activities, power production as secondary. Notwithstanding the prominent billing given to electric power in the years since 1933, it is important to remember that it is subservient to the primary purposes of flood control and navigation.
>
> Proof of power's secondary position is found in the method of operation of the river control system. Though the Office of Power is responsible for the physical operation of the system, the power people operate according to instructions from the division of Water Control Planning in the Office of Engineering. The latter organization determines the amount of storage space which must be provided at any given time in each reservoir in order to provide needed flood protection. It also determines the water requirements needed to provide the minimum required depth in the navigation channel. If the power managers can operate the system in such a way as to meet the navigation and flood protection requirements set up by the Chief Engineer and utilize the water to generate power at the same time, well and good; but if a conflict of interests develops, as it often does, navigation and flood control come first. It is frequently necessary during the winter months to spill water in order to maintain storage space in the reservoirs against the possibility of future floods. Spilled water is wasted water as far as power production is concerned, and a good deal of potential hydroelectric production is lost in this fashion nearly every year. This is the only way the system can operate if it is to provide flood protection and navigation, however, and this is the way it does operate.**

Mr. Lilienthal argued vigorously against building Chickamauga Dam, claiming that the TVA already had too much power, the supply of which should not be increased by building that dam. This was after he had abruptly and

*TVA: The First Twenty Years, ed. Roscoe C. Martin (Tuscaloosa, Ala.: University of Alabama Press and Knoxville, Tenn.: University of Tennessee Press, 1956), p. x.
**Ibid., p. 109.

The Making of the TVA

decisively declined to provide the Reynolds company with power that would permit it to compete with the Aluminum Company of America. (Throughout its history, Alcoa, under both its Republican founder, Andrew Mellon, and its Democratic president, Arthur V. Davis, had done everything possible to prevent the development of competition. At the beginning of World War II, when the government acted to break the aluminum monopoly, Reynolds became a large aluminum producer, but not with TVA power.) If we had built Chickamauga Dam at that time, flood control and navigation would have been improved, and the power needed by the Reynolds company to make aluminum could have been supplied. Mr. Lilienthal ignored the fact that power generation and sales were not the primary functions of the TVA but were secondary to navigation and flood control. He was willing to sacrifice both these primary concerns.

Wessel's account of the power program continues:

> The power business, regardless of who owns and operates it, is a public business. Where private corporations have undertaken the job of electricity supply, they have done so by reason of privileges granted by the public. They use public streets and highways as right-of-way for overland and under ground lines. They are given the right of eminent domain to secure land needed for their facilities. They are monopolies in the areas they serve, and are protected by their monopoly privileges by state regulation or by local franchise. Their rates are not set by competition but by government action, and are designed to assure them a reasonable level of earnings on the facilities they provide. These privileges are granted by the public, not as a mark of favor, but in order that the companies can do an efficient job of providing electric service.
>
> The public character of electric service is dictated by the very nature and function of electricity. Electric power is not just another commercial product to be placed on the commodity market at the highest price it will bring. Electricity is energy and in this modern age it is a basic necessity of life. It provides many of the comforts of modern living. Full development of a community's commercial and industrial economy would be impossible without a plentiful supply. Every community is entitled to an adequate supply at reasonable rates. It is an absolute requirement for minimum national strength and security.
>
> It is for these reasons, then, that the electric business is a public business. Where the public interest and the private interest conflict, as they sometimes do, the public interest must prevail. In the TVA Act, Congress recognized the public character of power supply and took steps to ensure that in the Tennessee Valley the public interest would be served.
>
> Section 9a of the act authorized the TVA Board of Directors to provide and operate facilities for the generation of electric energy in order to avoid the waste of water power, and to transmit and market the power produced. Section 10 empowered the Board to sell any surplus power developed by the TVA and give pref-

erence in the sale to states, counties, and municipalities, and to co-operative organizations not organized or doing business for profit but primarily for the purpose of supplying electricity to their own members. To make sure that the benefits of this power were actually realized by the people, the act also authorized the Board to include in contracts for sale of power such terms and conditions, including resale rate schedules, as were in its judgment necessary to carry out the purposes of the act. Section 11 reaffirmed the distribution policy set out in section 10, providing also that the power projects were to be considered primarily as for the benefit of the people of the region as a whole and particularly the domestic and rural consumers to whom the power could economically be made available. Sale of power to industry was to be a secondary purpose, to be utilized principally to secure revenue returns which would permit domestic and rural use at the lowest possible rates.

In sections 10 and 11 of the act, therefore, Congress made clear its intention to preserve for the people the benefits which would result from the development of the Tennessee River. This was a reaffirmation of a general policy first laid down by Congress in the Reclamation Act of 1906. These are the so-called preference provisions of the act and they are generally similar to the preference clauses contained in other laws relating to the sale of power generated at government-owned dams. Two categories of preference are set out: first, municipalities, co-operatives, and other public agencies not distributing electricity for profit were to have first call on the power TVA produced; and second, the power was to be considered primarily for the benefit of the domestic and rural consumer. The preference provisions, therefore, affirm the government's policy to produce and sell power for the benefit of the consumer, and continue the chain of responsibility for getting this power to the consumer through local agencies whose basic objectives are widespread use at low rates. It is worthy of emphasis that the act indicates clearly that Congress intended the function of distributing electricity to the ultimate consumer to be decentralized. TVA was to produce the power, but local agencies were to be given the job of distributing it to the ultimate consumers.

Section 10 contains another important provision which authorizes the TVA Board of Directors to make studies and experiments to promote the wider and better utilization of electric power for agricultural and domestic use and for small industries. This section also directed TVA to co-operate with state governments and their subdivisions, with educational and research institutions, and with cooperatives or other organizations, in the application of electrical power to the fuller and better balanced development of the resources of the region. Here is a clear statement of the principle that electricity was to be one of the tools to be used in helping the region to improve its economic status. This was to be accomplished by the application of low rates, the benefits of which were to be spread as widely as possible.

The act further provided that the proceeds from the sale of power were to be used to assist in liquidating the cost of the projects. Section 9a contains a preliminary statement on this subject which section 14 makes explicit in these terms: "It is hereby declared to be the policy of this Act that, in order, as soon as practicable,

The Making of the TVA

to make the power projects self-supporting and self-liquidating, the surplus power shall be sold at rates which, in the opinion of the board, when applied to the normal capacity of the Authority's power facilities, will produce gross revenues in excess of the cost of production of said power..." This policy was again affirmed by Congress in the Appropriation Act of 1948, which included a requirement that TVA pay into the federal treasury from net power revenue amounts which would equal all appropriations made for power purposes. *

These conditions were generally observed by Mr. Lilienthal. "One of the first big tasks confronting TVA was the development of a suitable market wherein its power could be sold. A few scattered municipal electric systems were operating in the region in 1933, and these were among the first to enter into power contracts with TVA."**

In general the policy under Mr. Lilienthal was "... for the TVA to buy the generation and transmission facilities and the local agencies—municipalities and cooperatives—to buy the distribution properties. The last major acquisition was in 1945, when properties of the East Tennessee Light and Power Company were acquired."†

The distribution systems have developed until "... there are 150 electric systems distributing TVA power—97 municipals, 51 cooperatives, and two small privately owned utilities."††

With great care, and with the help of a group of associates and coordinators of his choice, Mr. Lilienthal worked out a power contract between the TVA and consumer agencies that has remained practically unchanged since its first use in 1933. "One of the remarkable things about this contract is the fact that it has required relatively few revisions over the years. Modifications have been made, of course, to clarify certain points and to make the document more workable, but the contract of today is basically the same as the first agreement signed with the City of Tupelo, Mississippi, nearly twenty years ago..."‡

This comment on the lasting quality of the early TVA provisions regarding power sales is evidence of the generally high quality of the conditions of operation worked out by Mr. Lilienthal and his associates, particularly Llewellyn Evans, whom I recommended for this work. One possible exception to this excellence was the failure to create a "yardstick" by which the early efforts of

---

*Ibid., p. 111.
**Ibid., p. 111.
†Ibid., p. 112.
††Ibid., p. 112.
‡Ibid., p. 113.

the TVA power program could be measured.

The very essence of such a yardstick comparison between TVA- and private-power sales, which the President had asked for and which Mr. Lilienthal said he had provided, was the unit cost of power. But in fact a "yardstick" project was almost unfeasible in actual practice because of the difficulty of comparing only the one factor of price. Lilienthal should have responded to the President's request for a "yardstick" project by stating its unfeasibility; what he did do was to make a comparison that included numerous factors in addition to price, pointing to increased power sales. But to present the results to the President as though no factors were involved other than the comparison of price was misleading.

Before March 1934 the TVA's per-kilowatt-hour charge for power that it sold to distributors and the volume of its power sales were based on conditions existing before TVA power was available. Then a series of events took place that changed the conditions of sales and use. To begin with, a promotional campaign designed to draw people's attention to public power and to increase home-appliance sales was initiated in March 1934 and reached a peak in April 1934. Its major features were as follows. First, President Roosevelt sent a message to the city of Tupelo, Mississippi, drawing attention to the availability of cheaper public power. Second, a group of women, officials of land-grant colleges, went to Tupelo. Each was assigned to a particular area of the city, where she called on each family to make them aware of the advantages of electric power and electrical appliances in the home. Third, a distributor's organization formed by Mr. Lilienthal appeared in Tupelo and Athens, Alabama, with an unusual variety of electrical equipment for sale at exceptionally low prices. They offered these specially made, cheap home appliances to retail merchants on the condition that the merchants greatly reduce their margin of profit on sales. Some merchants complained bitterly about the small margin of profit, but they were not able to get low-priced appliances from Mr. Lilienthal's organization on any other terms. Fourth, through Mr. Lilienthal's effort, a department of the federal government, the Electric Home and Farm Authority, received ten million dollars, from which deferred payments could be made on purchases of electrical appliances supplied to the stores carrying the special line. Fifth, Mr. Lilienthal's staff of engineers and technicians toured the area to make people familiar with the installation and use of the new electrical appliances. Finally, with all this promotion and subsidy in the background, a period of test sales was inaugurated in March 1934 and ran until September. It resulted in a sizable increase in electric-power sales. However, in national publicity and in a report to the Presi-

The Making of the TVA

dent, Mr. Lilienthal gave the impression that the rise in sales was due almost solely to the reduction in the wholesale price of power. The publicity commonly cited the amount of revenue received by the city of Tupelo from the sale of power in March 1934 and then compared that figure with the revenue from power sales in September. No mention was made of the costly subsidized promotional campaign.

Following is the memorandum, dated November 16, 1934, sent by Mr. Lilienthal to the President.

> Memorandum to the President
> From: David E. Lilienthal
> Subject: Facts about Tupelo
>
> 1. Tupelo was the first city to sign a contract with TVA for wholesale power generated at Wilson Dam. The contract was signed on November 11, 1933, and current was initially supplied on February 7, 1934.
>
> 2. Upon receiving TVA-Muscle Shoals power, the City of Tupelo put into effect the new low TVA rates, which for residential consumers start at three cents per kilowatt hour and range downward to four mills per kilowatt hour. These rates represented a very substantial reduction to consumers of electricity, in almost every case more than 50%. Before TVA, residential consumers paid as much as ten cents per kilowatt hour for electricity, the average price being approximately seven cents. Under TVA rates the highest price is three cents per kilowatt hour and the average price has been two cents and less.
>
> 3. Before TVA, the City of Tupelo purchased wholesale power from a private company (Mississippi Power Company) at a rate of approximately 1.7 cents per kilowatt hour. Power from the same source over the same lines (purchased by TVA from the private company) is now sold to Tupelo at a rate which has averaged 5.4 mills during the past eight months. Since its contract with TVA, Tupelo has been able to save about 68% in its wholesale power bill. Because of this tremendous saving in the cost of power and by reason of a tremendous increase in use which has come about since the low rates were made available, the experience of the City of Tupelo has been a profitable one. Because of the increase in use and by reason of the excellent load factor, better than 50%, the City of Tupelo has been a profitable customer to TVA.
>
> 4. The experience which Tupelo has had under TVA rates illustrates how electric utilities can drastically reduce their rates, increase consumption and continue to prosper. Gross revenues for the City of Tupelo from its electric operations were only $5,600 in the month of March, 1934, at a time when the TVA program was just getting under way. By September, revenues had increased to more than $8,800, an increase of 57% in only six months. The rate reductions cut revenues in half, but with this reduction the people of Tupelo found that they could afford to make a wide and generous use of electricity in their homes and in their factories. By September, 1934, residential users had increased their consumption 126% as compared with September, 1933. They were using more electricity for lighting

their homes, for refrigerating and cooking their food, for heating their water, and for all kinds of purposes. They were using electricity, and in doing so, relieving drudgery in the home.

5. There has been much the same experience in other communities in which TVA rates have been put into effect. What has happened in the City of Athens, Alabama, for example, further illustrates the soundness and the benefits of this program. TVA rates were put into effect on June 1, 1934, in Athens. The immediate result was to cut residential bills by 50% and commercial bills by more than 40%. The consumer immediately responded to the inducement of fair and low rates. In the brief space of five months, residential consumption increased 79%, and commercial consumption increased 120%. These enormous increases can be attributed only to the fact that low and equitable rates have been appreciated by the public and that the low cost electric appliances will be in great demand whenever and wherever available.

Before TVA, the City of Athens purchased wholesale power from a private company (The Alabama Power Company). The rate paid by the City of Athens to the private utility was approximately 1.3 cents per kilowatt hour. Under TVA, the City of Athens saves about 49% in the cost of wholesale power, the average rate paid to the TVA being approximately six mills.

For the month of May, 1934, the last month before TVA, the City of Athens had a total revenue of approximately $3,000, out of which it paid approximately $1,400 to the private utility which supplied it with power. There remained to the City of Athens about $1,600 for covering its cost in distributing electricity. This situation can be compared with the month of September under TVA. During this month, the total revenues of the City of Athens were $2,790, out of which $940 was paid to TVA for wholesale power. There remained $1,850 for covering the costs of distribution. In other words, although Athens reduced its resale rates almost half, consumption increased at such a rapid rate that in four months the net revenues available for distribution were actually 15% greater than before.

6. *What the TVA rate method means to the country as a whole.* The actual revenue from residential consumers in the United States as a whole in 1932 was $650,000,000, for which approximately 11,790,000,000 kilowatt hours were supplied. If the United States as a whole were put on the same basis as Athens, Alabama, the total consumption would have been 21,000,000,000 kilowatt hours, and the total revenue would have been $463,000,000, an increase of 9,000,000,000 kilowatt hours, and a saving to residential consumers of approximately $187,000,000 per year.

Financial Result. The TVA rates will be criticized by all manner of special interests, but the fact is that *they work*. In actual practice in Tupelo, in northeast Mississippi, and in Athens, Alabama, it has been demonstrated that they work.*

O. S. Wessel explains the disposition of revenues as follows:

---

*Memorandum from Lilienthal to the President, Nov. 16, 1934, Roosevelt Library, Hyde Park, N.Y.

The Making of the TVA

>Another very important feature of the TVA power contract, and one quite different from anything found in most wholesale agreements, relates to the disposition of revenues received by the distributor. It is agreed that revenues may be used first for the payment of operating expenses—salaries, wages, materials, and supplies, the cost of power, and the like. Provision is made further for the payment of interest and principal on the long-term debt, for an allowance for depreciation of the properties, and for payments in lieu of taxes. Any accounts remaining after these requirements have been set are considered as surplus revenues and may be used for three general purposes: first, for new construction for lines to serve new consumers, or facilities to strengthen service to old; second, for the further reduction of rates; third, subject to the consent of TVA, for the retirement of system indebtedness prior to maturity.*

This provision prohibits the use of electric-power revenues for the general purposes of local government.

In Yellow Springs, Ohio, we do not have access to the cheap power of the TVA. The town buys power from a private company and then distributes it with its own facilities. Since a large part of the profits of private power-and-light companies comes from the charges made for distributing power, we save considerable money by distributing the power ourselves. The voters of Yellow Springs retained the right to use part of the receipts from power sales for meeting incidental expenses or exigencies not provided for in the budget. Thus, we avoid borrowing and paying the cost of loans or of going without until new tax provisions are adopted. The village finds that the use of surplus power revenue for general purposes of local government is markedly convenient and decidedly superior to the TVA's rigid rules on the use of power income. When a TVA-supplied community has undertaken to use surplus power revenue for other purposes, it has been prosecuted. Lenoir City, Tennessee, was compelled to stop using surplus revenues for education.

Most communities in the area served by TVA have special needs from time to time requiring emergency expenditures. "TVA has been subjected to criticism in some quarters because of the limitations which the power contracted places on the local use of electricity revenues." "Any municipality which considers the terms of agreement onerous has the option of rejecting it."** To reject the agreement, however, would mean to give up their source of power supply. Consequently few communities can make use of that course unless they have another power source.

*TVA: The First Twenty Years, p. 114.
**Ibid., pp. 115, 116.

In the years since *TVA: The First Twenty Years* was written, the power program has experienced continued and uninterrupted growth and has remained a major feature of the TVA.

Chapter Twelve

"Life to All Forms of Human Concerns"

The TVA conflict, in effect, was not between the directors; it was rather between the President's conception of government, as expressed in his message to Congress proposing creation of the TVA, and the more traditional concept of government held by David Lilienthal and Harcourt Morgan. To quote the President: "It [the TVA] touches and gives life to all forms of human concerns. . . . It should be charged with the broadest duty of planning for the proper use, conservation, and development of the natural resources of the Tennessee River drainage basin and its adjoining territory for the general social and economic welfare of the Nation."*

In this conflict of views, the other members of the board held that no TVA development projects were legitimate unless they were individually and specifi-

*The Public Papers and Addresses of Franklin D. Roosevelt, 1928-1945, vol. 2, p. 122.

cally described in the TVA Act. On the other hand, I was trying to implement the President's statement. Some of the most relentless opposition of the board majority was to actions directly in line with the President's specific illustrations to me of definite actions he had in mind. He had described, for example, how certain New England towns had developed local industries and how one community had departed from conventional methods of lumbering and had replaced them with selective use of timber for cabinetmaking, which was developed as a local industry. He wanted that same New England spirit of independent activity to characterize TVA projects.

When the various cultural and economic projects that I proposed were introduced into the TVA program, they were looked upon by some people as quite foreign to such a development and were referred to as "vagaries." However, the development of a program that was inclusive of all elements of cultural, economic, and legal values was not a temporary course. The efforts then made grew in variety and importance and have become important factors in the overall development of the Tennessee Valley. This part of the President's revolutionary hopes for the Tennessee Valley is well described in the study of those functions by Marguerite Owen in *The Tennessee Valley Authority*: "The people and their local institutions are involved in the Tennessee Valley, where a federal program continues to strive for achievement through a decentralized administration. Participation of citizens is wide, and local organizations are active. They share responsibility for power system operations, and for the development of recreation. They are engaged in fertilizer testing and in forestry improvement. Their role is basic in one program planned by TVA in the late 1930s, submerged during the war, revived in the post-war years, and by the 1960s matured and flourishing—Tributary Area Development."* This was all in accord with the President's enunciated policy, which it was my intense wish to implement. But the policy was forcibly rejected by the other two directors, who constituted a majority of the board. Later, however, it was adopted and fulfilled by the remarkable body of TVA employees.

That President Roosevelt's hopes for the TVA were not misplaced is evident in the wide variety of activities that have emerged in the Authority. In the course of time, the efforts to develop all-inclusive cultural and economic programs have been enlarged and expanded, and today the entire life of the people in the Tennessee Valley is enriched by such efforts. These many elements of value are described in a recent report from the TVA, "Tributary Area Development:

---

*Marguerite Owen, *The Tennessee Valley Authority* (New York: Praeger, 1973), p. 122.

The Making of the TVA

1971-72," which deals with at least 130 cases of about twenty different types of activities in twenty-seven area organizations, initiated largely as a result of the self-reliance that President Roosevelt's policy encouraged. The initial encouragement given by TVA engineering employees and the exceptionally able TVA personnel chosen from all over the United States by our initial Washington office staff has resulted in the formation of citizens' groups that cooperate in expressing their own aspirations, whether for health, education, transportation, growing food, or developing beautiful recreation areas.

The difference between the outcome of the TVA's developments and those that have generally accompanied the Corps of Engineers' work in similar fields is significant. Restriction of such development would have greatly checked the President's wishes. The active interest aroused by these "vagaries" was, to a significant degree, kept alive by the TVA employee work program, which ran in two shifts of five and a half hours, leaving a similar period free for training in various useful activities, largely under the direction of the hundreds of exceptionally able professional people whom we had assembled from all over the United States.

Mr. Lilienthal's view of the program is indicated in the following report from the Knoxville *News-Sentinel*.

> "I am against 'basket weaving' and all that it implies, except perhaps as a temporary expedient," Mr. Lilienthal told TVA employees recently.
>
> "I suppose," Mr. Lilienthal added, "it must be plain to you that I don't have much faith in 'uplift.' I suppose it is apparent that I believe deeply in the notion of progress and that I have great confidence in the general good sense of the average man and woman. I believe deeply in giving people freedom to make their own choice. It seems to me the duty of leadership to see that that choice is available, that it shall be a wise choice, if possible, but, in any event, a free choice. I hope it is apparent that no system seems to me worthwhile unless it is based upon the consent of men and women.
>
> "There is a great temptation to develop a kind of Alexander-the-Great complex among those of us who are carrying on this project. We are constantly looking at maps with a great area marked on them and blocking out this and that on these maps.
>
> "We are constantly reading articles by visitors to this project, written in a pitch of exaltation about the great opportunities you and I have on this job. There is a danger in all of this of losing our sense of humility. The cloth—the human cloth—at its widest is not very wide, and it is not much wider than it has been, by and large, for the last couple of thousand years."*

*Knoxville *News-Sentinel* (March 5, 1937).

As I pointed out in a speech in 1934, the realities involved other conditions as well as those mentioned by Lilienthal.

> I think one reason the President chose the Tennessee Valley area is because in the eastern part of it—the mountain area—there are six and a half million people that have never really had an economy. Before slavery was abolished, the economy of the South was based on slave labor. The slaveholders did not employ white men: a man could not work slaves and whites together. The man who could not afford slaves was out of it, and in the heyday of slavery only one family in four had as many as one slave. Only one family in four had any part in the slave system. The others—the three families in four who did not participate in the system—went to the hills. Because the slaveholders had all of the best land, these outcasts from the economic system had to catch hold where they could and try to live without adequate means. There was no market for their goods because the big plantations bought from New York, where they sold their cotton. So these white southerners lived from hand to mouth, sometimes almost like the Indians in the woods and often in poorer conditions than the slaves. When the war ended they were left without resources and with a lack of roads and railroads, and they have had a hard time. There are thousands of families in those hills that have never seen as much as one hundred dollars in cash in a year. This great area with six or seven million people has yet to get a decent economy. During the heyday of prosperity, they went north—to Detroit, Pontiac, Cleveland, Cincinnati, Columbus, and to other cities. They went by the hundreds of thousands. Then the depression came. From 1929 through 1930, 1931, and 1932, prosperity was "just around the corner." And they waited in Detroit, Cleveland, Columbus, and Pontiac for prosperity, until they had spent everything they had. Then the folks back home had to send money from their meager incomes to bring their boys home. They are back in the hills now with their cabins overcrowded and with no work to do. That mountain region is a relief station for our great industrial centers. It is supporting the people who were sent home when there was no further work for them in industry. Today the government is helping them. Otherwise there would be starvation on a large scale.
>
> The mountain country has been exploited. I have been making a study to show you the final fruits of rugged American initiative. Here is a county that years ago had the finest hardwood forest in America. If there had been a plan—if they had cut the right timber and had foresters to take care of the rest and had established little mills and manufacturing places—the area could have had prosperity for centuries. Instead of that, lumber companies bought the land for twenty-five cents to a dollar an acre, more or less, and they hired men for seventy-five cents a day, stripped the timber, and left the blackened stumps and the people behind. They had no sense of responsibility and made no effort to put those people on their feet. You have the same story in northern Wisconsin, where people sit in poverty after the stripping of the land.
>
> In some places they found oil and built pipelines. They hired some of the people for a few years, paying them perhaps one or two dollars a day in flush times. After

the oil was flowing they no longer needed workers, so the people were left "broke" again. The same thing happened when gas was discovered. Last fall, while the oil and gas were being piped out for use in northern cities, two-thirds of the people in one of the counties that produced it were on relief. Trachoma, tuberculosis, and pellagra exist everywhere. Schools and local government are breaking down financially. A man seldom sees conditions as bad in city slums as those that exist in that county.

I could give example after example from that area where the same thing has happened. Rugged individualism has abandoned these areas, and we must see what we can do to help them. We must, if possible, get these people off of government relief and help them to be self-supporting, self-respecting citizens. We hired a hundred men and put them on one of our construction jobs. They had been sitting in idleness for years. They were young fellows who did not want their lives to rust. They have made excellent workmen. In Chicago, Detroit, and Cleveland the problem is to get prosperity back; in many communities down here there has never been prosperity.*

THE TRIBUTARY AREA DEVELOPMENT REPORT

The spirit of the Tributary Area Development enterprise is captured in a quote its authors used from the noted conservationist Gifford Pinchot (1865-1946). "Suddenly the idea flashed through my head that there was a unity in this complication—that the relation of one resource to another was not the end of the story . . . seen in this new light all these separate questions fitted into and made up the one great central problem of the use of the earth for the good of man . . . " The cases discussed here are only a few examples of many instances in which individuals have been encouraged to initiate and direct some significant activity. They show how the President's desire to give "life to all forms of human concerns" is being realized even after a long period of intolerance and discouragement from within the board. The spirit of initiative that was stimulated in spite of such discouragement persisted through the years and found renewed expression when the discouragement had ceased. Personal and group initiative is again freely and actively encouraged.

Excerpts from the Report, 1971-72, follow.

A DECADE OF GROWTH, INNOVATION, AND PROGRESS

Through the Tributary Area Development program, TVA intensifies its resource development efforts in multi-county areas throughout the Tennessee Valley where local citizens have organized to accelerate social and economic progress. . . .

*From my speech to the Kiwanis Club, Madison, Wis., Oct. 1, 1934.

"Human Concern

At the time of its creation in 1961, the Office of Tributary Area Development worked with four organized local planning and development areas, representing only a small portion of the Valley. Today people in approximately 90 percent of the Valley counties participate through such multi-county organizations as citizens' associations, special state agencies, development districts, health districts, educational cooperatives, and others. These cooperative efforts between local citizens, their state and Federal governmental agencies, and TVA are demonstrating that people can help themselves when they organize and work together for their mutual benefit, and when they can obtain the necessary facts, technical know-how, and development assistance.

HEALTH CLINICS

"If we had some money, we'd be happy to pay a doctor—if we had a doctor." The statement reflects the complexity of a problem many of the people in the rural, five-county Clinch-Powell River Valley Association area have been facing in recent years. Many who have needed medical treatment couldn't have paid a doctor very much, if anything, if they had one to pay.

Nevertheless, literally thousands of the area's residents received examinations and treatment during the summers of 1970 and 1971. The service was free and it was delivered by mobile health clinics—"health fairs" as they became known locally.

For the past two summers volunteer medical and nursing students from Vanderbilt University, supported by members of the University's medical staff, TVA, and numerous additional local and national organizations and volunteer workers, have been busy meeting some of the area's medical needs through the operation of mobile health clinics.

In keeping with its goal to improve the quality of life for individuals in less developed areas, TVA furnished two mobile health vans normally used in TVA's employee health services program and equipped with sophisticated medical diagnostic and treatment equipment, as well as personnel, to the two eight-week health screening and treatment programs.

An estimated eight thousand persons, many of them children, benefited from the "fairs" during the summer of 1970, and thousands more were receiving examinations at the end of fiscal year 1971. Each person attending received an examination that would have, according to medical estimates, cost one hundred dollars or more if done in a hospital or clinic.

The impact of the mobile clinics on the small communities of Deer Lodge, White Oak, Clairfield, Habersham, Briceville, and Sneedville, has been dramatic. As an outgrowth of "fairs," community health councils have been organized in six east Tennessee communities and two additional communities are establishing their own clinics.

Many persons have been treated for a wide variety of illnesses and conditions, including diabetes, worms (particularly in children), black lung, tuberculosis, and other respiratory diseases.

EDUCATIONAL PROGRAMS

(A) *Educational Cooperatives:* In an innovative move to upgrade education in a predominantly rural four-county east Tennessee area, the Clinch-Powell Educational Cooperative began operations July 1, 1970. The cooperative, formed and sponsored by the school boards of Claiborne, Grainger, Hancock, and Union Counties, began formal operation after more than sixteen months of planning by the Clinch-Powell River Valley Association (CPRVA), local school officials, TVA, and many others.

The purpose of the new cooperative, the second of its type in the Tennessee Valley and one of the first in the nation, is to improve teaching methods and to make better educational opportunities available at the lowest possible cost. The organization provides a four-county pool of facilities and teachers that is made available to each school in the area on an individual basis.

Active since its creation, the cooperative moved into its second year in July 1971, sponsoring a wide variety of educational programs including driver education, early childhood education, teacher training, supervised student-teacher training, speech and hearing improvement techniques, and vocational guidance. Advanced educational practices, techniques, and materials include mobile teaching facilities, television, teacher training institutes, and the sharing of specialized teachers and facilities.

Through TVA assistance a training institute, originally planned for new teachers and aides, was expanded to include teachers previously employed in the system and nondegree teachers desiring to improve their educational qualifications. The headquarters, with a full-time staff of eleven, is located at Lincoln Memorial University in Harrogate, Tennessee.

TVA had been an active partner in the Clinch-Powell Educational Cooperative from its inception, offering technical and financial assistance in planning, creating and operating the new organization. The organization is being used as a model for both the state and the nation to demonstrate how an educational cooperative is planned, formed, and operated.

(B) *Adult Education:* During 1970 and 1971 the Hiwassee River Watershed Development Association Education Work Group continued its support of an area adult education project designed to prepare participating students to take the state-administered General Educational Development (GED) test. The test is especially designed to measure the educational power and attainment of adults.

During recent years many local adults, ranging in age from eighteen to fifty-five, attended night classes and received high school equivalency certificates following completion of the program. Several graduates continued their personal educational development by entering a local college and area trade schools. In recent years the program, begun in 1967 by the HRWDA with technical assistance from TVA, has sponsored adult education night classes in Cleveland, Copperhill, and Turtletown, Tennessee.

(C) *Innovative Schools:* A two-state, three-county school that would meet local educational needs and thereby eliminate the current practice of local students traveling about one or two hours each day over bad roads to attend classes in a distant location was proposed in June 1970. In 1971 a fifty-three thousand dollar grant was approved for facility-related costs. The sum, approved for fiscal year 1972 by the Georgia State Advisory Council under Title III Elementary and Secondary Education Act, will be used for research, planning, and development of the curriculum, and surveying existing facilities for coordination with newly designed programs. The proposed school, located atop Lookout Mountain, would serve Dade and Walker Counties, Georgia, and Hamilton County, Tennessee. No high school exists in the area at this time.

According to the proposal for the new facility, submitted by a contingent of local citizens to the Georgia State Department of Education in April 1971, the new school will provide an innovative environmental, individualized academic and vocational program for grades K (kindergarten) through twelve. The plan involves the close cooperation of local residents and school systems, several institutions of higher learning, and governmental agencies. TVA has provided technical, including pre-architectural, assistance in the project, and TVA Education Specialists worked closely with a local committee concerning such matters as the project's crossing of state and county lines and the arrangement for architectural services.

Additional aims of the new school include staff development, curriculum improvement, instructional program, facility utilization, community improvement, pupil-centered programming, and interagency coordination and cooperation. Both the indoors and the outdoors would serve as learning laboratories.

(D) *Area Vocational Technical Center:* Improvements continued to be made at the Tishomingo County Area Vocational-Technical Center in upgrading physical facilities, expanding the curriculum, and increasing enrollment. A 26,000-square-foot school addition, partially financed by a two hundred thousand dollar grant from the Appalachian Regional Commission, was completed about one year ago. TVA, working with the Yellow Creek Watershed Association, and two local school boards, identified and coordinated sources of financial and technical assistance and provided a landscape plan now being used to beautify the campus. A special feature of the plan is the creation of a mobile home beautification demonstration, designed to show that mobile homes, a particularly fast-growing segment of the local housing industry, can be made unusually attractive with a little added time and planning.

The center's expanding curriculum now includes such courses as adult general education, industrial drafting, auto mechanics, aviation ground school, and preclinical nurse's training. The center was started as a consolidated vocational school by the Tishomingo County Board of Education and the Iuka Separate School District Board.

The following excerpt from a report by Dr. James L. Craig, the officer in charge of TVA health programs, describes the present occupational health program of the TVA.

> TVA's occupational health program includes an automated central medical laboratory, an automated medical information system, computerized electrocardiography, multiphasic health screening, and mobilized medical services. These components have been found to comprise an effective system, in conjunction with medical offices and health stations, for providing occupational health care for employees scattered over parts of seven states. They allow health professionals to live in urban areas but to extend their services to employees in distant locations.
> As a regional resource development agency, TVA is interested in the health of the area's people as well as in the health of employees. In cooperative projects initiated by public and/or private health groups, TVA has demonstrated the adaptability of many of its occupational health testing techniques for community health care delivery. Mobile multiphasic health testing has been shown to be a method of improving rural medical care by serving as a point of entry for nonurban residents into the health care system and by raising the level of medical care through expanded diagnostic services. Mobile and automated systems may provide partial answers to the problems of medical manpower shortage in rural areas. However, it is important that such systems be developed in conjunction with comprehensive health care delivery concepts which include social and economic considerations.
> The health of employees was an early consideration of the first Board of Directors, which established an occupational medical service during the first year of TVA's operation. The Board's concern with the public health was also evidenced by one of its first charges to the medical service: that in conjunction with TVA engineering disciplines and other health agencies, the medical staff must work toward the elimination of malaria—a ravaging disease which at that time was a major hindrance to the lower Tennessee Valley's economic and social development. That the malaria control program succeeded is evidenced by the fact that no proved case of local-origin malaria has been found in the Tennessee Valley since 1948.
> Today the occupational health program provides health services for approximately 25,000 employees working in the 80,000-square-mile area of the Tennessee River Valley and its power service region. A wide variety of occupational health and safety hazards must be controlled in numerous work places, and we have found that an effective occupational medical care program must be mobile and adaptable to changing work conditions.*

The programs in health care and education are representative of some twenty areas in which the early stimulus of the President's outlook was expressed. Programs also exist for transportation improvements, help with solid-waste disposal, help with low-cost housing, recreation and tourism, vegetable growing

---

*James L. Craig, "Health Care Delivery Systems of the Tennessee Valley Authority," *Medical Progress Through Techology*, 1, No. 1 (1972), pp. 14, 24.

and canning, industrial expansion, improved water supply and sewerage, town-lift programs, young people's involvement in community activities and business, outdoor education, TVA interns, unique community regional improvement, improved living facilities, livestock improvement, a publicly owned port complex, and conservation.

In some areas, however, the prohibition of the other members of the board was absolute and the programs were never revived in any form. Prohibition of the forest policy, for example, substantially destroyed the kind of permanent local forest development that could have been the road to continuing prosperity.

Chapter Thirteen

The Basis of Conflict and Its Resolution

By the time I entered adulthood, I had decided upon a career in engineering. To me, the important factors in life were motives and the knowledge and skill to put one's motives into effect. I tried to find ways by which, with these motives, I could bring about a good spirit and desirable results. My resolve often failed me, but I had successes too. The problem of dealing with extreme self-interest and ill will arose frequently, and as I experimented with solutions, I found that near miracles were possible. A few typical cases will illustrate.

I succeeded as the head of a large organization a man who was not easy to work with. Just before I assumed the new position, the chairman of the governing board said to me: "I have one bit of counsel to give you. Don't continue the employment of your predecessor. He is a troublemaker; you will find him often at cross-purposes and undertaking to thwart you." The top member of the staff gave me similar advice. He said that he and his associates had found the former head to be the principal cause of dissension within the organization and that it would be unwise to continue his employment.

I made an exhaustive investigation and found that the man was competent; he simply had developed some bad life habits. His wife was a decided asset to the community, and his children, who seemed to possess most of their mother's character traits and only a few of their father's, had excellent reputations. Knowing that the man had no other prospects for employment, I asked myself if there was any way of dealing with the situation that would avoid ruining the prospects of this fine family. I decided to assume a risk. In a frank talk with the man, I pointed out my dilemma: if I were to continue his employment, I asked, could he change his habits that were undesirable? I offered to help him in any way I could, told him I would call his attention to his weaknesses as occasion demanded, and then suggested that he think about my conditional offer. After considering it, he told me he would try to do what was necessary. He made a sincere effort to be a desirable associate. There were problems, but he regretted his mistakes and tried to correct them. Within a reasonable time, he markedly changed his habits. I consider this experience to be one of the most satisfying of my life.

On another occasion, when I was searching for a person who combined the skills of design engineer and administrator to take charge of my organization's engineering-design staff, I found a man of extensive knowledge and great character. But his former employer strongly advised me not to hire the man, who he said was a troublemaker and, in addition, was detested by the rest of the staff. As I examined the man's work I found it unusual and of high quality. I decided that the rare quality of this engineer's work made it desirable to give him further consideration. During a forthright discussion of the situation, I asked him whether he would attempt to change his ways if he were hired. He said he would, so I employed him to head the design staff. Soon members of the staff complained to me that he was too difficult to work with and said that they wanted to quit. I told them that they were working for a genius and that if they would bear with him for a while I would work with them in an attempt to resolve the difficulties. After several trying months they learned to work together. Other examples could be given, but these will suffice to indicate that my previous experience had given me reason not to be overly fearful of difficult personal relationships.

At the time I was considering appointing him to a position on the TVA Board of Directors, Mr. Lilienthal was completing his term as a member of the Wisconsin Public Service Commision. It was common knowledge that he would

The Making of the TVA

not be reappointed, since the La Follette political organization with which he was associated had been defeated in a recent election. His political mentors and friends worked diligently on his behalf, with the result that he was appointed a TVA director by President Roosevelt with the consent of Congress.

During the first week of Mr. Lilienthal's service on the board, Dr. Floyd H. Reeves, the director of personnel, told me: "Dr. Morgan, the Lilienthal appointment will never work. He is going from man to man in the office discrediting you. The wise thing for you to do is to resign. If you do, the whole office will go with you." Although this news was disconcerting, I continued to hope that I could work out with him a mutually satisfactory working relationship. My earlier experience had demonstrated that fair and open dealing and persistent goodwill could often bring about desirable attitudes and working relations.

There were other reasons for my desire to bear with him. One was that I greatly admired Supreme Court Justice Louis Brandeis, who through information from his daughter had suggested that I investigate Mr. Lilienthal as a possible TVA director. Another reason was that I recognized the young man's latent abilities and his potential for public service. It seemed to me he should be afforded full opportunity to prove his worth as a director.

Even in 1933, when Mr. Lilienthal had undertaken to divide and assign the board's responsibilities for the TVA program without letting me know in advance, I believed that forthright and open dealing and goodwill on my part would be an incentive to him to develop a good working relationship with me. As evidence of my confidence and goodwill, I gave Mr. Lilienthal the opportunity to choose the person who would have charge of TVA's Washington office, one of the most important and powerful positions in the TVA.

As time passed, I realized that I was confronted by the most determined intent for domination and opposition in my entire career. It became clear to me that Mr. Lilienthal had set his course and would not deviate from it or change his attitudes.

In several histories of the TVA, it is stated that I threatened President Roosevelt with my resignation as chairman of the TVA board if David Lilienthal were reappointed when his term expired in 1936 and that I had backed down from this threat after his reappointment. In 1938, when the House committee investigating the TVA asked me about this, I denied that I had threatened the President, but I also asked to be excused from explaining the circumstances. I made this request out of loyalty to President Roosevelt and my concern that telling the whole story might harm the TVA and the New Deal.

When Mr. Lilienthal's initial term of three years was about to expire, I asked the President not to reappoint him. The President immediately agreed, saying that he had come to the same conclusion himself, and asked whom I would like to have appointed in Mr. Lilienthal's place. I suggested Neil Bass, then the principal assistant to Harcourt Morgan. Since both Dr. Morgan and I had full confidence in Mr. Bass, his appointment might bring harmony to the board. The President approved, and authorized me to speak to Mr. Bass. As I was leaving his office, the President called me back and told me warmly, "Arthur, it seems to me that you and I see things together just about 100 percent."

It seemed to me important that Mr. Bass know that his appointment was at my suggestion because that would indicate my personal confidence in him. I therefore mentioned the matter to him before telling Dr. Morgan. This was bypassing my fellow director, which was unwise and improper. I should have talked with the two of them together, but that course did not occur to me until later. This was only one of the various mistakes of my TVA years and, while the act probably did not change the course of events, it illustrates my capacity for error.

A week or so later the President called me in to see him again. He told me that Senator La Follette insisted on the reappointment of Mr. Lilienthal and that since he needed La Follette's support, he would have to reappoint Lilienthal. He said that after the election he would move Lilienthal to another position. He added that since Mr. Lilienthal had become identified with the battle for public power, to make a change at that time would make a bad impression on the public-power forces.

At this meeting the President was complimentary to me. He said that there were two agencies of which he was proud—the CCC and the TVA, "and you have done the TVA. Now, don't get out on a limb where I cannot use you in my administration." I left his office without expressing agreement with him. He later sent word by one of the men close to him that if I should like to leave the TVA, I could have almost any position in his administration that I asked for.

My wife, who knew of some of the difficulties I had faced, strongly urged me to resign and never ceased to believe that I should have done so. In trying to make my decision, I discussed the matter with one of our engineers for whose judgment I had much respect. Shortly thereafter I was visited by a group of our engineers and office staff. They said that they had come to the TVA in the expectation of working with me and that for me to resign would not be fair to them. The sentiments of this group and of other TVA personnel was a factor in my decision not to resign.

I met with the President again and told him I was under the impression that,

The Making of the TVA

between then and the time he said he would move Lilienthal, the majority of the board intended to carry through a series of organizational and personnel changes that would make it very difficult for me to continue serving on the board. One of those steps would be to appoint as general manager a man for whom I had little respect. Earlier that man had come to me and vigorously depreciated my opponents on the board. He argued that my position as chairman held power that I was not using and suggested that, if he should be made general manager, he and I together could rule and dominate the situation. I told him that I was not interested in his proposal. He turned very soon to the other two directors, and I knew that they were considering making him general manager (which they later did). I asked the President whether he would use his influence to maintain the status quo during the interval before Mr. Lilienthal was moved. The President asked me to write out just what action on his part I had in mind. When I brought him a draft of my suggestions, he went over it with me sentence by sentence, changing it in a number of details and then approving it.

When I talked with him again, in early 1937, a few months after the election, the President said emphatically that he and I were of one mind but that La Follette was obdurate as to Lilienthal and he needed La Follette's support. I would, he told me, have to be patient.

As the months passed and as I talked with the President from time to time, I came to the conclusion that he had no intention of moving Mr. Lilienthal. His decisions almost always supported Lilienthal, though he continued to tell me that he and I were in full agreement. Finally, when he had once again expressed his agreement with me, I said to him, "Mr. President, you always say that you agree with me, but your decisions do not indicate that is the case." His face took on an expression of innocent surprise, and he replied, "When have I made any decision against you?" At this point he commented, "I shall first have to put La Follette and Norris through the kindergarten."

When Mr. Lilienthal learned through Senator Norris that, according to the President's plans, he would soon be removed from his position, he proceeded to discredit me with the President. He made a series of false charges against me of which I was not aware and could not answer since they were made in private correspondence. (These papers are now available to the public at the Roosevelt Library in Hyde Park, N.Y.)

The contacts I had with President Roosevelt in the early months of 1936 do not confirm the story David Lilienthal tells in his *Journals* about the negotiations he had with the President regarding reappointment.

Recent examination of President Roosevelt's correspondence in the Roosevelt

Conflict and Its Resolution

Library confirmed and amplified my impression that Mr. Lilienthal, with the help of political associates and friends, had indeed engaged in a continuing and intensive campaign to discredit me with the President and other public figures, attempting to make it appear that I had betrayed the President and the cause of public power.

After receiving a letter from Mr. Lilienthal attacking me, Senator Norris reflected the assertions contained in that letter and wrote the President about me: "I had unlimited confidence in him. However, I cannot avoid feeling that he has completely changed . . . and against my will, I must reach the conclusion that he has gone over to the enemy . . . that Dr. [Arthur] Morgan has become sordid and . . . that he is willing to have this great enterprise injured, if not completely destroyed, in order to vindicate his own pride and his own selfish ambitions."* This radical change from the warm regard that Norris had for me was obviously caused by Lilienthal's communications. Senator Norris' statement shows the extent to which the most intimate friendship and cooperation was changed to complete mistrust.

To Senator La Follette, Lilienthal wrote that I "had gone over to the power boys, hook, line and sinker."** Norris' son-in-law, John Robertson, wrote to Senator Norris: "I am convinced that misrepresentations have been made to you and in some particulars you have been deceived, all in an attempt to prejudice you against Dr. Arthur E. Morgan."† The completely false statements concerning the reversal of my devotion to the President's program and the absolute falsehoods concerning any undercover association on my part with private-power interests was the central reason for my loss of standing with the President, and it ultimately led to my dismissal.

Although I was conscious of a deterioration in the President's relations with me, I was not aware of the intensity of the change in his attitude toward me. On March 11, 1938, President Roosevelt arranged a meeting with him of Mr. Lilienthal, Harcourt Morgan, and me. I had been away from my office for about seven weeks and was just recovering from a serious bout of pneumonia. I had informed the other two directors of my illness and the reason for my absence. But in mentioning it to the President and Norris, they simply said that I was taking a vacation and was not communicating with them. I did not feel physically or mentally equal to participating in a situation that was bound to be diffi-

---

*Letter from Norris to the President, quoted in Thomas K. McCraw, *Morgan vs. Lilienthal: The Feud Within the TVA*, p. 23.
**McCraw, p. 86.
†*Ibid.*, p. 86.

cult and trying for everyone involved. I wrote to the President advising him of my conditon and begging him to postpone such a confrontation until I had regained my health and strength. He responded with a peremptory demand that I appear at the time and place scheduled, so I complied. Mr. Lilienthal's impression of my condition, as recorded in his *Journals*, was that "Morgan looked like hell."*

At the meeting, President Roosevelt asked me to substantiate the charges I had made and to answer those made against me by Mr. Lilienthal and Dr. Morgan. Still quite ill, I hesitated to enter a discussion that would be characterized by antagonism and personal prejudice toward me. It would have been exceedingly difficult to defend myself under such unfavorable and prejudiced circumstances, especially when I was below par both physically and mentally and had had no opportunity to prepare documentation for my defense for such an unexpected hearing. I explained to the President that I did not feel able at that time to enter into the discussion, and I declined to respond to the charges. As I listened to President Roosevelt's comments, it dawned on me that he had come to believe that I had repeatedly betrayed him, as Mr. Lilienthal had charged. With the benefit of hindsight, I can see that I made a serious error in refusing to defend myself, but at that time, perhaps because of my illness, I did not fully realize the extent of the impact my refusal would have. It tended to further Mr Lilienthal's efforts to bring to an end my official connection with the TVA.

Because the circumstances of these presidential hearings of March 11, 18, and 21, 1938, seemed to be unsuitable for a true review of the facts and because, in the absence of an objective hearing before the President, the Congress had responsibility as representative of the people, I asked for a congressional hearing on the issues. At the hearings, which began May 25 and proceeded through the summer, I was given an opportunity to state my case, but politically and judicially the door was closed. I was barred from obtaining evidence from the TVA files. In a letter to me, John Pierce, who was in charge of engagements, stated that the files had been sorted out and the evidence I needed carted away under orders from Mr. Lilienthal's chief legal assistant, Lawrence Fly. Neither political party was interested in a true determination of the facts. The Democrats wanted to protect the Roosevelt administration and the Republicans hoped to discredit the TVA. (There was one congressman on the committee, Representative Charles Wolverton, who did act in a notably judicious and nonpartisan manner, with concern for establishing the truth.) The legal counsel to

---

*Lilienthal, p. 73.

Conflict and Its Resolution

the investigating committee, Francis Biddle, who was one of the President's loyal circle, refrained from following up the leads I presented, some of which I have discussed in this book. The record of these hearings contains significant evidence, however glossed over with misleading argument. Even though the hearings fell so far short of what they should have been, they do provide the opportunity to make some later evaluation of the issues.

The historians who have studied the TVA have lacked adequate information and therefore have failed to understand the nature of the conflict that existed within the TVA Board of Directors. For example, in one of the more perceptive books discussing the TVA, *The Tennessee: Civil War to TVA*, Donald Davidson wrote:

> The main issue was whether a public enterprise like the TVA ought to be guided by the conscience of an Arthur Morgan or the conscience of a Lilienthal and a Harcourt A. Morgan. The two consciences represented different philosophies of public duty. Both favored the broad conception represented in TVA ... This was a socialistic conception.
>
> But Arthur Morgan believed, apparently, that the socialistic conception required of administrators a moral scrupulousness far above the average in American affairs. He would not tolerate in himself or others any taint of politics or expediency. The public business must be an open book. He would not obscure issues or suppress facts—not even to win a victory over a power company or to appease an influential politician....
>
> To David Lilienthal—with Harcourt Morgan seemingly in agreement—this attitude represented a hopeless lack of realism. It was puritanical, as some TVA supporters openly said ... They had a cause to promulgate and would not sit around deciding nice ethical points while the cause waited ... They chose the path of expediency and glorified it with romantic talk in which they perhaps believed. The end which they thought good, justified the means, which did not seem too bad.*

Mr. Davidson did not sense the basic issue, which became more and more clear to me as I struggled with the TVA: it was not a conflict over two ways in which the public interest might be served but a more fundamental conflict between the public interest and a private interest concealed in the trappings of the public interest. The driving motive that seemed to underlie all of Mr. Lilienthal's actions is suggested in his self-appraisal in 1937, while he was a member of the TVA board.

---

*Donald Davidson, *The Tennessee. Vol. 2: The New River, Civil War to TVA* (New York: Rinehart, 1948), pp. 324-325.

> You have been carried along so far by an intense and absorbing desire for achievement; the contest spirit; make a place for yourself; get somewhere; etc. That you have done. It would be insincere to pretend that, at 37, you haven't a remarkable record, enough to satisfy the ambition of a lifetime. In five years of public life you have leaped from relative obscurity to a place near the top.
>
> What are you going to do with it now that you have what you have been driving for? It isn't only where do we go from here? But what do we do now we are here? Somehow there never seemed any problem on that score during the exciting climb. But here you are, and now what does it mean, what are you going to do with your accomplishment? *

After his appointment Mr. Lilienthal lost no time in sizing up his director associates. In almost the only lengthy conversation I ever had with him, shortly after his appointment, he inquired with concern about my prospects and intentions. He wanted to know how I expected to advance; how I would live on my salary as a director of the TVA, which he considered very small for a politician; and whether I had ways of increasing my personal income. He seemed preoccupied with the question of how I intended to go about extending my political influence; no other subject seemed of moment, and issues relating to the TVA were not mentioned. When he found that my mind was not centered on personal advancement, he lost interest in the conversation and never brought up the subject again. It seemed that he found out what he wanted to know about me.

In Harcourt A. Morgan, Mr. Lilienthal found a man of a different temper, who could be controlled with small effort. The excessive modesty that Dr. Morgan had displayed in our initial conversations was strikingly absent in his later association with me. I overlooked the well-known fact that extreme modesty is a standard means of working oneself into a position of importance and dominance. At first he acted as though he was impressed by my background as the chief engineer of several large water-control projects and as the president of Antioch College. He had also read some of my writings and apparently viewed my treatment of the subject matter favorably.

It did not take Mr. Lilienthal long to discover that Dr. Morgan's interests were surprisingly narrow in scope, limited for the most part to promoting the use of phosphate fertilizer in southern agriculture. So long as he could spend his time and energy in that effort and had sufficient funds to carry on the program, he would be satisfied. The ambitious program that the President had suggested

---

*Lilienthal, p. 67.

to me seemed unnecessary to him. Since his interest in water control, navigation, and power sales was minimal, he rarely concerned himself with problems involved in these major facets of the TVA program; usually, he was content to approve the recommendations of his associates.

President Roosevelt had set a condition that one of the directors must be a southern agriculturalist. Southern agriculture was largely controlled by persons of privilege (most of whom were descendants of large slaveholders), who were opposed in general to the President's ideas. In choosing a Canadian who had moved to the South, I thought I might have escaped this almost universal limitation found in southern political attitudes.

Harcourt Morgan had skillfully dealt with politics at the state level in Tennessee for many years. He had successfully worked his way into an important position in southern politics, holding a significant place in the land-grant-college bureaucracy. He possessed sufficient political acumen to recognize that, with the backing of President Roosevelt, Senator La Follette, Donald Richberg, and Felix Frankfurter, Mr. Lilienthal was likely to exercise much power. He accepted Mr. Lilienthal's leadership and ambition to gain control of the TVA, apparently believing that his own important but limited area of interest, phosphate fertilizer, might fare better as part of a limited program emphasizing power distribution than as only one of the broad range of interests that President Roosevelt had expressed.

Whether any informal agreement existed between Harcourt Morgan and David Lilienthal I cannot say, but it is significant that from the beginning they voted and acted as a unit, opposing the larger purposes of the TVA enunciated by President Roosevelt; they thus became the effective board majority and dominated the official TVA structure.

To Mr. Lilienthal's mind I was the obstacle to his establishing personal control of the TVA; therefore, it was essential that I be eliminated. The major part of his strategy to bring about my elimination was to convince President Roosevelt and Senator George Norris that my conduct as chairman of the TVA was improper and a hindrance to the Authority's progress. For instance, among the numerous letters from him to the President in the Roosevelt Library at Hyde Park charging me with conspiring against TVA interests, there is a ten-page letter dated January 18, 1938, which Mr. Lilienthal probably prepared and which he and Harcourt Morgan signed. In plausible language it depicts an alleged condition within the TVA that was completely at variance with the actual situation and charges me with various improprieties. Below are a number of quotations from this letter of January 18, each followed by my comments. The

The Making of the TVA

beginning of the letter is a tribute to the TVA staff. It reads:

> In 1933, when this project was set in motion, there were few guideposts for the administration of the enterprise. Its future course was largely uncharted. To carry out this undertaking, there was assembled a staff of thousands of trained men and women of scores of professions and occupations, drawn from all parts of the country and selected solely on the basis of merit. This staff has done a job of which Americans can be proud.

This statement makes no reference to the fact that for three months—while I was working alone—a staff was assembled under my direction by able, highly qualified assistants, who made a nationwide search for men and women of competence and character. The extensiveness of the search and selection strictly on the basis of merit were in marked contrast to the hiring practices prevailing in the federal service. The TVA personnel recruitment and selection practices were largely the outgrowth of techniques and procedures I had developed over the years, while serving as chief engineer of a number of water-control projects.

> From its creation in the summer of 1933 until the spring of 1936, the TVA was guided by a Board whose every corporate action was by unanimous vote of all three Directors. Since the spring of 1936, however, the Authority's work has been accomplished in spite of the repeated failure of Arthur E. Morgan to accept and cooperate in carrying out provisions of law and Board decisions. Much that has been accomplished since the spring of 1936 has been in spite of Mr. Morgan's continued efforts to obstruct Board decisions with which he disagreed. For more than a year, as a consequence, the undersigned majority of the Board of Directors have been compelled to assume responsibility for the project.

After a few meetings in Washington in June 1933, Mr. Lilienthal and Dr. Morgan announced that they would be absent for a time—on private business, they said. Meanwhile, President Roosevelt, who was deeply concerned about the severity of the depression, instructed me to get the major TVA programs under way as soon as possible so that people could be put to work. The engineering and construction staff and I began at once to carry out his instructions to the full extent of existing possibilities.

Early in July I received a telegram from my fellow directors asking me to meet with them in Knoxville. At that meeting they laid before me a plan for division of responsibility for TVA programs on which they had been working without my knowledge during the time they were supposedly transacting personal business.

This was little more than a month after their respective appointments. The TVA was just being born and their experience was minimal. I was extremely busy with TVA construction work, while Mr. Lilienthal had as yet few duties to interfere with his political designs. Moreover, the fact that I stood firmly against politically motivated appointments greatly reduced my potential sources of support. Whereas I had only the recommendation of Eleanor Roosevelt, and perhaps of Governor Cox of Ohio, to support my appointment, Lilienthal had surrounded himself with a number of politicians headed by the President's powerful favorites, Robert and Philip La Follette, and their numerous political associates.

I decided that I could live with Lilienthal's plan for the TVA, since it would place under the control of each director the particular aspects of the TVA program in which he was primarily interested. Hoping to avoid open conflict, I agreed to its adoption. Had I put my energies into a battle for control, the entire TVA project might have been destroyed.

I consistently abstained from voting on matters on which I did not agree, a practice that I followed until May 19, 1936, when, without advance notice, I was summarily informed by Mr. Lilienthal that he and Dr. Morgan were voting to take from me my responsibility as chief engineer of the Fontana Dam project. This action was a clear invasion of my major field of responsibility. I naturally protested, but to no avail; my protest was reported by Mr. Lilienthal as an intolerable failure on my part to accept the decision of the board majority.

On June 2, 1936, Mr. Lilienthal and Dr. Morgan held a meeting without my presence and without giving me notice, though I would have been available in two days. At this meeting they voted to suspend negotiations by the TVA to obtain the Fontana damsite but left open the possibility of negotiations with Alcoa relating to the interchange of energy. I have discussed at length how crucial TVA control of the Fontana site and its water was to the Authority's integrated management of the Tennessee River and its tributaries. In suspending negotiations by TVA to obtain Fontana, the decision of the board majority drastically compromised the position of the TVA as it related to the public interest in Fontana, and constituted what might be a serious violation of the most important physical aspect of the TVA concept.

After my responsibility as chief engineer of the Fontana Dam project was taken from me and given to Mr. Lilienthal and after the board majority had placed TVA's great interest in the Fontana damsite in jeopardy by reason of the action noted above, I felt compelled to put on record my disagreements with the majority of the board.

The Making of the TVA

Neither before nor after the spring of 1936 did a delay occur in the building of dams, power plants, reservoirs, navigation locks, and facilities for shipping, all of which was wholly under my direction. That work progressed uninterrupted except for occasional interferences, such as Mr. Lilienthal's refusal to approve a housing plan for TVA employees working on Norris Dam. For the two directors to assert that "for more than a year . . . [we] . . . have been compelled to assume responsibility for all projects" is fantasy.

Continuing his comments on majority rule, Mr. Lilienthal wrote:

> The process of accommodating conflicting views on particular issues is characteristically democratic. It roots from the conviction that in the give-and-take of discussion among independent men where viewpoints must be urged and defended on the basis of reasonableness, consideration of other viewpoints than one's own, the elimination of personal bias or personal ambition—a weighing and sifting and adjustment from which emerges a decision and action.

Mr. Lilienthal here states a classic ideal of group behavior as though it were a form of organization desired by the board. The statement might better have served as an expression of standards that the board habitually avoided, sometimes by extreme disregard for commonly recognized group procedure.

In the following excerpts from the letter, Mr. Lilienthal, with Harcourt Morgan's concurrence, was more specific in his charges, which were designed to discredit me and to destroy my effectiveness as chairman.

> When a board of public trustees, after weighing differing points of view, and after the fullest board discussion, has reached a conclusion by majority vote, how far may the dissenting trustee, while still continuing to hold his office, properly carry his opposition to these board decisions?
>
> We believe the following methods of opposition, which are among those employed by our associate since the spring of 1936, fall outside permissible limits.
>
> It is not permissible, as Arthur E. Morgan has done repeatedly in published statements, to attack the personal motives and good faith and impugn the integrity of his associates on the Board, not upon the basis of direct charges but by innuendo, indirection, and aspersion.

Very early in his TVA career, David Lilienthal began to make full use of just such tactics. This letter to the President, which Mr. Lilienthal probably wrote and Dr. H. A. Morgan joined him in signing, is one example.

Throughout my life, I have always striven to conduct my relationships with people on the basis of mutual respect and goodwill. I determinedly followed that practice while serving as chairman of the TVA, even after Mr. Lilienthal's tactics were made known to me. It seemed to me that I would be more effective if I concentrated on making the best use of the opportunities and responsibilities that were clearly in my hands, instead of diverting my energy to the struggle for personal power that so frequently characterizes bureaucracies. That belief accounts for the nearly three years during which "every corporate action was by unanimous vote of all three directors."

In a letter to me, George Chandler Harris, who was editor of the *Chattanooga Times* (and the son of Joel Chandler Harris, author of the famous "Uncle Remus" stories), took me to task because I refused to respond to charges that Mr. Lilienthal had made to the news media for widespread publication. He urged me to respond and offered his paper's help. I declined to do so, hoping that the exercise of goodwill would encourage Mr. Lilienthal to desist from his strategy. Mr. Harris seemed to assume that my refusal stemmed from timidity. He came to Knoxville and spent considerable time telling me that I was being grossly defamed and that I was on dangerous ground in not responding to such attacks.

After receiving many letters questioning public statements made in the name of the TVA board, I made a public protest in the fall of 1937 by means of articles published in the *New York Times* and the *Atlantic Monthly*. I made it clear that I did not approve of all that the TVA was doing, and these articles were the basis, I believe, of the charge quoted above.

Mr. Lilienthal went on to say:

> Such methods of expressing disagreement with the Act and with majority decisions of the Board, as have been employed by Arthur E. Morgan, are not permissible. Such methods are wrong because they violate the democratic principle of majority rule. They violate a spirit of good sportsmanship in public affairs; one should be a good loser in matters of opinion as well as in sports. We believe these methods to be wrong because they are not designed to persuade but to obstruct and discredit the carrying out of the law and of decisions duly reached after fair consideration.

But since on most matters H. A. Morgan invariably voted with Mr. Lilienthal, the "majority opinion" was in effect one-man rule by Mr. Lilienthal.

He further stated that: "It is not permissible for the Chairman of the Board after Board action has been duly taken, to fail and refuse to carry out explicit action taken by the Board." The basis of this charge of insubordination to the TVA board was my effort to get the board to reconsider its action ending negotiations with the Aluminum Company of America for acquisition of the Fontana damsite.

I had proposed a plan under which the TVA would acquire the Fontana damsite and in return would guarantee Alcoa the amount of electric power that the Fontana dam and dams that Alcoa had already built would produce if the TVA had not been created. Only this course would protect the public interest by establishing integrated control of the waters of the Tennessee River and its tributaries. Because the board's decision to discontinue negotiations with Alcoa to acquire the site placed the public interest in jeopardy and created an urgent need to resolve the issues, I deemed it mandatory that the TVA board reconsider its decisions. I therefore briefly discussed with Alcoa's president, Arthur V. Davis, the question of whether the primary obstacle in the negotiations—the company's demand for compensation for downstream use of Fontana water—was negotiable. I also asked him whether Alcoa would agree to reopening the negotiations. His answer to each question was in the affirmative. It was for these actions on my part that I was charged with insubordination.

Mr. Lilienthal also said: "It was not permissible for Arthur E. Morgan secretly to cooperate with a utility executive in the preparation of a memorandum, the express purpose of which was to show that a decision of the Board was wrong and activated by improper motives." The utility executive alluded to in this charge was the president of the Commonwealth and Southern Corporation, Wendell L. Willkie, whom I had personal contact with only three times in my life, as I explained in Chapter Eleven. The memorandum referred to by Mr. Lilienthal came about as follows. Prior to a TVA board meeting on February 2, 1937, that I invited him to attend, Mr. Willkie had conferred with Mr. Lilienthal about the possible purchase by the TVA of Commonwealth and Southern utility properties and about the sale and interchange of electric power. On January 29, 1937, Mr. Lilienthal addressed a letter to Mr. Willkie that presumably summarized the position of Commonwealth and Southern Corporation as it was stated at their conference. The letter was, however, in complete contrast to what Mr. Lilienthal had previously reported to the board. In it he stated that Commonwealth and Southern's position was that it would not contract for the sale and interchange of power to any other agency within the four states that it served.

During the board meeting, I pointedly asked Mr. Willkie if Lilienthal's letter correctly stated the Corporation's position. He replied explicitly and unqualifiedly that it did not and that, if the federal government through the TVA desired to acquire some of its distribution systems, the Corporation would sell

Conflict and Its Resolution

them with the understanding that there would be only one distribution system in any given area. That policy, he argued, would avoid the waste and inefficiency created by the duplication of facilities by two competing systems. After the meeting I wrote a memorandum covering what Mr. Willkie had said and asked him whether it accurately stated his corporation's position. He confirmed the memorandum sentence by sentence and authorized me to publish it if I should see fit to do so.

Mr. Lilienthal later issued a press release that again incorrectly stated the position of the Commonwealth and Southern Corporation. This was done notwithstanding Mr. Willkie's forthright assertion that Mr. Lilienthal's previous statement of the Corporation's position was wholly inaccurate.

Because I questioned Mr. Willkie about the content of Mr. Lilienthal's letter and checked with him the accuracy of my memorandum recording the Commonwealth and Southern position, I was accused of secretly cooperating with a utility executive for the purpose of showing that a decision of the board was wrong and activated by improper motives. Actually, my effort was directed solely toward making certain that the board fully understood the position of the Commonwealth and Southern Corporation. Except for my brief, general comments shortly after I became director, this was the only time I ever discussed the TVA with Mr. Willkie, although Mr. Lilienthal's letter to the President implied that I had done so frequently.

In another charge, Mr. Lilienthal stated:

> It was not permissible for Arthur E. Morgan to collaborate, in secret, with the former Chief Engineer of the Insull utility system, in the preparation of a detailed recommendation on power pooling policy, which report proposed evasions and violations of the TVA Act; nor was it permissible, during negotiations, for him to permit such report to be made available to the utilities.

President Roosevelt was very much interested in the possibilities of pooling public and private power-transmission capabilities. In order to explore the benefits to the public inherent in such pooling of power resources and to develop an appreciation for the problems involved, he scheduled a conference to which he invited leaders in the public- and private-power fields and others with special interests in electric-power generation, transmission, and distribution. As chairman of the TVA, I was invited to participate.

Mr. Lilienthal took the position that he should be the sole representative of the TVA at the conference, notwithstanding the fact that the President had specifically requested my presence. Recognizing my need to prepare for participation in the conference, I asked for engineering help. At first Mr. Lilienthal denied my request, but he later suggested that I use one of his staff men, Dr. Martin Glaeser, who had been associated with him on the Wisconsin Public Service Commission. The power-pool information Dr. Glaeser submitted to me was, in my opinion, grossly inadequate, and I found it mandatory that I prepare myself further.

The TVA had within its organization three men who could have helped me, particularly Llewellyn Evans. But since to take any one of the three away from his work at that time would have created a hardship, I chose to utilize the services of George W. Hamilton. At Mr. Lilienthal's request, the board had entered into a consultant's contract more than six months earlier with Mr. Hamilton, who was previously the chief engineer and a vice-president of the Middle West Utilities Company, a unit in Samuel Insull's utility empire. He was nationally known as an expert on switchyards, transmission pools, and distribution systems. When accusing me of collaborating in secret with the chief engineer of the Insull utility system, Mr. Lilienthal neglected to mention that Mr. Hamilton was then employed by him as a consultant, working on transmission problems under his direction.

The reason advanced by Mr. Lilienthal as to why it was wrong for me to utilize Mr. Hamilton's expertise was that, because he had a private-utility background, he was likely to have a biased point of view and might exercise undue influence over me. Actually, Mr. Hamilton had lost most of his personal wealth when the large block of Insull stock he owned became worthless in the stock-market crash. Furthermore, he was a litigant in an action against the Insull enterprises.

Mr. Hamilton and I worked together for a period of ten days, researching and assembling information that I needed for the memorandum I wrote for use at President Roosevelt's conference. Desiring that Mr. Hamilton's work and mine be reviewed before being put into its final form, I asked F. E. Schmidt, editor of the *Engineering News-Record*, the principal civil-engineering periodical in the country, to criticize a preliminary draft of the memorandum. He had just completed a study for Secretary of the Interior Harold Ickes of the Reclamation Service, which at that time controlled the largest federal power projects. He was, therefore, well qualified to criticize the draft.

I also asked Samuel Ferguson, president of the Hartford Electric Company, which was widely recognized as one of the most efficient and best-managed utilities in the country, to criticize my power-pool memorandum. Over the years, Mr. Ferguson had strongly and publicly supported the TVA, and he had also steadfastly refused to merge his company with a holding company or to consolidate. When he needed more power than he had, he made a pooling arrangement with another small company nearby. I thought his views on the content of my memorandum would be most helpful.

I did a very thorough job in preparing for the President's conference and made a copy of my prepared statement for each member of the commission appointed by the President.

Mr. Lilienthal concluded his condemnation of me with the words:

> And finally, we believe Mr. Morgan's methods are wrong because the doctrine of "rule or ruin" cannot exist alongside the doctrine of majority rule and minority responsibility.
>
> Having failed to persuade his colleagues to his viewpoint, no member of this Board may obstruct the work of the Board, as Arthur E. Morgan has done.

These two paragraphs are the capstone of ten pages of similar expressions.

CONCLUDING OBSERVATIONS ON LILIENTHAL

The measure of a man's character is not in what he started out with but in what he does with what he was given by heritage and background. In this light David Lilienthal's accomplishment, measured by the later maturing of his character and pattern of life, is extraordinary. Seemingly beginning with narrow personal motives and a limited view of his life and work, he broadened and clarified his purposes and understanding and grew in character to become a significant citizen and public servant. His intense ambition started him on a course that finally was characterized by a high order of social concern.

It is significant that in his book *This I Do Believe*, Mr. Lilienthal supports most of the objectives and values I sought for the TVA and for America. He emphasized, in one of the better statements I have seen on the subject, the responsibility and potential of all people for making their lives in their communities significant. If that book is an accurate measure of the development of Mr. Lilienthal's philosophy and character between the time I knew him and the ten or so years later when he wrote it—and I have been informed by some people who have been intimate with him, such as former TVA assistant chief engineer Harry Wiersema, that this is the case—then he has to a significant degree fulfilled the hope I had for him during that earlier period with the TVA.

There is one issue on which we were most centrally in disagreement. David

The Making of the TVA

Lilienthal assumed that the motives of people in general tended to be sound and that their primary need was for information and the opportunity, through the resources of communication, technology, and science, to give expression to their motives. In contrast, I believed that information and resources were not sufficient for human well-being because the mass of people, with selfish motives and purposes, are likely to put information and power to poor use. Further, the opportunities to misinform the people are beyond the people's abilities to cope with such misinformation. In 1936 I wrote in *The Long Road* about the critical need for character development and refinement of purpose among the people to whom knowledge, power, and resources are given.

Individual self-interest is not an adequate basis for an enduring democracy or a healthy society. The true interest of the constituent parts of society—individuals, races, classes, industries, nationalities, and religions—requires their right relationship to society as a whole. Lacking a sense of commitment to that larger interest, each part of society, in pursuing its selfish interests, comes into conflict, and the solidarity and harmony of society is deeply injured. Democracy can survive only in a society whose members have a sense and an understanding of their lives as parts of the ongoing totality of life and a loyalty to the totality that is greater than that to their own group and self-interest. Unless the members of society feel themselves to be parts of that larger stream of life, the meaning of their lives as individuals will fade into a retrogression of human well-being. We must respect and be loyal to the individual, the family, the community, and the nation; but we must recognize that the well-being of all of these depends upon their being linked in love with past, present, and future life and with the society of man, beast, and nature.

Chapter Fourteen

The Long Road

During my chairmanship of the TVA, the political manipulation I observed impressed me as symptomatic of the most serious problem confronting our country—that of ethics, motivation, and character. While confronted with such issues in the TVA, I wrote a book on the subject, *The Long Road*, published by the National Home Library Foundation, which was financed by Justice Louis Brandeis. This digest of its first two chapters summarizes the importance of the problem as I then saw it, and so it is a fitting conclusion to this book, written in retrospect about the TVA.

LIMITATIONS IN GOVERNMENT AND INDUSTRY

With the discovery of America, long-range navigation developed enormously. Yet the dread specter of scurvy followed every voyage. The joy of adventure was largely destroyed by this terrible malady of the sailor's life. When Captain Cook, on one of his voyages of exploration, with his men suffering from scurvy, stopped at a tropical island, his men ate the fresh fruit on the island and had remarkable recoveries. It was not until about a century and a half later, however, that biologists discovered the essential food elements called vitamins and their wonderful part in maintaining physical health. During the intervening years scurvy had been one of the chief menaces of polar exploration. A similar disease, beriberi, had wrought havoc in the Japanese army during the Russo-Japanese War, and another, pellagra, was known as a deadly malady in Europe and in our southern mountains. Still another related disease is commonly known as rickets.

The discovery of the functions of vitamins cleared up the mystery of these diseases. They were simply forms of starvation. A man might be living as a gourmand, eating twice as much as necessary; yet, if the essential vitamins were lacking in his diet, he would become seriously and perhaps fatally ill. A large quantity of food was not enough. Various specific food elements had to be supplied if health was to be maintained.

So, likewise, our social order today is plagued by some strange deficiency disease. Just as the discovery of America led to a great extension of navigation, and to long absences of sailors from the natural home supplies of food, so the discovery of the new worlds of technology and of business organizations has launched us on uncharted seas in economics and government. We have left the familiar home environment far behind and are losing intimate contact with the sources of our cultural nourishment. We must live on the cultural reserves that our foresight has led us to lay in store, or on the cultural resources that new and relatively artificial circumstances have supplied. Very evidently something is missing. It has become offensively trite to refer to our vast natural wealth, to our favorable climate, our great manufacturing plants, our transportation and communication systems, our banking facilities, and our millions of men and women eager to work. We have all of these resources, yet live in confusion and poverty, with many millions of our people denied the reasonable expectations of life.

There must be a critical deficiency of some essential social vitamins. What we face is real malnutrition—a scurvy of the social order, a political pellagra, a beriberi of business. Abundance of many things does not prevent a deficiency of others. Although in respect to some essentials we do have a great surplus, yet our deficiency is a real one. If we can discover what the missing elements are, we may find the way to supply them to give tone, health, and vigor to the whole social order. With the diseases beriberi, scurvy, rickets, and pellagra, we are no longer at the mercy of mysterious evils; we know our problems, and we know what is necessary to solve them. In my opinion we need no longer be in the dark as to what are the chief missing vitamins in our social order.

Though sheer corruption and graft are sometimes deeply entrenched, especially in our great cities, the chief weakness of government is not outright graft, but commitment to special interests and the routine, unimaginative inefficiency that results from bureaucracy, from machine politics, and from a lack of discrimination among voters.

During these years I have also seen much good government, with faithful, skillful men working without glory and for small incomes. Our attention is so often centered on governmental inefficiencies that we do not realize the extent to which our welfare is entrusted to faithful and loyal public servants. Nevertheless, I am not subject to the charge of undue pessimism in saying that American government—local, state, and national—for more than a century has suffered grievously from routine bureaucracy, political favoritism, machine politics, and explicit dishonesty, and in general from selfish ambition that puts private advantage before public good.

But political government is not the only part of American life that suffers from grave disorders. When we turn to Big Business, we find similar shortcomings throughout our history. The Revolutionary War was scarcely over when an economic disturbance, known as Shays' Rebellion, shook New England. I first became interested in making a study of Shays' Rebellion when reading John Marshall's *Life of Washington*. Marshall was a good conservative who deprecated any such disturbances on the part of the common people. Yet his comments throw light on a stirring and significant episode in our national life, accounts of which have been carefully expurgated in our school histories. Shays' Rebellion was caused by as cynical and ruthless oppression of the poor by Big Business as anything that has occurred since that time.

Follow the economic history of the United States through the era of national lotteries; of railroad building; of wholesale importation of cheap contract labor from Europe to break down efforts to achieve a decent American standard of living in the steel and mining industries. Continue through the corruption associated with privately owned utilities in our cities; to "frenzied finance," as described by Thomas Lawson; down to secret monopolies, railroad rebates, and restriction of output existing before the war; to the swollen profits of the war period; to the mad orgy of unloading inflated securites on the public during the 1920s; to exploitation by the electric-power industry, as abundantly documented in the reports of the Federal Trade Commission. We must conclude that business does not present a clean page.

Yet no inclusive indictment of business would be fair or truthful. The vigor and soundness of America have been due in large part to that mass of American business that has been skillfully, thriftily, and honestly conducted, with pride of workmanship, with intelligent and persistent striving after excellence of product and economy in production, and with "a decent regard for the opinions of mankind," at least so far as required by the accepted business code. So great and enduring a structure as American business could not have come into being except through the activities of a great many men of very substantial character.

This discussion of business and government might seem to imply that these two phases of our common life have peculiar defects from which most of our people are free. That is not the case. As a young man I worked in common labor gangs in several states and very often found among my fellow workers dull sensual inertness, without self-mastery or aspiration. Talk confidentially with intelligent and experienced men whose dominant interest is to bring about better conditions for labor and you will often hear the conviction expressed that the American labor movement has generally lacked responsible, public-spirited leadership. Repeatedly businessmen and public officials have found that they could not count on the responsible cooperation of labor leadership for achieving the common good. Such limitations have been no less striking in labor and in some of the professions than in business and in government. A discussion of character in business and government, therefore, does not imply that those activities are inferior to American life as a whole.

Both in government and in business, as in the general population, there is fine quality and there is low quality. Business points its finger at governmental inefficiency, yet at the same time government has been driven to intervene to protect the public against the sins of business in the form of adulterated goods, watered stocks, secret rebates, unfair treatment of weak competitors, and maintenance of unwholesome and indecent labor conditions. In many respects business did not clean its own house, and so it has been left for government to do it. Those who read Lincoln Steffens' *Autobiography* will realize more acutely what should already have been self-evident—that for every bribe taker in government there is also a bribe giver, often in business.

But where shall we turn for higher standards? When as a young man I went into engineering I felt considerably like a radical; I was determined to protect the common man against the encroachments of Big Business. Yet as I worked along through the years, over and over again I found that in practical affairs the ethics of men in big businesses were better than those of men who operated small businesses. In general, I found that I could have more straightforward and businesslike dealings with men of large experience than with men of small affairs. The difficulty, then, is not that Big Business has a lower level of ethics than small business but that defects of character, which in a simple society may be endurable as common weaknesses of human nature, may threaten to wreck the structure of our society when magnified to the dimensions of nationwide industries or continent-wide governments with the tremendous coercive power that size may bring.

Business, government, and labor are but different expressions of the single organism of our common life. Business recognizes the shortcomings in government and in labor; government recognizes them in business and in labor leadership; labor recognizes them in government and in business. The defects of each do not originate in its own particular activities. Rather, they are the symptoms of a general lack of social health, appearing in ways characteristic of the particular activities. It is then no longer enough for the pot of business and the kettle of government to call each other black. We must look below the surface phenomena to the common sources of our difficulty.

There are those who would undertake to cure our social ills by reforming government alone and by freeing business from discipline. In our present-day society, however, the expression "that government is best which governs least" is but a red herring drawn across the trail of our thinking. Our great corporations are in fact private governments and often have more intimate control of our lives than does public government. Through propaganda and advertising on a vast scale at the consumers' expense, they often determine not only what we will eat, drink, and wear, but also what we will think on public questions. Commonly, they discipline and regiment the lives of their employees, prescribing their duties, with small range of personal choice, sometimes preventing free expression of opinion and sometimes even dictating political action.

In the maze of specialized fields that exists today, a self-seeking person who gives the appearance of quick results by superficial work may win greater public approval than the straightforward person who quietly and thoroughly organizes for the effective mastery of his problem. That is true not only in public affairs but sometimes in private industry as well.

Throughout American industry there have been men in high places who have exploited the faithful, honest work of real builders and have advanced themselves by shrewdness in creating the appearance of rapid accomplishment. I know from personal experience that one of the most difficult aspects of carrying through public projects is to keep at bay demagogues and certain impetuous elements, while trying to lay the basis for efficient progress. Public suspicion and impatience may not give time for honest and thoroughgoing preparation.

In a simple society a relatively few checks and balances and restrictions may be enough to prevent gross abuses. In the extremely complex social and economic order that has emerged in the modern world, however, the kinds of inefficiency and antisocial action that are possible—and which in both public and private affairs may have the temporary appearance of success—are extremely varied, and laws, regulations, and supervision are increasingly difficult to apply. The checking of antisocial action by laws and surveillance becomes too involved for human management, and the whole process begins to bog down.

The time has come when enlightened self-interest fails, when we can no longer exercise enough shrewdness to protect ourselves from the maze of interests, powers, influences, propaganda, and other forces that surround us. Another kind of foundation, very different from shrewd self-interest, must be provided if modern society is to survive and advance.

With the failure of suspicion and vigilant inquisitions as safeguards to our common life, we are driven to rely on morale and on the character both of those who lead and of those who follow. We must count on each person to do his own work, of his own will, with skill and enthusiasm. That quality of workmanship is essential to keep society going. Character in business and in government will solve seemingly inextricable complexities; make unnecessary and meaningless vast systems of checks and balances, of laws, regulations, surveillances, inspections, and prohibitions; eliminate the need for constant exercise of shrewdness and suspicion; and release energies for constructive efforts. The limits of character mark the limits of good government and of good business.

To hold that the development of personal and community character is the primary essential is not to claim that it alone is sufficient for a better social order. Organized action, including political action, also is imperative. It is to a considerable extent true that an institution is but the lengthened shadow of a man, but it is also true that the character of a people may be largely the reflection of their institutions.

THE TENSILE STRENGTH OF MEN

Yet, although there is no single approach to a better social order, there are times when some essential quality has been so neglected that it needs dominant emphasis and for perhaps a considerable period should receive the major portion of our efforts. One might compare our capability to create a better human society with our ability to build great suspension bridges. The span of the bridges we can build is limited by several factors. One condition is our ability to finance the construction. A fifty-million-dollar bridge is within the reach of modern social effort; a ten-billion-dollar bridge would be beyond it. Another limiting condition is engineering design. The more skillful the design, the better the use that can be made of available money and materials. A third condition is the quality of the materials for building. The greater the tensile strength of the steel used, the less the weight of the parts required to provide a given strength, and therefore the greater the span that can be achieved. Our most recent great suspension bridges would have been impossible in the old days of low-grade steel.

In comparing the development of a social order to the building of a bridge, we may liken personal character to the quality of the steel of which a bridge is made. We may desire to create a bridge of greater span than ever has been built. Yet, if the only steel available is of very low tensile strength and of uneven and uncertain quality, no amount of fine design and no abundance of finance can overcome that limitation. By the time we have made the steel members thick enough to overcome the weakness of the material, so much steel has been added that the bridge will break down of its own weight. We reach a point where the making of more massive parts does not help, because it adds to the weight to be supported faster than it adds to the strength to support that weight. Then we have reached the limit of the span that can be built. Before that condition is reached we would do well to turn our attention from additional financing and additional refinements of design and to concentrate on improving the quality of the steel or other available metal. If we can produce steel or some other alloy that is four times as strong, then only a fourth as much of it is necessary to carry a given load. If the bridge is relieved of three-fourths of the burden of supporting its own weight, a much longer span is possible, an otherwise impossible financial undertaking may become feasible, and a new range of possibilities may be opened up.

Personal character in a social order is like the quality of the metal used in bridge building. If personal character is on a low level, then there comes a time when no refinement of social planning and no expenditure of public wealth, however great, will create a good social order. Additional complexities of planning and additional expenses for supervision, inspection, investigation, and enforcement finally begin to break down of their own weight. A point is reached where they add more difficulties than they relieve.

In my opinion, life in America is approaching that point. In the industrial and political worlds we have drawn far-reaching plans for great social and economic structures. Our ablest organizers and economists, both public and private, have made sweeping designs. To pay for those structures we have made vast levies on the stores of our natural resources. We are exhausting our soil five times as fast as we are replacing it, and even at our present rate of replacing fertility we are consuming mineral fertilizers a thousand times as fast as they were deposited in the rocks. We are cutting our forests faster than they can grow. We are using our coal ten thousand times as fast as it was created and our oil, iron, gold, and silver a million times as fast as they were deposited. For a truly unbalanced economic budget we must look to modern industry, not to government. And perhaps the greatest of all losses in a time of great inflation and expansion is in the waste of cultural reserves, for a rapidly expanding economy may consume character and culture faster than it creates them.

Notwithstanding all our fevered effort at design and this excessively prodigal expenditure of our irreplaceable wealth, our magnificently schemed social and economic structure breaks down, as it did in 1929, leaving us in confusion and distress. And that distress is but a foretaste of the decadence that may follow the exhaustion of our soil and mineral resources. It is time, I say, that we turn our principal attention from increasing intricacies of social and economic design to the quality of the social materials with which we build.

For perhaps the next half-century or more, the burden of our attention and of our loyalties and the full drive of our aspirations should be given to bringing about a revolution in the personal character of the American people. Not that I would stop economic production, or any other aspect of development. Men who are peculiarly equipped for service in these fields need not give up the work for which they are best fitted, whenever they can continue productive effort without compromise and without loss of self-respect. But for them, and for Americans as a whole, the great need of the coming years in whatever field they may work is the building of great character, the defining and clarifying of purposes and motives, the development of integrity and open dealing, the increase of self-discipline, the tempering of body and spirit to endure hardship, the growth of courage, the practice of tolerance, the habit of acting for the general good, and the growth of human understanding and of neighborly affection and regard.

During the past three or four decades sociologists and especially social workers have been inclined to minimize the influence of personal character, as compared with the influence of the prevailing social order, in determining personal conduct. It has been customary to say with Karl Marx that the moral deficiencies of men are due chiefly to a perverted social order. Create good economic conditions, they hold, and the limitations of character will largely disappear. That attitude originated as a reaction to extreme individualism and, especially in Europe, to political and economic oppression. To a degree it was a corrective to the laissez-faire philosophy.

Yet the dominant currents of American life and government drive one to a different conclusion. There has been in America a degree of political and economic freedom that has not been made full use of. There has been no legislation to prevent successful businessmen from setting examples of simple and modest living. Obstacles to the development of cooperatives, as a way of escape from economic exploitation, have not been insurmountable. The chief limitations have not been impressed upon them from without, except by the influence of prevailing opinion, but have been in the people themselves. There has been room for much more daring adventure in improving the quality of both public and private business.

I admit that economic and political organization are important. If they are not adequately developed, or if they are perverted, the normal expression of good character may be thwarted. But in the United States, in general, the form of government has been better than the people. The American form of government, imperfect as it is, has given greater opportunity for the creation of a good society than the character, vision, and intelligence of the American people have fully used.

Under these circumstances, while we continue to strive for more perfect and more effective forms of government, we would do well to recognize that the real frontier of American life is in the field of defining and stimulating the best possible drives and motives and disciplines of personal character and community attitudes.

Let no one think that this is counsel to withdraw from practical affairs or to avoid present-day issues. Character expresses itself only in dealing with actual problems. No sooner do we begin to define our ethical aims in relation to those problems and to discipline ourselves to act in accord with those aims than we find ourselves in the thick of current affairs. The change that I believe to be most necessary is not in the things we do but in the spirit and manner of doing them.

SPECIFICATIONS FOR A NATIONAL CHARACTER

It is obvious that character is not acquired solely as the result of any sudden change of attitude or of loyalty. It is a product of gradual growth, with increasingly clear definition of aims, constant strengthening and refinement of motives, steady improvement of methods, and gradually developing decision and discipline of drives and energies. The infection of great leadership and the changing currents of public interests, however, may greatly accelerate the development, and once a great movement gets under way, as much may be achieved in a year as is usually achieved in a decade or a century. It is probable, however, that a considerable period of relatively quiet and inconspicuous growth will be essential before there can be any sweeping change in our national character. As a rule, increase of genuine vigor and refinement of personality occurs primarily from the contagion of actual contact with the same qualities in others, though able persons enlarge upon and refine what they receive.

When I use the word "character" I have in mind three elements. First is purposefulness, or the pattern of desire—the vision of the life it would be well to lead, the kind of world that, so far as wisdom, judgment, and goodwill can determine, it would be well to live in.

Second, I include goodwill and the skilled and disciplined drive of desire that presses toward the realization of aims and purposes. Great insight into what would constitute a good life for oneself and for society has value only as expressed in well-considered action, though under the term "action" I should include the disciplined and carefully expressed thinking of the student and the work of the artist, as well as the more obvious activity of the laborer or the businessman.

Great vigor of action by itself, however, may have no more social value than the capricious force of a tornado, unless it is directed by a vision of what is desirable. A tornado may, by chance, break down harmful barriers as well as destroy values. The activity of Napoleon had some incidental value in breaking down what was obsolete in the structure of European government and society. While some of his actions were important constructive undertakings, they were largely capricious. What a pity his tremendous energy was not directed by a great vision of a good social order and by the ethical controls that would have led him to use suitable means.

The third factor is the ethical or moral quality, the habitual choice of means that are wholesome in their own effects. Even when the desired end is good and the disciplined energy great, it is important that the methods used shall be in themselves ethical or moral.

My definition of ethical or moral action is as easy to state as it is difficult to apply. An ethical act is one that is good when judged by its total consequences—that is good for the future as well as for the present, for society as a whole as well

The Long Road

as for ourselves. An unethical action is one that, while its immediate or personal result may be good, displaces action that would result in greater good, or has later effects on others that are undesirable and that outweigh the good. In practice "good" and "bad" must often be supplanted by the less absolute terms "better" and "worse," but that does not alter the argument. Our ability to judge the total effects of our acts is always limited and imperfect. It is increased by education and experience, by constant effort to use and to refine such discrimination as we possess, and by the leadership of men of exceptional insight.

When I speak of a pattern of desire or a vision of a good society, I do not think of some one type of social organization that is inevitably better than any other but rather of certain personal and social attitudes and traits that are good in any desirable society and of certain social conditions that are universally advantageous. I firmly believe that there are some common and universally good attitudes and conditions that mankind as a whole should seek to achieve.

We must come to recognize that all human activity is, to use a legal expression, "affected with a public interest." Social life in its evolution becomes ever more like a seamless fabric or a living organism. In a society without arbitrary barriers the inmost action of every person affects society as a whole. No activity of a man, either in thought or in outward act, is wholly private in its consequences. The recognition in law that some certain kinds of action are affected with a public interest is only an intimation and foretaste of the recognition that we must come to—that *all* action is of that character.

The justification for a large degree of personal freedom is not that some kinds of activities are solely private in their effect but rather that considerable freedom is good and expedient for practical reasons. External control and regulation of intimate personal matters by law is generally arbitrary and relatively undiscriminating. In respect to many activities a normal, intelligent person can direct his own affairs with greater economy and discrimination than can be secured by legislation or other external regulation. Free men working together for common ends are in the long run more effective than men regimented by outward authority, whether that authority be economic, political, or spiritual.

Moreover, a large element of personal freedom is good because free men are in some degree creative. Since no two persons are just alike, a man who originates his own action will give it some of the original quality of his own unique personality. Self-direction may interfere with the quick efficiency that uniformity of action sometimes achieves, but it adds variety and richness to life and constantly introduces new elements of excellence. We cannot wholly dispense with imposed uniformity of conduct, such as our traffic rules or as in the manufacture of uniform products like automobiles, but we would do well to strive constantly to increase the range and the capacity for self-determination.

For practical reasons a large degree of personal freedom is good—yes, essential—to all good social order, but this very fact makes all the more necessary the development of social-mindedness. It still remains true that all human activity is affected with a public interest, that "no man is an island" and "we are members, one of another." The conflict between those two great facts—the interdependence of men in society, and the practical value of self-determination and personal freedom—can be resolved only by personal character that directs free action to social ends. Under a regime of personal freedom, the first great principle of conduct is that a man's actions shall be determined by their probable total effect on society as a whole and not on himself alone.

As to the type of social order men shall adopt, there is room for choice and for honest differences of taste and of judgment. It continues to be true that the tendency of social organization is in some respects toward diversity and not toward uniformity. But it does not follow from this constant tendency to diversity that all ways of living are equally good or that selection is only a matter of taste or of prejudice. Great differences in value do exist, and efforts to select the better way have always characterized the human adventure. The method of open-minded critical inquiry and comparison, a relatively new technique in human affairs, promises to help greatly in the selection of the better among possible ways of living. Yet, diversity in social organization will be an increasing and not a transient phenomenon, unless uniformity should be brought about by some compelling influence, such as close association made necessary by the limited land area of the earth. Although certain elements of uniformity of social organization will gradually prove to be universally desirable and will become universally accepted by all peoples, as the postal service has in large measure become accepted, there probably will remain important variations in the way human societies choose to organize.

I have no other criterion for good conduct than the results. That is, good conduct is that which is expedient. But no expediency is fully sound that takes into account only the immediate consequences. The soldier who dies for his country gives expediency a larger meaning. The ultimate expediency is that which is good in relation to the whole of life and of time. There are attitudes of life and qualities of character that so nearly meet these conditions that within the limits of our judgment we may speak of them as ultimate expediency.

It is these universal expedients, I believe, that should provide the foundation for personal and social ethics. Given them, many and various forms of social order may contribute to the value and quality of living. In fact, as these universal qualities are developed, some of the present burning issues of the political, economic, and social world will shrink and fade until they become little more than matters of taste and convenience. Without these universal qualities of character, on the other hand, the most ideal structure of human society may be but a finely designed framework for hell on earth.

To a large degree in our present society, personal and social conduct is not the result of purposeful search and determined mastery but of a haphazard mixture of native impulse, early training, religious influence, the prevailing social habits, and one's own occasional contributions. Generally, these elements constitute a conflicting mass of factors, without unity of philosophy, outlook, or design. As a result, action is determined by the most immediate pressure or by the deepest-seated habits. Such patterns of action do not provide a foundation for a good social order.

It is possible and highly desirable that a common groundwork of personal and social life and action be developed that will give the fullest possible incentive to the growth of character, that will be universally expedient, and that will keep open the road to social evolution. It is obvious that such a common basis of personal and social action will not come spontaneously into existence and seldom will be acquired by chance. It is an achievement to be paid for by deliberate, consistent effort.

ELEMENTS OF AN ETHICAL CODE

If my assumption is sound that such a common groundwork of character is essential to any desirable social order, then its achievement should be a primary undertaking of every person. As the first element of such a universal framework of character, I have included the full and vital acceptance of the fact that each individual is an integral part of all human life, present and future, and that his actions should be determined by their possible total effect and not solely by their effect on him alone, or on his immediate circle, or for the immediate present.

Another principle, almost as important, is that there should be open-minded and free inquiry as to what constitutes the good life and ethical conduct. We have no final revelation of what is good but must achieve our concepts of values through cooperative search and trial. Unless our aims are constantly tested by open-minded criticism, and unless they are inclusive enough to provide room for human values in all fields, strong character may become an instrument of fanaticism and may do harm almost in proportion to its strength. Tolerance and humility of spirit must accompany great courage and great commitment to purpose. Without the attitude of critical, open-minded inquiry, convictions turn into dogmas, and social progress may be blocked.

Such critical inquiry in the long run does not mean increasing divergence of opinion but rather the opposite. In the field of science, where open-minded inquiry is the accepted attitude, consensus of opinion has been achieved over a greater area and to a greater degree than in any other field of vital concern. Where inquiry is inhibited, as in religion or government, conflict is greatest.

The present-day prohibition of free inquiry in certain Asiatic and European countries will hamper the gradual growth of insight and of judgment on which a good social order may be built. As a former college president, I know that a spirit of free inquiry in the field of human relations is not generally welcome in industrial America. I know that very dominant industrialists will go out of their way to express effectively their disapproval of small colleges where freedom of inquiry exists. A great university may tolerate a few unconventional inquirers, just as the emperor in his palace goes through the annual ceremony of washing a beggar's feet. The courtiers know that this rite is not intended to set a prevailing type of social action. The same difficulties await the minister, the professional man, or the corporation employee who has an active, open mind and applies himself to the dominant problems of the day.

It is not only in the economic field that open-minded inquiry is needed. Shallowness and flabbiness of personal living hide behind intolerance of criticism. It is not true in personal and social life any more than in science that one man's opinion is as good as another's. Rigorous, open inquiry drives men to necessary conclusions and is an essential factor in achieving sound unity of opinion.

Another element that I should include in a universal ethical code is the habit of honest and open dealing. The effort of men to withhold the truth from each other and to deceive each other mars many kinds of relationships, confuses issues, and leads men to use a large part of their energies in trying to circumvent each other. The general absence of complete and thoroughgoing integrity is one of the chief obstacles to a good society. There can be no good and stable social order without personal integrity.

Other very important elements of conduct are the habits of self-denial, foresight, and accumulation of reserves for times of stress. Periods of stress will come. They can be best surmounted by those who have kept themselves vigorous and tempered to privation, who have achieved poise and have learned to use their energies temperately, who have habitually lived within their means, who have reserves for an emergency, and who have planned in advance the steps to take when stress comes. Good intent needs to be skillfully and wisely implemented. Such character is not improvised. It is the result of a philosophy of living and of long, conscious discipline.

Another universally expedient principle is that a person shall not waste his biological resources. Regard for physical and mental health and an effort to increase one's energy and to refine one's capacity for insight and discrimination by wholesome living are desirable in any social order. Disregard for the best conditions of personal fitness is not evidence of open-mindedness or of tolerance.

Similarly, eugenic conscience is essential in any good social order. The greater part of our inheritance from the long struggle of life is in the biological and cultural gains we can pass on to our children. To waste that inheritance for trivial reasons or for pride of social status is one of the fundamental immoralities.

In addition to desirable types of action, of which I have endeavored to give examples, there is the underlying matter of the emotional drive that commits the whole personality to the achievement of such habits of action. Some persons and some organizations would approve the types of conduct I have described and yet make peace with personal and social habits that are fatal to any desirable social order. A great drive of desire that will lead men constantly to pay a great price for what they value most is essential. Emotional drive does not imply nervous tension or strain; it is at its best when associated with quiet reserve, poise, and conservation of energy.

We have then these three elements: a picture of the world as it might be, which gives purpose to our lives; our ethical principles, which determine our manner of action; and emotional drive, which leads us to put our whole energies into conforming our actions to our ideas.

Capacity to contribute to social wisdom, social purpose, and social values is not the possession of a few but in varying degrees is widely distributed throughout the population. To a still greater extent there is latent capacity that might develop under favorable conditions. It is social wisdom to keep open to all the opportunity and the incentive to take part in governmental and economic affairs. Any social, political, or economic stratification that rejects contributions from any competent source is unwise.

It is equally true that social wisdom and purpose are not *evenly* distributed through the population. Some persons have much ability to contribute, and some little. Some have the capacity to make one kind of contribution and some another kind. Almost irrespective of how far men may advance, that condition will remain. It will continue to be true that society does well to take full advantage of the leadership of men of exceptional insight and wisdom and that for a long time to come a few men will be leaders and many men followers. In any wholesome society, leaders will largely influence the direction of social action. The problem of how they will lead remains. Will it be as friends and as trustees of their special abilities in the service of the common good, or by using their exceptional ability to advance their personal interests?

If leadership shares responsibility and opportunity whenever such sharing can add to the growth of personality and to the general welfare, then we will have a good social order. Real democracy is not equal sharing of power and opportunity. It is equal commitment to the common good; it is a program of sharing opportunity and responsibility to the full extent to which the capacity exists to make good use of them.

A UNIVERSAL SOLVENT

The special abilities and special conditions of men are so infinitely varied and so changing that they can never be wisely classified and organized into any rigid social scheme. Life is far too complex for that. Self-interest and the will to power can take on subtle forms and mislead the mass of men. There is only one basis on which the universal play of abilities among men can work to the fullest extent. That is by the self-discipline of enlightened, social-minded character. Given such character, the infinitely varied capacities of men to contribute to the social good can be cumulative—or more than that, can be factors multiplied into each other—with resulting total increase in present welfare and in the rate and the range of social progress.

This being the case, the greatest of all social aims is that of developing the qualities of character and intelligence that will lead each person of his own volition to try to play that part which is best for society as a whole. Such an attitude would vastly simplify the processes of social adjustment. Enlightened character is a universal solvent of social evils.

One repeatedly finds that to act in a manner that would be normal in a good society and that would help set the stage for a good society is difficult or dangerous in the society that is. Enlightened self-interest will not bridge that gap. Repeatedly, it may be necessary to act in a way that is detrimental to the person involved but that in the end will be good for society as a whole. To provide a commonplace illustration, we have the old saying that "honesty is the best policy." Now as far as individual prosperity is concerned, no observant person can accept that saying as always applicable. We see both fortune and public honors acquired dishonestly and passed on to succeeding generations. We often see honesty heavily penalized. But most of us would agree that we would like to live in a world in which honesty would be the best policy. To make the transition from the present social order to a better one requires that many men work at laying the foundations for that better order at great cost to themselves. To do that is evidence of character.

Men who are engaged in such effort do not need our pity, any more than does the explorer who risks all he has to discover a new region, for they are doing what they prefer above all else. They have a zest for living that gives life interest and a sense of well-being that remains only with those who feel that their efforts may have enduring value.

Index

Alexander the Great, 41
Alexander, Will, 74
Aluminum Company of America (Alcoa), 104-117, 146, 175, 178
American Forestry Association, 63
American Society of Civil Engineers, 51
Antioch College, 4, 5, 8, 22, 27, 54, 65, 112, 118, 119, 128, 130, 172
Antioch Notes, 6, 8, 22
Appalachian Regional Commission, 161
Army Corps of Engineers, 5, 18, 26, 27, 50, 51, 75, 77, 93, 94, 98, 100, 104, 120, 129-130
Arrowhead Trail, 71
Associated Press, 47

Atomic Energy Commission, 135
Autobiography of Lincoln Steffens, The, 186

Barr, John E., 73
Bass, Neil, 167
Bear Creek Development Authority, 71
Berry Condemnation Commission, 82
Berry, George, 79-82
Biddle, Francis, 171
Bishop, Dr. E. L., 85-86
Bock, Carl, 30, 96, 139
Brandeis, Louis, 22, 165, 183
Briggs, Howard, 124
Broughton, Len, 34

201

Bureau of Mines, 68, 69
Bureau of Outdoor Recreation, 71

Capehart, Homer, 138
Cassells, Edwin, 22
CCC (Civilian Conservation Corps), 167
Chatuge Shores Recreation Area, 71
Chickamauga Dam, 100, 112n, 145, 146
Civil Service Commission, 122
Clapp, Gordon, 83-85, 130
Clinch-Powell Educational Cooperative, 160
Clinch-Powell River Valley Association, 159, 160
Commonwealth and Southern Corporation, 137, 139, 140n, 141-144, 178, 179
Community Service, Inc., 92
Congress, 3, 4, 7, 27, 57, 104, 108, 109, 112n, 113, 129, 132, 135, 137, 142, 146, 147, 148, 166, 170
Connery, Donald S., quoted, 138
Cottrell, Dr. C. G., 29
Cox, James M., 6, 175
Craig, Dr. James L., 161
Cumberland River, 99
Curtis, Dr. Harry, 133, 135, 145

Davidson, Donald, quoted, 171
Davis, Arthur, V., 109, 110, 115, 116, 146, 178
Dawson, J. Dudley, 118; interview with, 119-130
Dayton Flood of 1913, 5, 93
Democratic Party, 9, 10, 11, 16, 138
Department of Agriculture, 47
Department of Natural Resources, (Ohio), 92
Department of State, 134

East Tennessee Light and Power Company, 148
Eckel, Edwin, 80
Electric Home and Farm Authority, 149
Elk River, 70, 71
Elliott, C. G., 45, 47

Evans, Llewellyn, 21-22, 27, 32, 148, 180

Farley, James A., 9-17
Federal Trade Commission, 103, 185
Federal Water Pollution Control Act, 110
Ferguson, Samuel, 180
Fergusson, Douglas, 69
Florida Everglades, 47-48
Fly, Lawrence, 170
Fontana Dam, 37, 104-117, 175, 178
Forbes, Scotty, 126
Ford Motor Company, 112
Frankfurter, Felix, 173
Fry, Albert, 96

Georgia State Advisory Council, 161
Georgia State Department of Education, 161
Glaeser, Dr. Martin, 180
Goat Island Recreation Area, 71
Gould, Robert, 67, 68
Growden, James P., 116

Hamilton, George, 142, 180
Harper's, 126
Harris Clay Company, 68
Harris, George Chandler, 177
Hartford Electric Company, 180
Henderson, Algo, 22-23
Henry, S. T., 67
Hershey, John, 65-66
Hignett, Travis P., 133
Hill, Lister, 108, 109
Hiwassee Dam, 121
Hiwassee River, 70
Hiwassee River Watershed Development Association Education Work Group, 160
Home Extension Service (Tennessee), 125
Hoover, Herbert, 94
Hopkins, Harry, 72, 138
Horseshoe Bend Recreation Area, 71
House of Representatives Committee on Military Affairs, 110
Hoyt, Kendall K., 35

Index

Hull, Cordell, 81
Humphreys, A. A., 94
Hussain, Zakir, 91

Ickes, Harold, 180
Inman, Dr. Ondess, 65
Insull, Samuel, 137, 142, 179, 180
International Pressmen's Union, 79

Jacobs, Victor, 92
Jenkins, William L., 3
Jesus, 41
Jones, Barton, 96

Kahoe, Walter, 81
Kentucky Dam, 97, 99
Kettering, Charles F., 136
Kline, L. V., 66
Kruckman, Arnold, 29; letter from, 30-35

La Follette, Philip, 175
La Follette, Robert M., Jr., 23-24, 56; La Follette political organization, 166, 167, 168, 169, 173, 175
Lake Okeechobee, 48
Lawson, Thomas, 185
League of Nations, 138
League to Enforce Peace, 138
Lebanon Academy of Surveying, 43
Leiserson, William, 5
Lilienthal, David, 25, 26, 27-28, 29, 32, 35, 36, 55, 56, 57, 73, 90, 100, 108, 129, 131, 143, 154, 156, 157, 165, 166, 167; appointment to TVA board, 22-24; Berry marble case, 80-82; conflict with A. E. Morgan, 165-182; controversy over negotiations with Willkie, 137-144; Fontana Dam, 111-117; *Journals*, 23, 56, 115, 168, 170; patronage, 83-85; power sales, 144-146, 148-150; reappointment, 166-168; *This I Do Believe*, 181
Little River Drainage District, 49-50;
Little Tennessee River, 104-111, 113, 115

Locher, Charles, 96

Mafia, 120
Mann, Horace, 54
McBride, Don, 3
McCarthy, Charles J., quoted, 79
McCraw, Thomas, quoted, 79-81, 143n-144n
McIntyre, Marvin, 7, 13
Marsden, Anson, 47, 49
Marshall, John, 185
Marx, Karl, 190
Mayo, William B., 112
Meleager, 41
Mellon, Andrew, 117, 146
Miami Conservancy District, 6, 51, 93, 96, 118, 119
Middle West Utilities Company, 142, 180
Mississippi Power Company, 150
Mississippi River, 19, 20, 46, 50, 93, 94, 98, 99, 105, 106, 107
Mitraniketan, 91
Morgan, Arthur, 5, 15, 56, 80, 81, 82, 142, 143, 144, 166, 169, 170, 171, 174, 176, 177, 178, 179, 181; appointment to board, 6-7, 20; bean cooperative, 72-73; biographical information, 38-52; credit exchange program, 58-59; discussion with Dudley Dawson, 119-130; post-TVA "vagaries," 91-92; story about threatened resignation, 166
Morgan Engineering Company, 50, 52
Morgan, Griscom, 116
Morgan, Harcourt A., 20, 21, 25, 26, 28, 35, 36, 55, 56, 58, 65, 73, 76, 78, 80, 85, 111, 113, 124, 137, 143, 154, 167, 169, 171, 172, 173, 174, 175, 176, 177; fertilizer program, 131-135
Muscle Shoals, Alabama, 2, 3, 13, 112n, 132, 133, 134, 150
Muskingum Conservancy District, 5, 6

NAACP (National Association for the Advancement of Colored People), 74

203

National Ceramics Society, 69
Napoleon, 192
National Environmental Policy Act, 110
National Forest Service, 65, 75, 76
National Geographic, 126
National Home Library Foundation, 183
National Parks Association, 63
National Recovery Administration, 79
National Universities Commission, 91
New Deal, 90, 93, 166
Non-Partisan League, 79
Norris Camp, 83, 126
Norris Dam, 13, 26, 74, 78, 80, 81, 94, 96, 97, 121, 127, 128, 129, 176
Norris, George, 9, 32, 83, 84, 109, 111, 115, 137, 140, 144, 168, 169, 173
Norris Lake, 72
Norris, Tennessee, 124-125, 127

Obed River, 70, 71
Ocoee River, 70
Office of Drainage Investigation, 45, 46, 48
Ohio River, 5, 98, 99, 129
O'Rourke, Dr. L. G., 122
Owen, Marguerite, 29-30, 32, 155

Peace Corps, 134
People's Republic of China, 64n
Pickwick Dam, 119, 121
Pierce, John, 170
Pigeon Forge Pottery, 69
Pinchot, Gifford, quoted, 158
Power Pool Conference, 142
Princeton University, 139
Pritchett, C. Herman, quoted, 36
Prokop, Eugene, 98

Randolph, Isham, 47, 49
Reclamation Act of 1906, 147
Republican Party, 11, 14, 15-16, 17, 138
Reeves, Floyd, 27, 73, 74, 119, 122, 128, 166
Revolutionary War, 185
Reynolds, Richard S., 112, 146

Richards, Ned, 61
Richberg, Donald, 22, 173
Richey, Carl, 130
Ripley, Thomas H., quoted, 66-67
Rivers and Harbors Congress, see Water Resources Congress
Robertson, John, 169
Roosevelt, Eleanor, 4, 7-8, 87, 175
Roosevelt, Franklin, 1, 2, 3, 4, 6, 18, 19, 24, 26, 27, 31, 32, 33, 53, 54, 55, 57, 64, 65, 67, 79, 81, 83, 84, 104, 111, 114, 121, 123, 137, 138, 140, 141, 142, 143, 149, 150, 154, 155, 156, 158, 162, 166, 167, 168, 169, 170, 171, 172, 173, 174, 176, 179, 180, 181; life pattern, 7-9, 12; memorandum of conference with, 13-15

Schmidt, F. E., 180
Scientific American, 126
Shays' Rebellion, 185
Smith, Walter, 51
St. Francis River, 46-47, 50

Taylor, J. Porter, quoted, 70-72
Tennessee Power Company, 97
Tennessee River, 9, 20, 86, 97, 98, 99, 100, 104, 105, 108, 109, 110, 111, 116, 120, 145, 147, 155, 175, 178
Tennessee Valley, 7, 20, 33, 54, 55, 56, 57, 60, 61, 66, 69, 85, 122, 123, 124, 132, 137, 146, 155, 158, 160, 162
Tennessee Valley Associated Cooperative, 73
Tennessee Valley Authority, Act, 12, 16, 56, 83, 94, 129, 143, 144, 145, 146, 155, 179; annual reports, 57, 70-72; avoiding patronage, 7, 9-17, 83-85; board, 20-24, 25, 57, 129, 131, 132, 137, 138, 139, 140, 141, 142, 143, 144, 145, 146, 147, 148, 162, 166, 171, 176, 177, 178, 181; conflict with the cement trust, 100-103; division of board responsibilities, 35-37, 166, 174-175; education program, 160-161; employment prac-

Index

tices, 120-123, 129; FDR's conception of the TVA, 2-3, 6-7, 54-55, 154-156; forestry and forest genetics, 56, 59-67; health program, 9, 159, 161-162; housing program, 87-91; land-aquisition, 75-79; land development and recreation program, 56, 69-72; legislation to establish, 2, 18-20, 55; malaria-control program, 56, 85-87; negotiations with Alcoa concerning Fontana, 104-117, 178; race relations, 73-75; staff, 56, 94-100, 119, 174; Washington office, 27, 28-35, 166
Time, 126
Tims Ford Dam, 71
Tims Ford Lake, 71
Tishomingo County Area Vocational-Technical Center, 161
Tishomingo County Board of Education, 161
Trail of Tears, 71
Trainor, John, 103
Tributary Area Development Report, 156, 158; quoted, 158-161
Truman, Harry, 117
TVA Ceramics Research Laboratory, 68
TVA Chemical Department, 133
TVA Forestry Agency, 66, 123
TVA Industry Divison, 68

TVA Personnel Divison, 119

Upton, Nellie, 128
U.S. Office of Experiment Stations, 85
U.S. Reclamation Service, 26-27, 51, 94, 95, 180
United States Steel Corporation, 92
U.S. Weather Bureau, 51

Volta River, 91

Wagner, Aubrey J., 3, 108
Walker and Dade County Development Association, 72
Water Resources Congress, 130
Weigel, F. W., 68
Wessel, O. S., quoted, 145-148, 151-152
Wheeler Dam, 26, 74, 78, 94, 97, 119, 121
White, Marie, 125
White, Ross, 96, 127
Wiersema, Harry, 75, 96, 181; letter from 75
Willkie, Wendell, 137-144, 178-179
Wilson Dam, 132, 150
Wolverton, Charles, 170
Woodward, Sherman, 94, 96
World Congress of Religions, 40

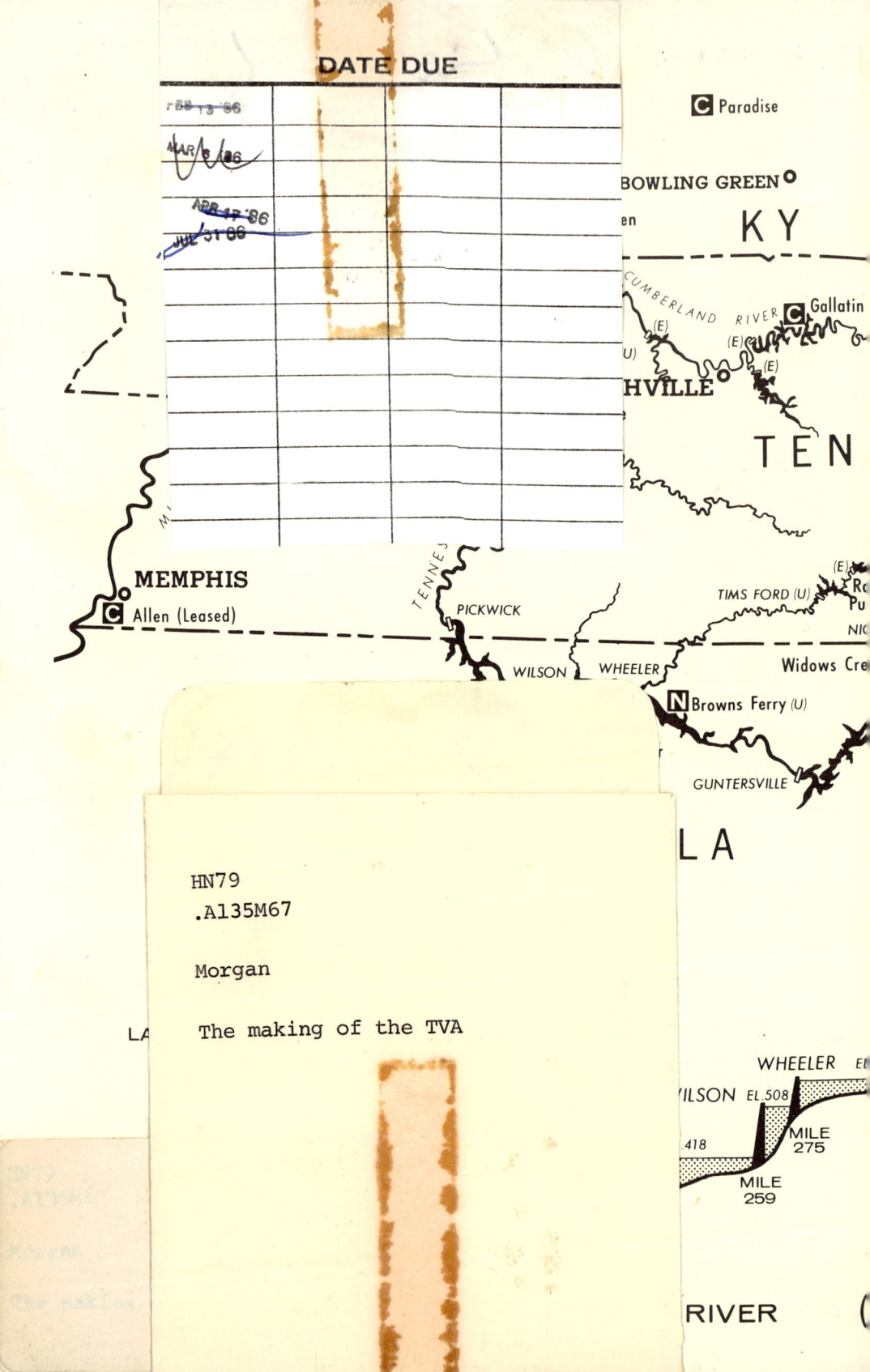

DATE DUE

FEB 13 '86		
MAR 6 '86		
APR 17 '86		
JUL 31 86		

HN79
.A135M67

Morgan

The making of the TVA